# That Which Is Just in the Church

## Other Books of Interest from St. Augustine's Press

Maurice Ashley Agbaw-Ebai, *Light of Reason, Light of Faith: Joseph Ratzinger and the German Enlightenment*

Maurice Ashley Agbaw-Ebai, *Africae Munus: Ten Years Later*

Peter Kreeft, *Ha! A Christian Philosophy of Humor*

Peter Kreeft, *If Einstein Had Been a Surfer*

Peter Kreeft, *A Socratic Introduction to Plato's Republic*

Peter Kreeft, *The Platonic Tradition*

Peter Kreeft, *The Philosophy of Jesus*

Peter Kreeft, *Socratic Logic (3rd Edition)*

Marvin R. O'Connell, *Telling Stories that Matter: Memoirs and Essays*

Richard Peddicord, O.P., *The Sacred Monster of Thomism*

Josef Pieper, *Exercises in the Elements: Essays–Speeches–Notes*

Josef Pieper, *A Journey to Point Omega: Autobiography from 1964*

John von Heyking, *Comprehensive Judgment and Absolute Selflessness: Winston Churchill on Politics as Friendship*

Gabriele Kuby, *The Abandoned Generation*

Gene Fendt, *Camus' Plague: Myth for Our World*

Roger Scruton, *An Intelligent Person's Guide to Modern Culture*

Peter Fraser, *Twelve Films about Love and Heaven*

Roger Scruton, *The Politics of Culture and Other Essays*

Roger Scruton, *On Hunting*

Anne Drury Hall, *Where the Muses Still Haunt: The Second Reading*

Allen Mendenhall, *Shouting Softly: Lines on Law, Literature, and Culture*

Chilton Williamson, *The End of Liberalism*

Marion Montgomery, *With Walker Percy at the Tupperware Party*

Charles R. Embry and Glenn Hughes, editors, *The Timelessness of Proust: Reflections on In Search of Lost Time*

# That Which Is Just in the Church
## An Introduction to Canon Law
CARLOS JOSÉ ERRÁZURIZ
TRANSLATED BY MICHAEL JOSEPH MAZZA

ST. AUGUSTINE'S PRESS
South Bend, Indiana

Manufactured in the United States of America.

1  2  3  4  5  6   28  27  26  25  24  23

**Library of Congress Control Number: 2023937582**


Hardback ISBN: 978-1-58731-894-8
Ebook: 978-1-58731-895-5

∞ The paper used in this publication meets the minimum requirements of the American National Standard for Information Sciences – Permanence of Paper for Printed Materials, ANSI Z39.48-1984.

St. Augustine's Press
www.staugustine.net

# Table of Contents

# Chapter I
## RIGHTS, JUSTICE, AND LAW IN THE CHURCH

### 1. The existence of an authentic law in the Church of Christ

#### 1.1. The objections to the existence of ecclesial law throughout history

**1.** No one doubts the empirical-factual existence of the historical phenomenon called "canon law." Present since the dawn of the Church, the juridical order proper to the Catholic Church assumed extraordinary importance in the Middle Ages and has remained alive, without interruption, to the present day. Nevertheless, a phenomenon that could be termed "anti-juridicism" has continually presented objections to the very notion of such a law, denying the nature of ecclesial law as such, and questioning both the authenticity and the legitimacy of a law existing in the Church. Such an attitude can be derived from either of two presuppositions: According to the first, the true essence of the Church founded by Christ does not admit the presence of a "law" within it; in fact, the "law" represents an element that is in contradiction to the life and mission of the Church. A second presupposition comes from the idea that law is a reality that by its nature can only exist in non-ecclesial spheres; that is, in civil society alone.

The first type of objection, a *spiritualistic anti-juridicism*, had its origin in those Christians who for various reasons rejected the institutional and juridical Church, considering it to be in contrast with the true Church of Christ, one that would be of an exclusively spiritual nature. This tendency, already operating in movements of the first centuries (*e.g.*, the Gnostics, Montanists, Donatists, etc.) and Medieval (*e.g.*, the Cathars, Waldensians, Albigensians, Beghards, Fraticelli, Hussites, etc.), found its greatest historical expression in the Protestant Reformation. The famous gesture by

Martin Luther remains emblematic of this spiritualistic anti-juridicism, beyond whatever other interpretations that may be given to the act. In 1520, Luther publicly burned, along with other documents, the *Corpus Iuris Canonici*—i.e., the set of books containing the universal law of the Church united to the Roman Pontiff. The leading theoretical exponent of this line of thought, though often not followed in its radicalism by Protestants themselves, was the Lutheran jurist Rudolf Sohm (1841–1917). Sohm maintained the existence of a clear contradiction between, on the one hand, the law of the Church, considered as a worldly reality of a formal nature and linked to force and to merely human social power and, on the other hand, the essence of the Church, seen as a spiritual and invisible reality.[1]

In this sense, the power of the Hierarchy, especially that of the Pope, as the source of ecclesiastical laws, constitutes the primary object against which this anti-juridicism moves. Rather than being a means by which one can unite with Christ, that power would be a purely human dominion, compromised with worldly interests, and contrary to Christian freedom and the development of charisms inspired by the Spirit. But this rejection of the hierarchical aspects then extends to any causal link between the external actions of the Church (a visible reality) and the gift of salvation (an invisible, spiritual reality). Indeed, spiritualism realizes that to admit seriously the existence of an ecclesial law means also recognizing an intrinsic link between the visible aspects of the Church (the sacraments, the word of God, laws, etc.) and its invisible aspects—that is, the very salvation of man in Christ through the Church. The basic problem is not the mere recognition of the need for an external disciplinary order in the community of the faithful, something that almost all concede in practice as a consequence of man's social nature and the needs and difficulties of any human coexistence. The real question appears when this ecclesial order is related to the salvation of the Christian. Spiritualism denies in principle that there can be such a relationship, which would contradict the exquisitely spiritual and individual nature of the grace that each person receives from God. In a word, *the very sacramentality or mediation of the Church is challenged—namely, the causal connection between its visible and invisible aspects.*

From this point of view, the sacraments are conceived as external actions of a purely symbolic nature, performed in the Church with the aim of teaching mankind what God accomplishes in people independently of the sacraments themselves. According to this idea, the sacraments cannot in any way be the cause of grace. Consequently, the juridical questions concerning the sacraments lose their substantial importance; that is, being linked to the salvation of persons. In fact, little or no relevance can be afforded to questions such as those surrounding the validity of the administration of the sacraments if such administration is considered to be devoid of truly salvific causal effects. After all, if one thinks that the obtaining of grace, the remission of sins, and the incorporation into the Church are not intrinsically connected with the external act of baptism, questions regarding the validity of the way in which such a sacrament was administered lose their juridical import.

As for the word of God, it too could not be viewed as an object of any truly juridical relation, as it remains totally transcendent, above and beyond any human act of proclamation or interpretation. Viewed through a spiritualistic anti-juridical lens, there cannot be an objective point of reference constituting a firm criterion for the authentic interpretation of the Scriptures for the Church on her pilgrimage through history. To admit otherwise would be to replace the divine word with a human word. From this follows the decisive denial of the possibility of any ecclesiastical magisterium, whose interventions would consist of nothing other than human words. Even were it a charismatically enlightened word, it cannot have a binding value different from any other manifestation of faith by any member of the faithful moved by the Spirit. Without any authority that gives it certainty in the Church, it is understood that the divine word remains a good that is seen as outside of the juridical realm, and not susceptible in itself of any relationship of obligation or right between the faithful. On the contrary, the faithful are seen as having to coexist peacefully in the free and necessarily pluralistic understanding of the Christian faith, of a divine word which, given its transcendence, remains completely inaccessible to that objectification that any juridical order requires.

As far as the canonical norms are concerned, the sacred Pastors could not arrogate to themselves the prerogative of issuing ecclesiastical laws binding the conscience of Christians; not even the customs of the community could have such a value. While certainly recognizing the need for rules for regulating the discipline of the external life of communities, such norms would in no way, however, be seen as giving rise to moral duties connected to the path of Christian salvation (the Sunday obligation would not constitute a duty in conscience, for example). It would be understood then, as was demonstrated especially in the early days of Protestantism, that the help of secular powers could be used to organize and protect Christian confessions externally, including even securing their assistance when resolving juridical issues within such confessions, notwithstanding the serious dangers that arose from such state interference with respect to the authenticity of Christianity. Over time, such risks were ultimately noted, as was the widely perceived need to put these questions back into the ambit of the self-regulation of the various confessions.

The second kind of anti-juridicism, the *statalistic* one, begins with *the exclusive attribution of all juridical power to the authority of civil society.* As a result, canon law in this view is conceived of as a mere internal order endowed with moral value for the members of the Church, but as lacking that juridical efficacy which is necessarily associated with civil norms that are endowed with sanctions enforceable through the use of compulsion. In the medieval context of the struggles between the Empire and the Papacy, the most famous author in this denial of any juridical power of the Church, and specifically of the Pope, was Marsilius of Padua. In his book *Defensor Pacis*, published in 1324, he argues that it is precisely this interference of the Church in the temporal sphere of law—including, according to him, even those norms concerning the internal life of the Church (e.g., the appointment of ecclesiastical authorities)—constitutes a threat to peace. Marsilius argues for the reduction of the task of ecclesiastical authority to the mere administration of the sacraments and preaching of the word of God on clearly spiritualistic conceptual bases. In favor of his thesis, Marsilius invokes Jesus' answer to Pilate: "My kingdom is not of this world" (John 18:36). On this basis, Marsilius attempts to argue that all visible power in the Church was thus denied.

This anti-juridicism *calls into question the legitimate autonomy of the Church in the performance of its own mission*, insofar as it tends to attribute juridical competence over internal ecclesiastical matters to civil authority. Such a trend has materialized in different ways in various historical moments, sometimes in ways that appeared to be favorable to Catholicism (e.g., in Spanish regalism), and sometimes in ways decidedly contrary to the faith (e.g., in secular liberalism) or, with unprecedented ferocity (e.g., Marxist-inspired totalitarianism).

*1.2. The defense of canon law by the Church*

**2.** In the face of anti-juridicism, the Church has invariably reaffirmed its own law as an irrepressible aspect of her being on this earth. Against spiritualism, the existence of the Hierarchy was proclaimed in particular, as being instituted by Christ himself and as being endowed with true power regarding salvation, the administration of the sacraments, the authoritative teaching of the revealed word, and the governance of the Church through the promulgation of laws binding the conscience of the faithful. In a special way, the primacy of jurisdiction belonging to the Pope as successor of Peter was reaffirmed. To confront statalism, the sovereignty of the Church over all human power was heralded, a sovereignty that was inherent to the Church by virtue of its own divine foundation and indispensable to it so that it might fulfill its mission with due independence, and without undue interference of any sort.

On both of these fronts the Church's *magisterial activity* has been particularly intense since the Protestant Reformation. In fact, the ecclesiastical magisterium proclaimed several truths that were at the center of the controversy with Protestants in matters juridical. One example of this can be seen in the teaching on the sacraments, so amply set forth by the decrees of the Council of Trent (1545–1563), in themes decisive for the law of the Church such as the following: the *ex opere operato* effect of the sacraments; the sacramental character deriving from the reception of the sacraments of baptism, confirmation and holy orders; the obligatory nature of the precepts of the Church for the baptized;[2] and the Hierarchy founded on the sacrament of orders.[3] Another teaching which is especially relevant is the definition of the primacy of the Pope at the First Vatican Council. This definition included the full and supreme power of jurisdiction of the pope not only in matters of faith and morals, but also in the discipline and governance of the universal Church, as well as the infallibility of his solemn definitions in matters of faith and morals.[4] With regard to relations with civil society, there has also been a magisterial emphasis on the independence of the Church as a sovereign society, endowed with a juridical power of divine origin, radically autonomous from the power of political authority.[5]

In the same period, theologians and canonists worked to defend canon law as one of the dimensions of ecclesial life most threatened by the attacks of both Protestantism and secular liberalism. The 18th century saw the development of a *discipline dedicated to the apologetics of the Church from a juridical point of view*. This was the so-called "Public Ecclesiastical Law" (*Ius Publicum Ecclesiasticum*), which had its initial phase in Germany, appearing as an attempt to make use of the legal culture of the time—the school of rationalistic natural law of the 17th century of Hugo Grotius, Samuel Pufendorf, and others—in order to defend the Church within the framework of public law then in place for civil society. The discipline reached its maturity in Rome in the 19th century and lasted until the first half of the 20th century. Among its most well-known scholars were authors closely linked to the Roman Curia, such as Cardinals Tarquini, Cavagnis, and Ottaviani.[6] In this context, the famous notion of the "juridically perfect society" was developed; that is, a society that is fully autonomous in both its ends and in its means, a concept that was then applied to the Church in its own order, just as it was applied to the State in its own order. The emphasis on the hierarchical aspect, and especially on the papacy, was strong, given that canon law (understood by these authors as the collective body of ecclesiastical laws) was linked to the power of the Hierarchy that issued it.

It would be misleading to attribute this defense of canon law, and therefore of the hierarchical power and autonomy of the Church, to temporal and worldly interests. It is sufficient to recall that, as in other moments in history, the so-called Counter-Reformation (or, rather, "the Catholic Reformation"), was driven by a real impulse to revitalize the faith and customs of the clergy, religious, and all the faithful, producing lasting fruits in many countries with a venerable Catholic tradition as well as in many new mission territories. This occurred not only because of the charisms aroused by the Holy Spirit (as should be obvious), but also in close connection with the juridical structure of the Church, strengthening canonical discipline and the unity with the Bishops and with the Roman Pontiff, the cornerstone of ecclesial unity. *Concern for the laws, for obedience, and for the visible unity of the ecclesial structure has always been perceived by the Church as something inseparable from its own mission of salvation.*

Without denying the inevitable shadows, deriving from the human element that accompany her earthly journey, *the Church's constant defense of canon law as part of her self-understanding must be recognized as a good, as an aspect of her fidelity to the foundational plan.* In fact, this defense is not simply a matter of defending a more or less contingent cultural product, much less some kind of pretense in artificially keeping alive a dated model such as the one that existed during medieval times. Behind the defense of canon law, when it is understood in its essential aspects, there is in reality a defense of the Church herself: of her authenticity, unity, independence, and indefectibility.

Despite the merits of this apologia of the law advocated by the *Ius Publicum Ecclesiasticum*, it is worth noting here its limitations. A particularly important limitation in this sense was the identification of the juridical realm in the Church too closely with the corpus of ecclesiastical laws themselves, and therefore with the Church's hierarchical dimension as well. As a result, the juridical importance of every human person in the Church was not sufficiently acknowledged. (This is closely connected with the very notions of right and law, on which we will speak in numbers 5–8, *infra*). Furthermore, the theoretical justification of canon law was rather poor, a one-sided approach based heavily on the need for authority and laws for the common good of a society. Such notions were essentially valid for any human social grouping; that is, they were situated rather on the level of natural law, and therefore took little account of the supernatural specificity of the People of God. It was, moreover, also a doctrine that more than anything else appeared to correspond to the maximum public dimension of human sociality (i.e., the binomial "State" and "Church"), and thus was not very sensitive to the juridically active position of the faithful and their associations. Even when the link between law and Christ's saving power was deepened, as was seen in the 1943 encyclical *Mystici Corporis* by Pius XII on the doctrine of the Church as the Mystical Body of Christ, there remained a perspective of the law that focused more on the power of governance of Pastors. As a result, there was a certain inability to integrate other aspects of ecclesial life (for example, the legitimate freedom and the rights of the faithful, the influence of charisms and of a healthy ecclesial pluralism, etc.). These limits help explain the crisis of meaning that afflicted canon law in the years around the most recent ecumenical council, Vatican II.[7]

**3.** The convocation in 1959 of a Conciliar Assembly by St. John XXIII was explicitly linked from the beginning to a reform of the Code of Canon Law. In fact, after the celebration of the Council (1962–1965), which ended during the pontificate of St. Paul VI, a great deal of time was spent working on a new Code, which was ultimately promulgated in 1983 by St. John Paul II as a document closely tied to the Council. Despite this, it is clear that, especially in the years immediately after the Council but also afterward, *canon law has gone through an unprecedented crisis within the Church itself.* This crisis does not concern only one or another aspect of the ecclesial juridical order, but affects the very *raison d'etre* of the law in the Church, first accepted with equanimity, but then viewed with impatience, if not with open hostility. This climate has certainly diminished since 1983, but there remains an atmosphere of indifference regarding canon law, almost as if it were some kind of lesser evil to be endured, or something that in any case is of interest only to specialists; that is, to canonists.

How can this crisis of the notion of ecclesial law be explained? Certainly there is nothing in the conciliar texts that can justify it. Indeed, the Council itself, in its decree on priestly formation, *Optatam Totius*, famously maintained that the teaching of canon law "should take into account the mystery of the Church, according to the dogmatic constitution *De Ecclesia* promulgated by this sacred synod" (n. 16). This reference to the constitution on the Church *Lumen Gentium* shows a fundamental method for a deepening of one's conception of canon law.

The ecclesiological teachings of the Council with juridical significance are manifold. One thinks, for example, of those that concern the hierarchical constitution of the Church itself: the Council highlighted episcopal collegiality, the sacramentality of the episcopate, the power proper to bishops in their dioceses, as well as the two-part dimension of the Church—that is to say, both its universal and particular elements. All this was done in such a manner that is in no way opposed to papal primacy and the demands of the unity of the Church. *The most important novelty of Vatican II with respect to juridical matters, however, concerns the comprehensive presentation of the Church as the People of God*, adopted by *Lumen Gentium* when expounding its doctrine regarding the Church as a whole. The fact that this

Constitution discusses first that which concerns the entire People of God (in chapter II)—that is, before moving on to what specifically concerns the hierarchy (in chapter III) and the laity (in chapter IV)—is extremely significant for the conception of the notions of right and law as they relate to this People of God. In fact, *a plan of equality for all the faithful in the Church* is clearly outlined, prior to any hierarchical distinction and one not altered by such a distinction. "The state of this people is that of the dignity and freedom of the sons of God" (*Lumen Gentium*, n. 9b). This condition of *dignity and freedom* possesses in itself an undoubtedly juridical relevance, one that is reflected in the renewed conciliar awareness of *the rights of the faithful* (see, e.g., *Lumen Gentium*, n. 37, *Apostolicam Actuositatem*, n. 3d).

Yet the crisis in the life of the Church regarding canon law has been and continues to be real. It is true that the crisis not only does not find a foundation in the teachings of Vatican II, but that it should be overcome precisely on the basis of the Council. Nevertheless, it must be recognized that the conciliar documents lack an overall exposition on the law and rights in the Church that would apply the ecclesiological doctrine of *Lumen Gentium* to it. In our opinion, this lacuna is simply due to the fact that at the time there was not a sufficiently mature doctrinal elaboration in this regard. During the years of the Council there still prevailed a notion of the juridical domain of the Church understood as simply a set of laws emanating from the power of jurisdiction. In this framework, it was truly difficult to translate the new insights (or, rather, the rediscoveries) of Vatican II into juridical concepts.

Indeed, *this same conception of rights and the law so tied to authority alone was the primary object behind the crisis of canon law.* The newfound awareness of the equality among the faithful, and of their liberty and their rights, led in many ecclesial circles to a sharp reaction against canonical laws, and ultimately to an attitude of opposition towards hierarchical authority. The law appeared to be an obstacle to the freedom of Christians and of communities as they tried to follow the charisms of the Spirit. Thus existed a widespread and popular climate in which the traits of rigor, uniformity, and formalism were often emphasized in law—traits that were to be overcome in a simplistic manner through mercy, pluralism, and spontaneity. These latter terms reflected an absence, or at least a drastic decrease, of the sense of law and all of its typical points of reference: norms, trials, sanctions, etc. In all of this, the reaction against the disciplinary order and authority that had been for so long insistently emphasized was of considerable importance. Still, it should not be forgotten that in the 1960s the entire Western society was involved in a profound crisis of values, which often included the rejection of anything reflecting authority, institutions, and traditions.

*1.4. The post-conciliar debate on fundamental questions regarding ecclesial law*

**4.** Parallel to the work of drafting the new Code, an unprecedented and still ongoing scientific debate took place with respect to the existence and the foundations of the law and rights in the Church. The very depth of the crisis provides the background for the appearance of the debate as one of the positive effects of the crisis. While some authors continued to be more or less bound to older positions, new approaches emerged. Although some of these innovative approaches had already begun before the Council, in the post-conciliar phase they marked authentic *currents in canonical science.*

A sector of canonical doctrine, close to the so-called "progressive" tendencies and marked by *pastoral* concerns, sought to make the Church's legislation as flexible as possible, as well as its interpretation and application, in order to make it more suitable to the pastoral needs of each person and each group. This current retains the view of the juridical domain as a set of laws or norms, but removes the traditional sense of obedience to authority and its connection with morality, and tends to relativize the precepts of divine law and their authentic interpretation by the ecclesiastical magisterium.[8] From this point of view, the rights of the faithful take on a variable content, depending on the alleged pastoral needs in each circumstance. Obviously, this approach, while maintaining the external aspects of juridical technique, not only does not overcome the crisis of canon law, but uses juridical instruments to counter the cornerstones of rights and law in the Church, thereby preventing the finding of authentically pastoral solutions. A crystal-clear example of the consequences of this approach is evidenced by declarations of matrimonial nullity seen simply as manipulable instruments in the face of certain pastoral problems. Under such an approach, one proceeds as if the "solution" could ignore the truth about the existence (or not) of the matrimonial bond; at the same time, this truth is manipulated in different ways, thus tending to reduce marriage to a mere form of living together.

Another current insisted on conceptualizing ecclesial law as a *theological reality*, thus attempting to go beyond any approach based merely on the natural law. Special importance was given to the school which is based on Klaus Mörsdorf, a professor in Munich in Bavaria.[9] In response to criticism of Sohm, Mörsdorf emphasized the fact that the law intrinsically belongs to the Church, and argued that the juridical dimension exists in the same elements with which the Church is built; that is, in the Word and the Sacrament. Word and Sacrament, therefore, appear as intrinsically juridical realities, thus explicitly refuting the notion that the concept of law is something extrinsic to the salvific-ecclesial reality. Canonical science is, therefore, under Mörsdorf's view, a theological science that operates with a juridical method.

Among the disciples of Mörsdorf, Eugenio Corecco radicalized this vision.[10] Corecco, in fact, went so far as to emphasize the total detachment of ecclesial law from secular law, arguing that they were not law in the same sense, but only in an analogous way. In positing that ecclesial law and secular law were essentially different realities, Corecco pointed to the fact that the theological virtues (especially charity) refer to the first, and that the cardinal virtues (including "justice" in the sense of the *ius suum cuique tribuendi*, which in the Church would be surpassed by charity) refer to the second. Corecco viewed ecclesial law from the perspective of *communio*; that is, the reciprocal immanence between different elements (as an individual person and Church, the common priesthood and the ministerial priesthood, the universal Church and the particular Church, etc.). As such, under Corecco's view, canonical science is a theological science with a theological method. This school has certainly contributed to the awareness of the supernatural nature of the concept of the law in the Church of Christ. Its main limitation, however, comes from its lack of an in-depth analysis of the specific reality of the law, so that the essence of the law in the Church remains obscure.

A third trend is represented by those authors who have tried to better understand the authentically juridical character of canon law. The school headed by Pedro Lombardía and Javier Hervada, professors in Pamplona (Navarra), stands out here. In these authors there has been an interesting process of clarification and deepening of the essence of the juridical phenomenon. Distancing themselves from any juridical positivism (which reduces law to positive human norms), they first became aware of the truly juridical nature of divine law (both natural and positive), as an integral aspect that, together with human law, constituted one juridical order of the Church. Then they realized that canon law was not reducible only to a discipline and an authority, but also denoted a reality arising from the legitimate freedom of the faithful. Thus, they saw that the fundamental rights of the faithful are founded on the truth of the Church, and therefore were not opposed to discipline and authority. In recent years, Hervada has proposed to review canon law in the light of the classic concept of right as the object of justice.[11] The following exposition is rooted in this juridical realism, since we consider this approach to be a fundamental prerequisite for finding a renewed sense of rights and the law which, avoiding many misunderstandings, is able to enhance the implementation of the dimension of justice within the People of God.

## 2. The concepts of right and law in general

### 2.1. The various meanings of the word "diritto" (law, right)

**5.** In Italian, as well as in many other languages, the term "diritto" has different meanings, among which the best known are that of a *set of rules governing social relationships* (or the *science that studies these rules*) and that of an *ability or a claim by which one can demand something from others.* In the first sense we speak of Italian "law," or of "commercial law"; in the second, it is said that someone exercises or claims a "right." In some languages, this phenomenon does not exist and the two meanings correspond to two distinct words, as happens in English with the words "law" and "right."

In this way of conceptualizing the notion of right and law, a long and complex historical process is crystallized, which inexorably leads to the *separation of law from justice.* In fact, the "law as norm" (and also the "power to demand" that it must be based on) tends to appear more and more as an instrument of command and sanction, admitting of any content, so that the nature and juridical validity of the norm does not depend on its substantial conformity with the demands of justice deriving from human nature. These "demands of justice" are not only considered to be largely relative and open to debate, but are thought to be an extra-juridical matter.

For example, the "law" could establish the beginning (and the end) of the limits for the protection of human life, as well as what forms of sexual unions that could be socially accepted.

Wholly different from this notion is that concept of right (*ius*) handed down to us by Aristotle (*to díkaion*; i.e., that which is just in an objective sense[12]), by the Roman jurists ("justice is the constant and perpetual will to give to each that which is his own right,"[13] according to the text of the jurist Ulpian), and by St. Thomas Aquinas (who speaks of right (*ius*) as "*ipsa res iusta*," or "the right thing itself"[14]). In this tradition, the enduring validity of which has been shown by authors such as Michel Villey and Javier Hervada,[15] *the concept of right is inseparable from justice, as it is precisely its object, that is to say, that which is just.* Acting according to justice means giving to each one that which is his right. Consequently, *this right (this just thing) precedes justice,* the latter being defined by this presupposition.

In order to better understand the juridical world, it seems essential to us to recover this classic vision of realism. It is not a question of ignoring other concepts (i.e., law as a norm or as a set of norms, or right as the ability to demand something), but rather to situate them as *subordinate to the idea of "that which is just."* Norms are juridical insofar as they really constitute rules of justice; the ability to demand exists as a consequence of a right; that is, of a just thing that really belongs to the subject. It is interesting to note, after all, that in the concept of *human rights,* so present in contemporary culture, a content of justice is clearly insinuated, and this content is a substantial value that cannot be reduced to a "power to demand" that is merely legal or founded on force and subject to arbitrariness.

*2.2. Analysis of the right as that which is just*

**6.** *The concept of right understood as that which is just* can be described as: a) *a thing or reality or good,* understanding these terms in a broad sense, which includes not only physical goods external to man but also dimensions of the person himself (life, freedom, reputation, work, etc.); b) *that belongs to a human person or to another subject that transcends the individual, as "his";* that is, as an object that is in the sphere of his competences (obviously the same thing can be the right of different subjects, but under different aspects: for example if one owns a house, and the other rents it); and c) *insofar as it is owed to him by another subject,* such that the latter must "give" to the other that which is his, in order to allow him the effective exercise of his dominion over the thing (this "giving" can mean transferring or giving something back, acting in a certain way or simply respecting the rights of others, a very important modality for coexistence according to justice).

This means that the concept of right always connotes a relationship between at least two subjects, in which *the existence of a right on the one hand and the existence of a juridical debt or duty on the other are inseparable*. For the actual existence of a right, the relationship of domination between the first subject and that which belongs to him is not enough; what is required is the actualization or conservation of that relationship which depends on the human action of another subject. From this perspective, the juridical order appears as that totality or network of multiple juridical relationships of justice, the holders of which are, in the last analysis, human persons (inasmuch as the other social subjects are always constitutively dependent upon human persons).

The classic *essential properties of right (ius)*, i.e., *otherness or intersubjectivity, obligatoriness, demandability, as well as coercion or an ability to be coerced*, find in this vision a natural explanation, inasmuch as they correspond to those characteristics deriving from the essence of the object of the juridical relationship. In fact, "that which is just" always postulates the existence of at least two subjects (otherness or intersubjectivity), one of which has a debt to give to the other—the *ius suum* of the latter (the obligatoriness). The social demandability, which can include, in case of necessity, even the legitimate use of coercive force, is a consequence of the particular obligation of the debt of justice, which is not only moral but also concerns the respect or satisfaction of the rights of others. However, it is important to emphasize here that the duty of justice, based on rights, exists regardless of whether the person entitled to the respective right exercises his or her right to demand compliance. There are holders of certain rights who are, unfortunately, completely defenseless, of whose protection the law and authority should take special care (think, for example, of human persons not yet born).

The relations of justice are given above all between individual human persons, as they must mutually respect the rights of one another, including those deriving from mutually agreed-upon contracts as well as those relating to the reparation of damages caused to others (these contractual and compensatory obligations are considered part of the ambit of the classical concept of *commutative justice*). The existence of the community—understood in the broadest sense, from the State to the most elementary of associations—entails new juridical relationships between the community and its members. On the one hand, given that every social group is at the service of people, who retain their autonomy with regard to the whole, there are relations of *distributive justice*, according to which the community must assign social goods to its members, who are holders of corresponding rights. The criteria for such distribution are proportional in nature and vary according to the types of community. On the other hand, the members of the community must do what is required for the common good, which must be determined by the laws (understood in a very broad sense, and not limited to those of the state) that regulate social life. As a result, this type of *justice* is called *legal*.

### 2.3. Right as a reality proper to the human person as such

**7.** The essential features of right that we have just indicated allow us to penetrate the anthropological, and ultimately metaphysical, presuppositions of juridical reality. In the first place, the concept of right understood as that which is just presupposes that *the human person is the holder of rights*; that is to say that rights are something that belongs to the human person as such. Only people (or collectivities ultimately made up of people) can have rights, because only they are beings in the earthly world endowed with a dignity of their own that never permits them to be exploited for the good of others or the community. Personal being implies the ability to have a certain dominion over one's own being, as well as over one's acts and external objects. This dominion can be put into action by those who are able to exercise their freedom and responsibility, but there exist circumstances—either transitory or habitual—that can impede such an exercise of dominion. Therefore, the active (or actual) dominion does not belong to the essential constituent of man's personality, which also exists in people unable to understand and choose or who suffer from any limitations or illness. *Being a holder of rights is essentially linked to being a human person*. In the right to life of every human person at any moment of his earthly existence, the personal nature of the right is seen in all its radicality and simplicity as that which is just.

15

The concept of right also presupposes the existence of at least two human persons. What belongs to one of them—that is, his right—is right or just if and to the extent that the other is obliged to respect it or to render it if it were within the other's sphere of power. Thus, *the concept of right is a personal reality with a relational nature*. In it, that interpersonal relationality which is intrinsic to the very essence of the human person becomes present and operative. In the ambit of rights and the law, human persons enter into a relationship, given that rights and the correlative juridical duties are relational realities of a personal nature. The fact of being the holder of a right to life that everyone is obliged to respect, or the fact of being two persons obliged to reciprocal performances established by means of a contract, are everyday examples of the juridical relationality inherent to the nature of any person in this world. The concepts of right and law are best understood in the perspective of human coexistence and relationality, as a specific form of relational coexistence.[16] Seeing as how interpersonal relationships are placed on multiple levels (solidarity and charity, friendship, various associative bonds, including those pertinent to the political community, etc.), which are then intertwined, it is worthwhile to determine the specific content of a given *juridical relationship*. It can be described as relationality according to justice, which means that a person's possession of a good that is the object of right depends on the personal action of others; that is, of the one who has a debt of justice related to that right.

Human juridical reality certainly presupposes the personal being of man and his relationality as a person. However, rights and the law are also essentially linked to the corporeal existence of man, given that social relationality concerns the external activity of people. Performing juridical duties or enjoying one's rights are human actions and situations that involve *the dimension of exteriority*. This does not mean, however, that only material goods can be the object of rights. On the contrary, the principal juridical goods are those inherent in the person himself and pertain to his most spiritual activities (life, liberty, good reputation, privacy, truth, etc.). The juridical specificity of these goods is certainly linked to their external and perceptible dimension, but this dimension cannot be separated from the overall human reality of these goods, which otherwise would become mere appearances, and not real. For example, when the rights of freedom of the person are recognized and protected, the objective juridical good is the same spiritual freedom of man in its visible manifestations. Justice is not satisfied with a false appearance of freedom, which hides a reality of unjust conditioning by refined and hidden forms of moral compulsion.

*2.4. Natural right and positive right: distinction and unity; the role of the legal system*

**8.** If the reality of rights and the law is brought into focus in such a way that juridical relationships are seen as a modality of interpersonal relations, and not as a mere system or technique for organizing the social life of man, then the decisive premise has already been set for the admission of *natural right,* that is, the right founded on the person in his natural essence, in his dual dimension as an individual being who is inherently social. This is true first of all because respecting what belongs to each means recognizing the dignity of the person, whose being is capable of having something as his own. It is also valid because the person is the holder of fundamental goods that are not attributed to him by any social system or by any agreement between the interested parties, but come from his nature itself (understood in a metaphysical sense, as the essence) of man: life, integrity, freedom, reputation, the ability to have assets, etc. In this sense, the best of the legal culture of our times recognizes the existence of *human rights*, which exist prior to any positive norms that might declare them. The substance of these human rights can find an objective, universal, and permanent foundation only in the nature (in the metaphysical sense) of the human person. It should also be noted that this conception is radically different from any sort of individualism. Indeed, human rights are inseparable from the correlative fundamental legal duties of the person. Nor should it be forgotten that every human right is a concrete reality, intrinsically often limited by the rights of others and by the needs of the common good, and that the competent juridical actors must participate in determining these limits, including those relating to public authority, to custom, and to agreements between the people themselves.

*The problem of whether natural right is recognized or not depends above all on the way of envisioning the concept of right in general:* if rights and the law are seen as power structures extrinsic to persons; that is, within the framework of legal positivism, natural right is considered *a priori* to be logically and structurally inadmissible. If, on the other hand, the concept of right is understood as pertaining to the reality of justice intrinsic to the human person, it appears as a reality inherent in the nature of the human person. This perspective on the concept of right obviously presupposes, in turn, a vision of man, with notions as person and nature that imply an anthropology based on the metaphysics of being.

*Legal positivism*, among its variety of forms, tends to see rights and the law as mere techniques for regulating social life, compatible with any content, and whose juridical value depends on the ability to effectively impose itself, resorting to force if necessary. In this way, rights and the law are understood as *extrinsic realities* with respect to the human person and man's actual relationships. Juridical regulation, in this view, does not depend on the demands of justice inherent in the social reality itself and in the being of man, given that these requirements would be only relative, and their translation into legal norms would only rely on social consensus or on the strength of those who impose such norms. Beyond being merely theoretical doctrines, such views are, unfortunately, often accepted in life and in juridical science today. It is clear that such perspectives not only prevent the acceptance of natural rights and of *objective* human rights—to use the expression of St. John Paul II[17]—but ultimately do not grasp the true meaning of juridical reality, which is thus subject to manipulation according to any interest, even against the most fundamental goods of the person and of society.

Juridical reality, however, is never purely natural. Multiple human interventions, by individuals and by communities, are required to recognize that which is in conformity with or appropriate to the nature of the human person, to make decisions within a wide range left to freedom in the way human life is organized, and to protect existing rights and the observance of corresponding duties. Positive rights and positive law are *inseparable from natural rights and natural law, and all these juridical phenomena constitute a single unitary reality.* The juridical order or set of juridical relationships includes both natural elements and positive elements. The distinction between the two levels—that is, between what proceeds from the nature of man and of things in relation to him natural rights and natural juridical law)—and that which comes from the competent and legitimate human will—(positive rights and positive law)—is certainly necessary, given that natural law represents the foundation and the inviolable limit of positive law. But the concept of right as that which is just is always something concrete, in which the natural and positive aspects are inseparable, seeing as how they are mutually required: it is not consonant with the historical reality of man to hypothesize a situation in which the nature of man and of things would be sufficient to resolve all juridical questions; and identifying rights and the law with positive law alone, detaching it from natural rights and natural juridical law, as legal positivism does, leaves the juridical reality devoid of any true anthropological and ethical foundation.

A very important aspect of positive law is the *juridical system* (more or less culturally developed) for the declaration or determination and for the protection of the rights and correlative duties of everyone. The very peculiarity of the concept of right, with its classic properties—its otherness, its exteriority, its obligatory nature, its demandability, and its coercibility— requires the existence of such a system, which overcomes the uncertainties and risks of spontaneous self-protection of one's rights. This system, composed of rules or norms, procedures, bodies, and also of concepts, principles, reasoning, etc. constitutes that world with which the ideas of right and the law are usually most immediately associated. It is the subject of a human specialization, represented by the social figure of the jurist (judge, lawyer, teacher, etc.). There is a danger of considering this specialized world as the substance of the phenomenon of law, consisting especially of norms, procedures, sanctions, etc. In such a way it would be forgotten that the juridical system, and the profession of the jurist, refer instead to an underlying and primary reality: the relationships of justice between persons (or between them and social groupings). Consequently, it cannot be argued that rights and the law are something essentially instrumental. That which is instrumental is the system or the technique that serves to render operational rights and duties, by means of their declaration, determination, and protection (through rules, procedures, sanctions, etc.). As we have seen, the existence of *the juridical domain prior to the juridical system* must be especially affirmed; that is, the existence of natural rights, which precede human rules and procedures.

## 3. Ecclesial right as that which is just in the Church

*3.1. The revealed truth about the Church, a prerequisite for the understanding of its juridical dimension*

**9.** *The understanding of ecclesial rights and the law rests on two foundations: the revealed truth about the Church, and an adequate conception of right and law.* Indeed, it is not possible to know what is meant by rights and the law in the Church if one does not have a knowledge of the essence of the Church. An external description of the Church founded by Christ is not enough, in the same way as any religious phenomenon of a social nature. Even less convincing would be those approaches that limit themselves to pointing out similarities with other social realities, such as associations or States. The only way to adequately grasp the essence of canon law is to situate it in the mystery of the Church, according to *the Church's own self-understanding.* As we have already mentioned, the conciliar direction on the teaching of canon law in priestly formation is often cited, which can be applied by extension to any attempt to understand rights and law in the Church: "[T]he teaching of canon law . . . should take into account the mystery of the Church, according to the dogmatic constitution *De Ecclesia* promulgated by this sacred synod" (*Optatam Totius*, n. 16). "I believe the Church": it is precisely in this article of the Christian and Catholic faith that the place of canon law must be sought. It is therefore logical that the conciliar passage just mentioned refers to the teaching on the Church of the same Council in the dogmatic constitution *Lumen Gentium.* Only in the light of the faith, inseparable from the authentic guidance of the Magisterium of the sacred Pastors, is it possible to discern what ecclesial right and law are in their proper essence.[18] Otherwise there are only superficial and partial approximations, based on aspects that are common to other social realities, which focus on peripheral issues (organizational, formal, patrimonial, etc.) or, worse still, claim to transfer to the Church models incompatible with its own foundational characteristics (challenging, for example, its hierarchical dimension).

Attempts were made during the years after Vatican II to establish canon law on the basis of various aspects of conciliar ecclesiology: the Church as the People of God, the Church as sacrament or as communion, etc. In reality, these are complementary ways that shed light on various aspects of the juridical dimension of the Church. But in order for these attempts to bear valid fruit, one must never lose sight of *the existence of right and law.* Just as there is the risk of uselessly seeking to base ecclesial law outside of the essence of the Church, there is the opposite risk of simply identifying it with this essence, as if it did not correspond to an intrinsic and specific dimension of the same essence. We would then fall back into the false contrast between juridical reality and theological reality, such that the sacramental and communal essence of the juridical would be affirmed, but in such a manner that this essence would remain in the shadows or, even, risk being conceived of something other than truly juridical.

Two ecclesiological notions that appear particularly helpful for understanding right and law as an intrinsic aspect or dimension of the Church of Christ are those of the Church as communion and of the Church as a sacrament.

*3.2. Ecclesial rights and law as aspects of the Church as communion*

*3.2.1. The relationship between right as that which is just and ecclesial communion*

**10.** Right as that which is just and ecclesial communion: these are the two realities that need to be put in relation in order to understand canon law. On the one hand, right is a personal and relational reality. It involves the existence of at least two people, between whom there is a specific relationship according to justice: one has the right, and the other has a correlative debt. The right of the first person is a true right, precisely because the other person must render it or respect it. The right, therefore, entails a well-determined modality of coexistence of persons, in which they mutually recognize themselves as persons insofar as they act in a just manner towards others.

On the other hand, communion is also a personal and relational reality. Before relating it to the right, however, it is advisable to distinguish between the *vertical dimension* of communion; that is, the communion of the human person and of the whole Church with God the Father in Christ through the Holy Spirit, and its *horizontal dimension*; that is, the one existing between human persons themselves, as the fruit of their common union with

God. These are two inseparable dimensions, given that the horizontal aspect is not a mere union on the human level, but is given only in the context of that overall reality which is communion with God and with one's brothers and sisters: the love of God requires the love of one's neighbor, and if this is to be lived out with respect to all, it obliges in a particular way with respect to one's brothers and sisters in the Church.

Within the horizontal ecclesial communion, the fundamental relationship is undoubtedly that of fraternal love. There are, however, other types of relationships in the Church, which are also always called to be lived out in love. In this sense, if there is something in the Church that belongs to every believer who is a member of it, and that is due to him by others according to justice, then in the Church there is that reality called right (as that which is just), and, as a result, there necessarily exist duties of intra-ecclesial justice.

Therefore, the existence of rights and justice in the Church appears when the very being of ecclesial communion is examined in its horizontal dimension. In this regard, another classical distinction must be introduced, corresponding to the soul-body composition of a human being; that is, between the *internal* and *external* aspects of communion, which are inseparable from each other. "Ecclesial communion is at the same time both invisible and visible. As an invisible reality, it is the communion of every human being with the Father through Christ in the Holy Spirit, and with the others who are fellow sharers in the divine nature, in the passion of Christ, in the same faith, in the same spirit. In the Church on earth, there is an intimate relationship between this invisible communion and the visible communion in the teaching of the Apostles, in the sacraments, and in the hierarchical order. By means of these divine gifts, which are very visible realities, Christ carries out in different ways in history his prophetical, priestly, and kingly *function* for the salvation of mankind. This link between the invisible and visible elements of ecclesial communion constitutes the Church as the *Sacrament* of salvation."[19] Later we will describe these visible elements of communion, traditionally enunciated in the following triad: the bonds of the profession of faith in the word of God, of the sacraments, and of ecclesiastical governance (see *Lumen Gentium*, n. 14b; canon 205). Viewed from a juridical perspective, these three elements of communion constitute the fundamental juridical goods in the Church.

*3.2.2. Juridical goods in ecclesial communion*

**11.** *Visible salvific goods, especially the word of God, the sacraments and the service of charity, are therefore the principal juridical goods in the Church.* Salvation in Christ and in the Church is universal, destined for all men: juridically this means that every human person has the right to receive the proclamation of the word of Christ entrusted to the Church, as well as the sacrament of baptism if he or she is well disposed. The baptized, in turn, have the right to receive the other sacraments, especially the Eucharist, the center of ecclesial communion, given that Jesus Christ himself is really present in it, offering himself as a sacrifice and giving himself as food under the species of bread and wine. The juridical good of the service of charity consists essentially in an activity of the faithful and of the Church institution which seeks to meet the material or spiritual needs of one's neighbor in an evangelical spirit, and is configured as the right of the faithful to participate in such service and the institutional duty of the Church to do so.

The reference to the Eucharist is decisive for understanding the juridical significance of the sacrament of Holy Orders, which enables some of the faithful to sacramentally represent Christ above all in the Eucharistic celebration, which constitutes an essential prerequisite for the Christian to be able to exercise his right to participate in the Eucharist. The right of the faithful to receive the goods of salvation from the sacred ministers, especially the word and the sacraments (see canon 213), shows the importance of *ecclesial juridical relations between pastors and the other faithful.*

The rights of the faithful exist also with regard to the entire Church, though, and therefore to one's brothers and sisters. There is a level of equality among the baptized, insofar as they share the same dignity as Christians and are entitled to the same fundamental rights and duties. On this level *there are true ecclesial juridical rights and duties among all the baptized as members of the Church.* It is sufficient to note here the obligation on the part of all the faithful to be in communion of the faith in the Church, an obligation that is correlative to the right of all of the other faithful to live in that communion; that is, not to be led into infidelity to the doctrine of Christ through the spreading of ideas that are contrary to the deposit of faith by other members of the faithful.

To the three main salvific juridical goods—i.e., the *word of God,* the *sacraments* and *the service of charity*—we must add two other salvific juridical goods that are of particular importance for the operation of the juridical sphere: the *liberty of the human person in the Church* and *the power of the ecclesiastical hierarchy*.

In the first place, "the glorious freedom of the children of God" (Romans 8:21), that liberty founded on the truth which is Christ (see John 8:32; 14:6), is an essential aspect of the condition of the faithful in the Church (see *Lumen Gentium*, n. 9b) and implies a right on the part of every believer, before all of his other rights, to lead a Christian life. This right of liberty pertains above all to the area of his *legitimate intra-ecclesial autonomy*, in accordance with the very personal determination of his Christian vocation (e.g., the election of one's state of life, the possibility of associating himself with others in the Church, the different modalities of participation in ecclesial life, making decisions in matters of legitimate debate, among others). This autonomy of the faithful within the Church, based on divine law itself, implies an area left open to the initiative and self-determination of each believer, without juridical obligations beyond those inherent in communion itself.

It is nevertheless advisable, however, to caution that this freedom of the Christian in the Church is also exercised by the observance of intra-ecclesial duties. These include not only those fundamental ones relating to communion, but also, and inseparably, to all those duties which involve determinations of a contingent nature, legitimately derived from ecclesiastical laws, customs, agreements, etc., Christian liberty is always vitally connected to *legitimate ecclesial discipline*, indispensable *hic et nunc* for the practical realization of the truth of being a Christian, which includes the observance of the concrete determinations required for the ecclesial common good and for the respect of the rights of others. Autonomy is, in a certain sense, *preeminent* over discipline, given that the greatest possible juridical autonomy of the faithful must be recognized and protected in the Church—befitting that inestimable personal dignity linked to the condition of being a child of God—precisely for the better realization of the Church's mission. Nevertheless, there is no real "right of autonomy" in the face of legitimate disciplinary requirements.

Along with the good of freedom, that of the *power of the Hierarchy in the Church* must be mentioned. Such a power embraces all aspects of the mission of the sacred Pastors: to preach and interpret the word of God with authority (*munus docendi*), to celebrate worship and to administer the sacraments (*munus sanctificandi*), to govern the People of God (*munus regendi*). In this third area, there is an aspect that is of singular importance from the juridical point of view: it is the power of governance (i.e., the *potestas regiminis*, which is more frequently called, in the canonical tradition, the *potestas iurisdictionis*; that is, the power of jurisdiction). The juridical relevance of this aspect derives from its own effects, directly connected with the declaration and determination of intra-ecclesial juridical relations, both in general (with laws) and in particular (by administrative acts and judgments). In this way, the holders of the power of government declare, determine, and protect that ecclesiastical discipline to which the faithful must freely adhere, mindful of the power conferred by Jesus on the Apostles: "Amen, I say to you, whatever you bind on earth shall be bound in heaven, and whatever you loose on earth shall be loosed in heaven" (Matthew 18:18).

The ecclesiastical authority integrates the traditional triad of the bonds of communion (see *Lumen Gentium*, n. 14b; canon 205), manifesting its particular operational relevance in the service of the principal goods of the word, the sacraments and the service of charity. The government of Pastors appears to be in an instrumental position with respect to those principal goods, but it is an unavoidable and essential means, of divine foundation, without which the true Church of Christ cannot exist. This good of hierarchical governance is juridical in this sense: the duty of obedience to such authority on the part of the faithful is correlative to the right of the Church and of the other faithful. In other words, it is just that ecclesiastical laws and other legitimate manifestations of this hierarchical power be observed, and it is unjust if they be disregarded. To be sure, the same hierarchy is the holder of juridical duties in the exercise of its power, and the faithful are holders of their own respective rights, including—though this is often not emphasized—the right of being able to effectively rely, at any time, on a structure of laws and on a government that is ecclesially just.

To penetrate the core of canon law, this consideration of the juridical dimension of salvific goods is fundamental. Nevertheless, it would be misleading to reduce canon law only to juridical relations immediately concerning these goods. The Church is composed of human persons with a natural juridical patrimony, which continues to exist in the canonical context. As a result, such rights of each and every person in the People of God must be recognized as such; *natural personal goods* (e.g., life, liberty, good reputation, privacy, etc.) exist also in intra-ecclesial relationships. It would obviously not make sense to invoke such goods against the ecclesial communion itself, as if, for example, the natural rights of freedom that belong to a person could be legitimately exercised in the Church independently of the faith and ecclesial discipline. This would contradict the very membership of the faithful in the Church, and would mean ignoring that natural freedom which is harmoniously integrated in Christians as their supernatural freedom as children of God—a good which is inseparable from ecclesial communion. Moreover, to justify the existence of the duties of a Christian within the Church, a consideration of simple natural law will suffice: active participation in any social grouping requires by its nature the observance of the respective duties with regard to the body as a whole and to the other people who belong to it.

Furthermore, given that the Church lives in this world, canon law also concerns *temporal goods* that serve the mission of the Church. These include not only patrimonial assets, but also other human means of various types (organizational, formal, procedural, or those relating to communication, among others). These goods can be the object of relations of justice in the Church, insofar as they fall within the juridical dimension of communion. From a juridical point of view, those means that are aimed precisely at the configuration, realization, and protection of that which is just in the Church (norms and juridical acts, sanctions, trials, etc.) have special importance. Ignoring or undervaluing these technical means would render canon law inoperative, making it appear as mere theory and not as an essentially practical reality in ecclesial life.

*3.3. The relationship between right as that which is just and the sacramentality of the Church*

**12.** Another perspective from which ecclesial rights and law can be considered, complementary to that of communion, is offered by the sacramentality of the Church. At the beginning of *Lumen Gentium*, it is stated that "the Church is in Christ like a sacrament or as a sign and instrument both of a very closely knit union with God and of the unity of the whole human race" (n. 1). We are not dealing here with the notion of sacrament in the strict sense, applicable exclusively to the seven sacraments of the New Covenant instituted by Christ, but with an analogical extension of the concept to the whole reality of the Church. In effect, only the sacraments properly so-called produce their effects with that maximum objective efficacy called *ex opere operato*; but every ecclesial action participates in some way in the sacramentality of the Church. In fact, in every action two aspects can be distinguished, one perceptible and another imperceptible, being the first sign and instrument (in a broad sense) of the salvation wrought by Christ and, in Him, by the Church. This sacramental structure rests on the sacramental nature of Christ's human nature itself, as an instrument of salvation in the unity of the person of the Word (see *Sacrosanctum Concilium*, n. 5a).

The sacramental perspective is intertwined with two other ecclesiological concepts of a dynamic type: that of *mission*, and that of *mediation*. In fact, the mission of the Church, which throughout history continues the mission of Christ in the Holy Spirit, is carried out in a sacramental way (in the broad sense of the term; that is, without limiting itself to the paradigmatic case of the seven sacraments), given that it involves an activity in which visible and invisible aspects intertwine. "All power in heaven and on earth has been given to me. Go, therefore, and make disciples of all nations, baptizing them in the name of the Father, and of the Son, and of the Holy Spirit, teaching them to observe all that I have commanded you. And behold, I am with you always, until the end of the age" (Matthew 28:18–20). In these words of Jesus to the Apostles, applicable to the Church of all times, the substance of the mission of salvation entrusted to the Apostles is manifested, and the connection appears between the presence and power of Christ, on the one hand, and, on the other hand, the faithful fulfillment of the works through which He makes himself present and active: the teaching of the Gospel, the administration of baptism (and the other sacraments), the practical observance of the doctrine of Christ. It thus appears clearly that in those works there is a real mediation of the Church with respect to the salvation of men accomplished by God. And it is also clear that this ecclesial mediation is a participation in that of the only mediator between God and men, Christ Jesus, true God and true man (see 1 Timothy 2:5–6).

How do ecclesial rights and law participate in the sacramentality of the Church; that is, in the mission of sacramental mediation entrusted to it by Christ? In this regard, the following passage from *Lumen Gentium* is often quoted: "The society made up of hierarchical organs and the Mystical Body of Christ, the visible assembly and the spiritual community, the Church of the earth and the Church now in possession of heavenly goods, they are not to be considered as two realities, but form a single complex reality resulting from a human element and a divine element. By a not weak analogy, therefore, it is compared to the mystery of the Incarnate Word. In fact, just as the assumed nature is at the service of the divine Word as a living organ of salvation, indissolubly united to him, in a similar way the social organism of the Church is at the service of the Spirit of Christ who vivifies it, for the growth of the body (cf. Eph 4:16)" (n. 8a).

These general considerations must be applied to the specific reality of rights and the law in the Church. However, it is necessary to try to determine more in what the sacramentality of ecclesial rights and the law consists precisely from the juridical point of view.

From the point of view of its finality, canon law participates in the sacramentality of the Church insofar as its ultimate goal, as has been traditionally asserted, is the salvation of souls (*salus animarum*). To testify to this, an explicit reference to the *salus animarum* as the *suprema lex* in Ecclesia was included in the last canon of the CIC (cf. c. 1752). In more recent times this truth has been expressed through the idea of the intrinsic *pastoral dimension* of law in the Church.

This teleological consideration must, however, be completed through the specific consideration of what canon law is, so as to discover not only the ultimate purpose to which it tends, but also the *way* in which rights and the law in the Church, as juridical realities, are dynamically ordered to that same end. To describe this way, it should be remembered that the juridical ecclesial dimension, understood as what is just in the Church, belongs on the one hand, like every juridical reality, to the visible and external sphere, and on the other hand it concerns, as its main specific object, precisely those salvific goods to whose diffusion the activity of the Church is directed (word of God, sacraments, etc.). *The sacramentality of the juridical in the Church highlights precisely the intrinsic link between the observance of what is just in the Church and the fulfillment of the saving mission.* In the context of the dimension of justice in the People of God, there is therefore that intrinsic connection between visible ecclesial actions and the invisible effects of grace that is described through the concept of sacramentality, or sacramental mediation, of the Church. This connection exists both in the person who holds the right to receive salvific goods, and in the holder of the corresponding duty of justice. In fact, the right to salvific goods depends on one's own sanctification and on the possibility of actively participating in the apostolic mission of the Church; the corresponding duty—to give or respect the rights of others and of the whole Church to salvific goods— is a juridical requirement which, like any true duty but for a reason strengthened by the importance of its object, represents for the obliged Christian himself a fundamental way for his own salvation, through which he also contributes to the implementation of the Church's mission.

According to spiritualistic anti-juridicism (see n. 1), the denial of canon law is based on the denial of the sacramentality of the Church, or of some constitutive element, since in this way law remains meaningless in the saving economy. It can continue to be defended as an organizational requirement, or as an inevitable lesser evil, but it is impossible to situate it intrinsically in the mystery of the Church. Justice between brothers, or between Pastors and their own flock, ends up being a relative question, since the same points of reference for the visible objectivity of communion and its consequent juridical requirements are lacking. This explains why the efficacy *ex opere operato* of the sacraments, the function of the ecclesiastical magisterium in authentically—and sometimes infallibly—declaring the word of God, and the ability of the Church to establish a truly binding discipline, are so decisive in founding one's own right according to the self-understanding of the Catholic Church. Equally objective as well as truly sacramental is the legitimate freedom of the faithful in the Church, insofar as the authentic freedom of the person—in no way opposed to the bonds of communion—is what allows it to correspond to the divine plan of salvation.

Even when juridical relations concern purely human goods, such as patrimonial ones, there is no doubt that these goods are a matter of intra-ecclesial justice only in so far as they are linked with the Church's mission of salvation. Therefore, even in this case the juridical-ecclesial dynamic belongs to the salvific dynamic of the Church.

*3.4. Divine law (positive and natural) and human law: the perspective of what is just*

**13.** To adequately understand the juridical in the Church, it is necessary to deepen the distinction between divine law and human law. The approach from the point of view of the law boasts a consolidated tradition in the canonical context. It is connected to that fundamental distinction, concerning any juridical sphere, between the law founded on the very nature of the human person in his own sociality (natural law), and the law constituted by the legitimate decision of men (positive or human law). Divine law in the Church includes natural law: ecclesial law, as a supernatural juridical order, incorporates and strengthens what God himself as creator has imprinted on human nature as his essential order of justice. But the constitutive core of ecclesial law is of a supernatural nature (while always assuming natural elements): it is the positive divine law, which constitutes the dimension of justice of the saving economy established by Christ the Redeemer. This law is positive because it comes from a gratuitous intervention of God, who in the fullness of time sent his Only Begotten Son, whose saving work the only Church founded by himself is a perennial sacrament. Finally, in the Church there is a law of human origin, called "human," "ecclesiastical" law (not to be confused with the so-called "ecclesiastical law of the state," i.e. the state law on religious matters) or simply "positive" (in the usual usage this term designates the positive human law, not the positive divine one). Summarizing these distinctions, *canon law is partly divine, natural or positive law, and partly human law.*

This distinction considers the juridical from the point of view of its origin or source. We try to clarify what is the efficient cause and the foundation of what is juridical. The importance of this doctrine consists above all in recognizing that *there are juridical aspects that derive from the very being of the Church and of the human person.* They are essential and permanent aspects, and therefore no one can change them. The Church herself, by virtue of her *fidelity to Christ* her Lord, not only cannot contradict divine law, but must actively commit herself so that it is implemented and lived in the realization of the mission of salvation.

As we said, in the exposition of many authors the distinction between divine and human juridical aspects is normally formulated from the perspective of law: we think respectively of the divine and human norms that regulate ecclesial life from a juridical point of view. This perspective is certainly valid, but it can be integrated into the more essential one, namely, of the right as that which is just. *Divine right is that which is just in ecclesial reality itself (including the aspects of natural right present in it).* For example, the rights of the faithful and of the Church, the hierarchical constitution of the Church, the content of the salvific goods (word of God, sacraments, etc.), possess an essential and permanent nucleus, which the Church must preserve and make fruitful, without ever being able to modify it, much less eliminate it. Of course, in all these cases there are norms of positive divine law, promulgated through divine revelation (Sacred Scripture and Tradition). However, it is important not to lose sight of the fact that divine law and rights are inherent in visible ecclesial realities: they possess, according to God's saving plan, an essential juridical dimension. We must avoid any idea according to which their divine juridical dimension would depend on the voluntaristic application of an extrinsic norm. Seen in this way, divine law risks transforming itself into a mere external limit, which one seeks above all to diminish and relativize, as if it were an obstacle to the freedom of the Church and of Christians, when the truth is that divine law is that which makes the human person free in the juridical field (cf. John 8:32).

The rights in the Church that have a human origin represent what is just because it is legitimately established by a competent human actor. Normally, in this field the intervention of the Hierarchy is considered almost exclusively, which through ecclesiastical laws or other positive norms determine ecclesial rights. And it is true that the function of authority is of great importance, because it has the task of protecting divine rights, which are declared by human norms, and of introducing those universal and particular determinations required by the common good. But the role of all the faithful should not be underestimated, both in the knowledge of divine rights and law through their sense of faith (not in opposition to the Hierarchy, but vitally united with it), and in the determination of the historical aspects of human rights and law. Just think of the juridical relevance of the behavior of the faithful in the Church (cf. n. 62), or of everything that falls within the sphere of legitimate juridical autonomy of the baptized (for example, in the configuration of associative initiatives in the Church).

The realistic consideration of right as an object of justice also helps to understand that the divine and the human in the juridical domain are not two parallel systems. Rather, they are *two dimensions of the same juridical realm understood as a unitary reality*, made up of elements of divine origin and others of human origin. In reality, the divine and the human do not exist as complete and separate realities, since the former always requires a historical realization, in which necessarily there are contingent elements, and the latter necessarily postulates a divine foundation, without which it would have no real juridical value. With this the distinction is not denied, nor deprived of relevance, above all because one must always act with a sense of profound respect for divine law and rights, adapting oneself to the declarations of the authentic magisterium of the Church. The danger of a reductive vision of divine law is avoided, as if it were limited to some rare fundamental questions, and instead did not affect the whole order of intra-ecclesial justice. Law and rights whose source is human must be constantly interpreted and, if necessary, improved in the light of divine law and rights.

### 3.5. Canon law and secular law[20]

**14.** Another crucial aspect for a correct understanding of canon law is its comparison with secular law. In the period following the Second Vatican Council, much emphasis was placed on the specific nature of canon law, perhaps as a reaction to a previous tendency that was not very sensitive to this aspect. Beyond the positions of the various schools of thought, there is wide agreement that *ecclesial law is neither conceivable nor enforceable if its constitutive and permanent reference to its ecclesial specificity is ignored.* Consequently, trying to indiscriminately transfer concepts, institutions, and experiences from other juridical spheres to the canonical field would preclude any true understanding of the law and rights in the Church. Just as it would not make sense to develop, for instance, a science of maritime law by uncritically applying results from terrestrial activity; that is, without taking into account the reality of the sea and of man's relationship with it, so too with canon law. In other words, it must be placed in the context of the Church, which is constitutively supernatural, and therefore accessible as such only through faith.

*This does not mean in any way whatsoever, though, that canon law is law in an essentially different sense from that of secular law* (as Corecco's thesis of analogy would argue; see number 4, *supra*). If it were so, not only would there be a direct opposition to the canonical tradition, which has always recognized its common affinity with secular law (represented above all by Roman law), in the juridical world, but the value of law itself from a human and a Christian perspective would be thrown in doubt, given that it would not be considered assumable in the ecclesial sphere. These views, of a spiritualistic nature, contrast with those expressed by the pastoral constitution *Gaudium et Spes* when it affirms that "the very Word made flesh willed to share in the human fellowship," and that the Lord, in "willingly obeying the laws of his country, He sanctified those human ties, especially family ones, which are the source of social structures" (n. 32b). In the conciliar text such human solidarity is in continuity with fraternal communion, which is the Church as the Body of Christ (cf. n. 32d).

The tendency to purify canon law from any contamination with realities incompatible with the being of the Church is very understandable if we keep in mind to what extent the legal culture of modernity has conceived of notions of right and law in such an inadequate way. Positivism, compatible with either the liberal or the collectivist view of rights and the law, has dominated the scene, and continues to largely dominate it in practice, despite the fact that its radical inability to offer a convincing explanation of juridical phenomena has now been established. Nevertheless, it should be emphasized that *positivism, liberalism, and collectivism are inadequate to understand any right and law, not just ecclesial right and law.* The right as the object of justice is neither positivistic, nor liberal, nor collectivistic: it is an intrinsically personal and relational reality. Therefore, rights and the law belong to the realm of authentic human realities, to which the salvation of Christ extends. Nothing therefore prevents them from also being assumed within the People of God, logically in a manner consistent with the specific—and indeed unique—character of that People.

Their common membership in the juridical world allowed in the past for reciprocal and fruitful *exchanges between canonical juridical science and experience and that of the secular.* For this reason as well canon law occupies a place of honor in the global history of rights and the law. In the current situation, these interdisciplinary relationships are both very desirable and advantageous. The canonist can learn from the valid developments in the various branches of contemporary juridical science, without however yielding to the temptation of a simplistic mimicry, ignoring the juridical needs of the Church as well as of her true situation in every place. At the same time, there is no doubt that the secular jurist can benefit greatly from that human and Christian patrimony of juridical culture taught by the ecclesiastical magisterium and contained in the living canonical tradition.

On the other hand, it is certainly necessary to reaffirm that *knowledge of canon law requires supernatural faith,* without which its object—intra-ecclesial justice—remains deprived of a certain point of reference, as it is seen as something merely human and contingent. Without faith, one can certainly know a great deal about canon law, but its very substance is ignored, given that at most it is taken as a highly respectable cultural product, without realizing instead that it is a source of objective justice or injustice in the area of the salvific economy. On this constitutively supernatural basis, the field of canon law is vitally linked to theology, especially ecclesiology as well as sacramental theology, moral theology, among others. But it always remains a juridical science, whose formal object is that which is just in the Church. The methodological confusion, which tends to convert canonical science into a theological discipline in the strict sense, loses among other things its practical sense of direct service to the implementation of the order of justice in the Church. Therefore, expressions such as "the theological nature of canon law," despite the aspects of truth that such articulations can convey—in the sense of affirming the supernatural nature of the juridical dimension of the Church—should be better specified, so as to avoid any interpretation that might imply even an indirect denial of the scientific specificity of juridical knowledge in the Church, or a positivistic understanding of this specificity.

*3.6. Canon law in the life of the Christian and of the Church*

*3.6.1. Intra-ecclesial justice as a moral and juridical requirement of the faithful; canonical equity*

**15.** It is very frequently believed that canon law concerns canonists exclusively; that is, specialists in juridical-ecclesial science and technique. The need for specialization in this field, as in so many others concerning the doctrine and life of the Church, is beyond doubt. However, we must not lose sight of the fact that canon law, especially if understood as that which is just in the Church, is an ecclesial reality which by its nature is of compelling interest to each and every Christian and to each and every community of the faithful. *They who must be just in their ecclesial actions are, above all, the baptized themselves.* The precepts of the Church mentioned in the catechesis point out some particular duties of every Catholic,[21] which at the same time possess a personal dimension (of minimal participation in the salvific goods) and a communal dimension (of the ecclesial common good). This last dimension implies the existence of true duties of intra-ecclesial justice.

On the other hand, every member of the faithful is bound to respect the rights of his brothers and sisters, first and foremost the right to live in ecclesial communion and to exercise legitimate freedom in the Church. From this point of view, the faithful themselves play a leading role in canon law. In fact, *the faithful have rights inherent in their status as baptized persons.* Such rights concern, above all, the salvific goods of communion: the word of God, the sacraments, the service of charity, the legitimate freedom of the faithful person himself, the power of the Hierarchy. Sometimes it is feared that these rights are understood in terms of contrast with the needs of communion and of the hierarchical constitution of the Church, as if they were subjective and arbitrary claims, and possibly even contrary to the goods of communion and set against obedience to the Hierarchy. This approach is favored by a vision of the concept of right as a simple faculty of demanding or claiming (i.e., a subjective right), detached from its object—i.e., from that thing which is objectively just, which establishes and limits the claim. Such an approach also forgets that the right establishes in every case, and therefore also in the Church, something that which is owed to a person, a debt towards him (given that the demandability by the holder of the right is only a consequence of the debt, and not the constitutive element of the right as that which is just). In the Church that which is due to each one is directly in the service of the salvation of the one to whom Christ has destined the saving goods. Depriving someone of the authenticity and integrity of the word of God, or of the sacraments when there are no obstacles posed by the same subject, or of legitimate freedom, constitutes an injustice of particular gravity.

*Being just in relation to the Church and to one's brothers and sisters in the faith constitutes a juridical and moral requirement at the same time.*[22] The duty of justice on the part of a member of the faithful is also juridical insofar as it is based on a right of others. The same duty of justice is moral because the personal good of the same obliged faithful depends on it; if he acts unjustly, he damages himself in the first place, in that by his own action he does not respect the demands of that communion within which he is being saved. In fact, acts that juridically contradict communion; that is, acts in which a member of the faithful becomes unjust with respect to his brothers and sisters, rupture the external bonds that bind someone to the Church and that are a part of the individual's own personal path of salvation.

Consequently, being faithful to the doctrine of Christ authentically taught by the Church, participating in divine worship and receiving the sacraments according to their saving truth, fulfilling the laws legitimately issued by the hierarchical authority, are obligations of conscience for the faithful, expressions of their fidelity to Christ and to the Church. Canon law cannot be seen as a purely external order to ensure efficacy in common action and the absence of conflicts among the People of God. The order of canonical justice, rather, concerns the very center of the salvific economy: salvific goods, starting with the word of God and the sacraments. For every Christian, this order is therefore an essential part of his vocational commitment. This means that the juridical aspect, in its essential elements, not as a specialization, must be part of the formation common to all the faithful. In preaching and in catechesis, this juridical dimension of Christian life within the Church must be taught to all. When we talk about the requirements of the virtue of justice, attention almost always focuses on those that pertain to civil coexistence. Without taking anything away from this, it is also important to form also a sense of intra-ecclesial justice, with the goal of discovering its salvific importance.

Despite their intimate interpenetration, *it is necessary to distinguish law and morality*, avoiding undue confusion. The juridical perspective possesses its own legitimate autonomy, as it examines problems from the point of view of that which is externally just; that is, inasmuch as the right is respected by others. Social demandability cannot go beyond, even in the Church, the scope of what is a juridically obliged. On the other hand, the demands of the moral good far exceed the juridical ones. Additionally, the rights, by their very nature, need human determinations of a historical and contingent nature; these determinations are often foreseen by general rules. Judging the juridical and moral value of these determinations in individual cases is not always an easy task, which we will discuss later (see number 51, *infra*).

*The intra-ecclesial justice of the Christian, like every other virtue, must be animated and surpassed by charity.* Being just in the Church is an aspect of the Christian vocation to holiness and to the apostolate, and therefore it must be enlivened by love for God and neighbor, a love that will lead to a generous self-giving that goes far beyond the rights of others and of the Church. But *charity does not eliminate justice*; the virtue that is characterized by having the right as its object. Considering charity to be an immediate principle of canon law would prevent us from grasping the juridical specificity of the latter. It is true, however, that at times the holder of the right is morally obliged in charity not to make use of some of his rights, if he judges that more serious damage for the Church could result from such exercise. Furthermore, in some cases charity itself may require that he modify the juridical relations that are in his power. These are cases in which *equity* operates (often called "canonical equity" within the Church), understood as the virtue that tempers, out of kindness or mercy, the rigor of justice alone.[23] This occurs, for example, when a debt is forgiven (in a matter that allows it), or when the authority itself establishes some exceptions to the laws (dispensation, privilege, etc.), or when penalties are subject to remission or mitigation, without however injuring the good of the community. However, under no circumstances is it permissible to authorize injustice in the name of charity, as would happen, for example, if a valid marriage were to be declared null in order to allow the parties to remarry. In such cases there would be neither true justice nor true charity.

### 3.6.2. Justice in the community life of the Church

**16.** After having examined the juridical domain from the perspective of the faithful, it is helpful to consider its intrinsic communitarian dimension. This dimension is inherent in the very being of the right, as a relational reality between people (property of intersubjectivity) accompanied by the other classic essential properties of juridicity (exteriority, obligatoriness, enforceability, etc.). This involves a specific social operation, which gives rise to the existence of a juridical system (composed of bodies, rules, procedures, sanctions, etc.) tending towards the effective realization of that which is just in social life.

Rights in the Church, because they are true rights, possess the essential properties of every right, and thus require their own operative juridical system. Naturally, the singular characteristics of the Church have implications regarding this, so that, for example, one cannot think that the enforceability provisions or sanctions in ecclesial law are a simple transposition of those found in the laws of states or other secular social realities. There exists, nevertheless, an essential core, representing that which is found in common concept of right (*ius*), the negation of which would question the very existence of rights in the Church.

For example, the ecclesiastical penal system requires a way of proceeding that is appropriate to a reality such as the Church, which seeks not only to ensure justice internally, but also the salvation of all, including those of the faithful who are guilty of a gravely unjust action in the ecclesial sphere. Thus it is understood how the most typical canonical penalties, the medicinal ones (or censures), are directly aimed at the conversion of the guilty, which must be remitted when the guilty person has truly repented of the crime and has done as much as possible to repair the damage or the scandal (see canon 1358 § 1, in relation to 1347 § 2). Regardless, it would be contrary to the true spirit of justice which is essential in the canonical penal system to remit the medicinal penalty for a member of the faithful who refuses to repent (see the same canon 1358 § 1). On the other hand, there are also canonical expiatory penalties (the most serious of which is dismissal from the clerical state), the operation of which is independent of the conversion of the offender, given that they seek above all to protect the rights of the ecclesial community.

*Intra-ecclesial justice is inserted, as an intrinsic dimension, into the life of the Church as a whole.* This life cannot be conceived without the juridical, not in the sense of human norms (which, however, have always existed), but in the sense of that which is just in the Church. An ecclesial life on earth without rights and the law is simply an impossibility, a utopia contrary to the demands of Christian vitality itself, personal and communitarian, which could conceal all kinds of injustice. Equally, it would be completely misleading to want to limit ecclesial life to juridical aspects only. The defect of juridicism derives precisely from an exaggeration of law, which would overlook the other dimensions of the Church, starting with the priority of charity. Such an exaggeration would also translate into the pretense of resolving pastoral problems by means of the juridical system alone. This would be extremely dangerous, because it could often lead to the opposite extreme; that is, to claiming to resolve them without taking justice into account. Charity must inform everything, even the life of justice, which, however, is an indispensable prerequisite for being able to broadly advance the service of the Church and of souls.

**17.** *Rights and the law are closely linked with governance and the administration of justice in the Church, but they are not identified with these functions.* Such an identification more or less clearly accompanies a normative conception of the juridical, in which it would be considered a set of laws and other norms and acts with which the governing power (i.e., those with the power of jurisdiction) directs ecclesial life. The functions of legislating, administering, and judging, integrating the aforementioned power, are certainly very relevant in the juridical-canonical work. Ecclesiastical laws determine rights and duties with regard to the ecclesial common good; singular administrative acts ensure that the government practically affects concrete situations, in everything that belongs to the jurisdictional power of those governing; sentences of ecclesiastical courts declare what is just or decide upon sanctions. Nevertheless, the essential juridicity of these functions rests not so much on the ecclesiastical power that is exercised in them, but rather on their connection with the rights and duties of the faithful and of the Church. Thus, these functions are juridical to the extent that they contribute to the configuration and protection of the rights of persons and institutions in the Church. What is more, these rights depend above all on divine law, and the freedom of the faithful themselves also plays a very significant role in them, by means of which they marry, follow other vocations in the Church, associate, choose (to a large extent) where and how to participate in the salvific goods, etc.

That said, it should be remembered that the government of the Church includes many aspects that are not attributable to functions strictly belonging to the power of governance. At all levels, governance involves aspects of planning, promotion, and verification, which in turn require the use of various means, among which personal dialogue, collegial study, and institutional communication stand out. It is a question of generating an environment of mutual trust, based on the common interest of the authority and of all the faithful that supports the entire work of the Church. Given the fact that Pastors, as members of the faithful themselves, are recipients of the pastoral concern of the Church, this working together for the Kingdom of Christ is naturally and obviously opposed to any conception that would put into opposition hierarchical governance on the one hand and the freedom of the faithful on the other. All this in the Church is then inseparable from its being a community that celebrates the sacramental Sacrifice of Jesus and that prays with Him. Governing the Church includes many human and supernatural aspects, intimately linked in the unitary reality of the ecclesial mystery.

It follows that the prudence of those who govern in the Church requires at all times a careful consideration of the various aspects of justice, including the more formal or technical ones such as the precise formulation of norms and of acts, procedural and formal requirements, etc. (which are also indispensable for the human operation of any system of law). It would be a very harmful illusion, though, to think that this was enough to really govern the Church. Pastoral problems require people to be kept in mind above all, as well as concrete circumstances, in order to be able to take appropriate government measures. Furthermore, one must always govern with a sense of the whole, which unites the smallest community of the faithful with the universal Church. *Juridical-canonical prudence must therefore be integrated into a broader and more comprehensive prudence of governance. In this way pastoral justice is in turn inserted into pastoral charity.*

Similar considerations apply to the other aspects of the ecclesiastical ministry, and concretely to those which have care for souls as their object. The juridical dimension of their pastoral work includes the dimension of justice inherent in the ministry of the word, the administration of the sacraments, the leadership of their communities, and all aspects of the pastoral function. *A sacred minister must always respect and promote the rights of all the faithful with whom he enters into a relationship, indeed of all the human persons he meets, inasmuch as they are holders of the right to receive the Gospel of Christ.* The juridical aspect of the ministry cannot therefore be reduced to certain formal or bureaucratic acts, however necessary they may be, but encompasses rather the entirety of their ministry, in which the virtue of pastoral justice must be lived out day after day. This justice must then open itself to the horizons of Christian charity, and specifically of pastoral charity, which requires from the Pastor a complete dedication of his life to all of the persons entrusted to him.

The life of the Church herself as an institution must always be governed by charity, not only with respect to the participation in salvific goods, but also in the sphere of goods linked to the natural life of human beings (food, health, education, etc.), first of all in the service of needy brothers and sisters, and then to all people in need. As Benedict XVI taught in his first encyclical,[24] the organized expression of works of charity constitutes a specifically ecclesial task, being inseparable from the proclamation of the word of God and the celebration of the sacraments. Such work cannot simply be left to others, although collaboration with all religious and civil institutions engaged in similar fields is highly desirable. This gives rise to multiple questions of true intra-ecclesial justice vis-à-vis the entire Church, beginning with those concerning the Catholic identity of charitable organizations linked to the Church. In this aspect there is also therefore a special inter-relationship between justice and charity.

### 3.7. Knowledge of canon law as knowledge of that which is just in the Church

**18.** It is usually thought that the canonist; that is, one who knows canon law, is the expert in canonical norms and in their application. The essential knowledge in this field would be that of the canons, to find those relating to each matter or case and to be able to interpret them in such a way so as to identify plausible solutions to problems that emerge.

This description of juridical-canonical knowledge undoubtedly captures at least one true aspect, but is unable to capture it entirely, given that it loses sight of the essence of the concept of right as that which is just. In this latter perspective, *what the canonist—as a jurist—seeks to know is this: the relations of justice that exist in the Church, and, therefore, the just solution that should be given to the questions posed by ecclesial life.* To this end, familiarity with canonical norms is certainly necessary, as they are precisely rules of justice, which declare divine rights and law and determine positive rights and human law (see chapter III, *infra*). However, it must not be forgotten that the fundamental point of reference for the interpretation of the same rules is the intrinsic justice of intersubjective relationships. This realism makes it possible to understand the true meaning of the rules, and to ascertain the limits proper to every human norm, before which justice itself recommends separating oneself from the text in order to better identify the substance of canon law: intra-ecclesial justice (on the interpretation of the laws, see numbers 53–55, *infra*).

Knowledge of canon law is of various types. There is a basic knowledge, which must be part of the formation of every Christian. In addition to general scientific preparation on rights and the law in the Church, sacred Pastors need particular familiarity with the practical aspects most connected with the exercise of their ecclesiastical ministry. Therefore, courses on canon law are compulsory in seminaries.[25] More specialized knowledge is necessary for those who work in the administrative or judicial sphere of the Church, or who dedicate themselves to teaching and research in this field. It is for this very reason of scientific rigor that canon law, as a discipline of study, was born in the medieval university (see number 30, *infra*), and that, in addition to its presence in some civil law faculties, it is at present fostered in the ecclesiastical faculties of canon law that exist in various countries.[26] Various factors must be included in the formation of a canonist, corresponding to the very nature of canon law: the knowledge of rights and the law in general and the consequent possession of an authentic juridical mentality, a solid philosophical and theological preparation in full harmony with the Catholic faith, as well as the specific competence required of a canonist.

There are different *levels* within canonical knowledge.[27] In the first place, there is the immediately practical knowledge of that which is just in the individual case: it is *juridical-canonical prudence*. The ecclesiastical judge, whose function consists precisely in declaring what is just in concrete situations, is the one who must exercise this prudence par excellence. But it is also proper to all those who work in the judicial field (defenders of the bond, advocates, etc.), each according to his or her role, and also extends outside trials, so as to resolve all the questions of justice that arise, with good sense and with a truly Christian spirit. Although the practical canonist must know canonical science, his prudence can never be reduced to a mere application of theoretical notions, given that it requires contact with concrete reality, and the discovery of the demands of justice inherent in it. As a result, the canonist is often called on as a consultant to collaborate in the configuration of human law when juridical documents of various kinds are being drafted.

The second level of knowledge of canon law is that of *canonical science*, concerning the development of an abstract and systematic knowledge on rights in the Church. At times juridical science takes into account the essential and immutable principles of an ontological nature, such as when it is affirmed that every man is the holder of rights based on his dignity as a human person.[28] But juridical science, in its peculiar abstraction, must take into account the contingent historical realities and the cultural creations of man, especially those related to the operation of the juridical system itself. In this way, a set of concepts, principles, and rules come into play with respect to scientific concepts called "institutions" (for example, trials, benefices, prescription, etc.), which represent the intellectual resources that the jurist then uses in practice. The legacy of juridical science has a progressive historical configuration, and includes aspects of a rather permanent nature, belonging to the more or less common juridical culture of humanity, as well as certain aspects that are more contingent and circumscribed. It should then be borne in mind that, alongside concepts, there are "types" (of acts, entities, crimes, etc.); that is, ideal patterns or models that describe and regulate concrete reality through a reference to some generally found characteristics—a type—thus rendering possible a link between that reality and certain juridical effects, with the consequent advantages of economy and legal certainty. In the demarcation of administrative or jurisprudential juridical types, juridical science plays an important role, as a critical instance, both when proposing the creation of new types and when evaluating existing ones. The technique of the type itself requires constant attention to the evolution of social realities in order to reflect them as best as possible—naturally within both the natural and positive demands of justice—and to implement the appropriate correction mechanisms in individual cases. It should never be forgotten, in fact, that the type corresponds to a general description so as to simplify the attribution of some juridical effects, such that the search for just solutions based on types requires always taking into account the needs of justice of the concrete case.

Throughout history and even at the present time, the activity of canonical science has focused a great deal on *the exegesis of normative texts*, especially laws. This operation of legislative hermeneutics is certainly essential, but it must be integrated, as in fact occurs in juridical science in general and also in the more developed canonical science, into a *treatment of a systematic nature*. Such treatment means that juridical matters are presented on the basis of doctrinal concepts and principles, which while certainly taking into account a current juridical system, also involves distinguishing between the methodology for drafting normative texts, and that for deepening the knowledge of the order of justice in which a given text operates. An adequate systematics ultimately favors a much more lucid and coherent exegesis.

The third level of the integral knowledge of canon law postulates a level of a fundamental or ontological nature, such as the one that was prevalent in this chapter, and which will often be present throughout the book. This is an authentically juridical knowledge, but one that is aimed at the essential principles of ecclesial rights and law. This *theory of the foundation of canon law* does not constitute a part of theology in the proper sense, given that its formal object remains in the sphere of right and justice. Of course this does not mean denying the legitimacy of a properly theological discourse on rights and law in general, and on that of the Church in particular. In such a discourse, which is divided into the plurality of specializations of theological science (e.g., ecclesiology, moral theology, pastoral theology, etc.), the formal perspective is constituted by the relationship of rights and law with the mystery of God itself, and therefore does not concern a formally juridical knowledge.

The three levels of knowledge indicated above are closely linked to each other, and cannot proceed separately. Prudence requires not only an awareness of the results of science, but even more so a mindfulness of the principles of a fundamental nature. Science is nurtured by both the knowledge of practical cases and the deepening of the foundations: otherwise it is an exercise in sterile, self-referential reflection. A theory that regards the foundational aspects remains faithful to its object only if it positively takes into account the entire dynamics of knowledge and of juridical practice: otherwise, it turns into empty speculation. Indeed, although there are certainly important propositions at each of the levels described, it must be borne in mind that in reality the three types of knowledge, in different doses, always work together. When one insists on sealing off one of the levels from the others in order to absolutize it, the epistemological status of true juridical knowledge is immediately lost: prudence is transformed into arbitrariness, science into an auto-referential abstract, and a theory on the foundational aspects into lucubration that has lost its harmony with its object—that is, with rights and the law.

In turn, juridical-canonical knowledge, like any true knowledge, must be open to other knowledge that can illuminate and enrich the knowledge of rights and the law in the Church. In the case of canon law, this need for *interdisciplinarity* is particularly evident. Traditionally, canonical science has been viewed in a kind of intermediate position between theology and the science of civil law. From both of these sides, canon law can and must receive a great deal, but can never renounce its own specificity. A similar need for fidelity to one's object on the part of the canonist occurs today in the relationship with the psychological and psychiatric sciences in the context of the causes of matrimonial nullity concerning consensual capacity.

**19.** Bibliography

a) on the vision of right and of justice in general on which this book is based:

Aristotle, *Nicomachean Ethics*, Book V.

J. Hervada, *Critical Introduction to Natural Right,* Wilson & Lafluer, Montréal, 2020.

J. Pieper, *The Four Cardinal Virtues*, University of Notre Dame Press, Notre Dame (IN), 1966.

J.-P. Schouppe, *Le réalisme juridique*, Story-Scientia, Brussels, 1987.

S. Thomas Aquinas, *Summa Theologia*, II-II, q. 57 ss.

M. Villey, *La formation de la pensée juridique moderne : cours d'histoire de la philosophie du droit*, edited by S. Rials, Presses Universitaires de France, Paris, 2003.

b) on diverse positions regarding the foundations of canon law after the Second Vatican Council:

*Il concetto di diritto canonico*, edited by C.J. Errázuriz M. e L. Navarro, Giuffrè, Milan, 2000.

J.M. Bahans, *La nature de droit canonique. Essai de théorie et de théologie du droit*, Les Presses Universitaires—Institut Catholique de Toulouse, Toulouse 2019.

E. Corecco, *The Theology of Canon Law: a Methodological Question*, Duquesne University Press, Pittsburgh, PA, 1993.

P. Erdö, *Teologia del diritto canonico. Un approccio storico-istituzionale*, Giappichelli, Turin, 1996.

C.J. Errázuriz M., *Justice in the Church. A Fundamental Theory of Canon Law*, Wilson & Lafleur, Montréal, 2009.

J. Hervada, *Las raíces sacramentales del derecho canónico*, in *Sacramentalidad de la Iglesia y sacramentos. IV Simposio Internacional de Teología. Pamplona, abril de 1983,* EUNSA, Pamplona 1983, pp. 359–385.

Id., *Pensamientos de un canonista en la hora presente*, Servicio de Publicaciones de la Universidad de Navarra, Pamplona, 1989.

G. Lo Castro, *Il mistero del diritto*, 3 vol., Giappichelli, Turin, 1997–2012.

K. Mörsdorf, *Lehrbuch des Kirchenrechts auf Grund des Codex Iuris Canonici*, I, 11a. ed., F. Schöningh, Munich—Paderborn—Vienna, 1964.

Id., *Schriften zum Kanonischen Recht*, edited by W. Aymans—K.-Th. Geringer—H. Schmitz, F. Schöningh, Paderborn—Munich—Vienna—Zürich, 1989.

L. Örsy, *Theology and Canon Law: New Horizons for Legislation and Interpretation*, The Liturgical Press, Collegeville, MN (1992).

C.R.M. Redaelli, *Il concetto di diritto della Chiesa nella riflessione canonistica tra Concilio e Codice*, Glossa, Milan, 1991.

## Notes

1   See R Sohm, *Kirchenrecht*, 2d ed., Duncker und Humblot, Berlin 1923 (reprinted, 1970), I, pp. 1–2.
2   See, respectively, canons 8 and 9 in *De sacramentis* and canon 8 in *De baptismo* of the 7th Session, 3 March 1547, in Denzinger—Hünermann and Fastiggi, Ignatius Press, San Francisco 2013, 1608–1609 and 1621.
3   See Session 23a., June 15, 1563, *in ibidem*, 1763–1778.
4   See the Dogmatic Constitution *Pastor Aeternus*, June 18, 1870, *in ibidem*, 3050–3075.
5   Among the many magisterial documents that defend the Church as a sovereign society with respect to the state, we should especially remember *Immortale Dei*, the November 1, 1885 encyclical of Leo XIII (in ASS, 18, 1885–86, pp. 162–175).

6   *See,* e.g., A. Ottaviani, *Institutiones iuris publici ecclesiastici,* 4th ed. emendata et aucta iuvante prof. I. Damizia, Typis polyglottis vaticanis, 2 vol., Civitas Vaticana 1958–1960. On the historical development of this science, see A. de la Hera—Ch. Munier, *Le Droit Public Ecclésiastique à travers ses définitions,* in *Revue de Droit Canonique,* 14 (1964), pp. 32–63.

7   Nevertheless, as should be obvious, the question of power remains absolutely key to the understanding of rights and the law in the Church. Moreover, the real task of the *Ius Publicum Ecclesiasticum,* adequately renewed, continues to require specific scientific treatment.

8   Among the most well-known theorists of this line was the Dutch Peter Huizing and the North American Ladislas Örsy, the latter of whom was more moderate in his statements but employed the same basic approach. See, e.g., Örsy, *Theology and Canon Law: New Horizons for Legislation and Interpretation,* The Liturgical Press, Collegeville, MN, 1992.

9   On his doctrine, see K. Mörsdorf, *Lehrbuch des Kirchenrechts auf Grund des Codex Iuris Canonici,* I, 11a. ed., F. Schöningh, Munich—Paderborn—Vienna, 1964, pp. 1–26; Id., *Schriften zum Kanonischen Recht,* edited by W. Aymans—K.-Th. Geringer—H. Schmitz, F. Schöningh, Paderborn—München—Wien—Zürich 1989. Among the most important disciples of Mörsdorf in the field of fundamental questions are the German Winfried Aymans, the Swiss Eugenio Corecco and the Spaniard Antonio Rouco Varela. The Polish Remigiusz Sobanski occupies a similar position to this school.

10  See E. Corecco, *The Theology of Canon Law: a Methodological Question,* Duquesne University Press, Pittsburgh, PA, 1993.

11  See J. Hervada, *Las raíces sacramentales del derecho canónico,* in *Sacramentalidad de la Iglesia y sacramentos. IV Simposio Internacional de Teología. Pamplona, abril de 1983,* EUNSA, Pamplona, 1983, pp. 359–385; Id., *Pensamientos de un canonista en la hora presente,* Servicio de Publicaciones de la Universidad de Navarra, Pamplona, 1989, pp. 27–63.

12  See his *Nicomachean Ethics,* Book V.

13  "Iustitia est constans et perpetua voluntas ius suum cuique tribuendi" (*Digest,* 1,1,10).

14  *See* his *Summa Theologiae,* II-II, q. 57, a. 1, ad 1. An excellent presentation of the Thomist doctrine is found in J. Pieper, *The Four Cardinal Virtues,* University of Notre Dame Press, Notre Dame (IN), 1966.

15  *See* M. Villey, *La formation de la pensée juridique moderne : cours d'histoire de la philosophie du droit,* edited by S. Rials, Presses Universitaires de France, Paris 2003; J. Hervada, *Critical Introduction to Natural Right,* Wilson & Lafluer, Montréal 2020. As an historical-systematic exposition of this line of thought, see J.-P. Schouppe, *Le réalisme juridique,* Story-Scientia, Brussels 1987. In the following exposition I closely follow Hervada's doctrine.

16  From this perspective, see the philosophical investigation of S. Cotta, *Il diritto*

*nell'esistenza. Linee di ontofenomenologia giuridica*, 2nd ed., Giuffrè, Milan, 1991.

17 The expression "objective human right" was used by John Paul II in the programmatic encyclical of his pontificate, *Redemptor Hominis*, 4 March 1979, n. 17.

18 For an introduction in ecclesiology, besides the exposition of the *Catechism of the Catholic Church* (nn. 748–975), it is advisable to read the two fundamental magisterial documents of the 20th century in this area: The encyclical of Pius XII, *Mystici Corporis*, on the doctrine of the Church as the Mystical Body of Christ (29 June 1943), and *Lumen Gentium*, the dogmatic constitution on the Church from the Second Vatican Council.

19 Congregation for the Doctrine of the Faith, *Communionis Notio*, "Letter to the Bishops of the Catholic Church on some aspects of the Church understood as communion," May 28, 1992, n. 4. We cite it below with the abbreviation *CN*.

20 The discussion that follows addresses only the fundamental problems regarding the proper understanding of both laws, and not the questions relating to their mutual relationship, which must be dealt with in the context of relationship between the Church and civil society.

21 See *Catechism of the Catholic Church*, nn. 2041–2043.

22 Sometimes this distinction between law and morality in the Church is expressed through the formula "external forum" (juridical) and "internal forum" or conscience (moral). However, the more proper meaning of this terminology is different, referring instead to the different modalities, respectively public or occult, of exercising the power of governance (see canon 130).

23 The definition that Hostiensis attributes to St. Cyprian is famous: "aequitas est iustitia dulcore misericordiae temperata" (*Summa*, Scientia, Lugduni 1537/Aalen 1962, Lib. V, *de dispensationibus*, 1, p. 289r). It must be borne in mind that with the name of equity (or *epicheia*), one can also see an aspect of the same virtue of justice. It is a question of the justice of the particular case, which arises because of the imperfections of the general human rules (on this point see number 51, *infra*).

24 See the second part of the encyclical *Deus Caritas Est*, "On Christian Love," December 25, 2005, especially #25.

25 See *Optatam Totius*, n. 16d; canon 252 § 3; Congregation for the Clergy, *The Gift of the Priestly Vocation. Ratio Fundamentalis Institutionis Sacerdotalis*, December 8, 2016, n. 174.

26 See the apostolic constitution regarding Ecclesiastical Universities and Faculties of Pope Francis, *Veritatis Gaudium*, December 8, 2017, articles 77–80; Congregation for Catholic Education, Norms for Application for the Faithful Execution of the Apostolic Constitution *Veritatis Gaudium*, December 27, 2017, articles 60–63. These documents embrace the changes introduced to

the apostolic constitution *Sapientia Christiana* of St. John Paul II (April 15, 1979), by the decree of the Congregation for Catholic Education of November 14, 2002, which among other things extended the program for a license in canon law from two to three years.

27  On the levels of juridical knowledge in general, see J. Martínez Doral, *La estructura del conocimiento jurídico*, Universidad de Navarra, Pamplona 1963; J. Hervada, in *Exegetical commentary on the Code of Canon Law,* edited by E. Caparros, Wilson & Lafleur—Midwest Theological Forum, Montréal—Chicago (IL), 2004, vol. I, pp. 27–38.

28  Although even in this case there are cultural aspects in the conception and formulation that go beyond the purely ontological level. One thinks, for example, of human rights as a way of presenting the natural rights of the person. These rights in the past were perhaps less well known, but they were certainly also considered under other classifications and points of view, starting with those pertaining to the realm of natural law and natural rights, of the virtue of justice and of the commandments of the second table of the Decalogue.

# Chapter II
## *CANON LAW IN HISTORY*

### A. INTRODUCTION: CANON LAW AS AN HISTORICAL REALITY

### 1. *The special relevance of the historical dimension in the canonical area*

**20.** *Law in an historical reality.* Every right, every law, exists over time and participates in the historicity of the human person and of his relationships and social groupings. Rights and law entail an interpersonal and institutional dynamic: the juridical world is never a fixed network of invariable relationships, but implies the continuous evolution of these relationships, which are born, transformed, and die. Furthermore, every juridical relationship always contains something unique and unrepeatable: no human history, not even juridical history, is a mere repetition in a series. On the other hand, juridical culture is also historical, because, like any human knowledge, it is vitally inserted into a tradition, and being a system of knowledge of a practical nature, it remains always closely tied to the experience of life. Of course, the historical evolution of the juridical legal world can demonstrate both progress and regression, both from the substantial point of view of justice itself and from the point of view of the technical effectiveness of the means used in the juridical system.

In the case of canon law, the importance of its historical dimension is unique. This peculiarity can be illustrated by two complementary considerations. In the first place, *the dimension of justice belongs intrinsically to the history of salvation.* It enters the historical scene of humanity in the "fullness of time" (Galatians 4:4), as the fruit of the redemptive Incarnation of the Word of God. That is, it is *linked to the same historical process of the foundation of the Church by Jesus Christ.* Therefore, it is a radically new law, not a simple human realization of the social dimension of natural religiosity. This novelty also exists with

50

respect to the proper law of the Old Covenant with Israel, which prepared the way for a new, definitive, and universal Covenant (see number 22, *infra*).

The special relevance of the historical dimension of canon law derives also from the fact that *the Church remains itself over time*. This reflects its divine being, given that not only its foundation but also its subsistence on earth until the end of time depend absolutely on divine action on the supernatural level of salvation. Christ expressly promised this indefectibility of the Church (see Matthew 16:18). "This Church," teaches the Second Vatican Council, "constituted and organized in the world as a society, subsists in the Catholic Church, which is governed by the successor of Peter and by the Bishops in communion with him, although many elements of sanctification and of truth are found outside of its visible structure. These elements, as gifts belonging to the Church of Christ, are forces impelling toward catholic unity" (*Lumen Gentium*, n. 8b).

The historical continuity of the Church of Christ renders particularly relevant the knowledge of the evolution of its law, as it is always connected to the same institution which transcends time. With two millennia of multicultural experience, the Church has learned how to distinguish between the unchangeable essential and the accidental contingent; in legal terms, between divine law and human law (see number 31, *infra*). The same experience shows the human contribution to ecclesial law; that is, the effort to live and configure in every time and place an order of justice in the Church that corresponds to the foundational plan of Jesus Christ. This effort is not a mere succession of unconnected moments, but represents a true tradition, the so-called *canonical tradition*. Along with the courage to recognize the human errors of the past—a "purification of the memory"[1] in the context of ecclesial rights and laws—it is necessary to take advantage of the valid achievements of the canonical tradition. Such achievements, while intended to bear fruit even in the present, are not, however, mechanically transposed. Rather, what is required is a process of constant revitalization and enrichment of an inherited patrimony. The Church is conscious of its absolute duty to faithfully preserve all that has been entrusted to it by Christ himself; for the same reason, the Church wants to keep what has been shown to be useful for that faithfulness, and wants to introduce prudently those changes that are demanded by the needs of that same faithfulness in every situation. The Code of 1983 itself, seeking to introduce the innovations of the Second Vatican Council, explicitly reaffirmed its continuity with the canonical tradition, and the hermeneutical function of the latter (see canon 6 §2).

## 2. The setting of the study of the history of canon law

**21.** Canon law can be conceived as the set of Church norms, or as what is just in the Church (see numbers 2–3, *supra*). These concepts give rise to two ways of understanding the history of canon law: as *a history of canonical norms*, and as *a history of intra-ecclesial justice*.

According to the first approach, the essential point of reference would be ecclesiastical norms; that is, the canons. What would be considered most relevant here would be knowing the historical origins of the canons, the transformations they underwent, their cessation, and their replacement by other norms. Of course, the reality to which they apply would be considered in some way, but always subordinate to the normative point of view, which would remain the real juridical reality. This logic leads to the conclusion that the early Church would have had a very limited law; the Church would be viewed as becoming increasingly juridical as the norms and specialized culture developed, historically culminating in the Middle Ages with the classical age of canon law.

The second approach, the one based on the right (*ius*) as the object of justice, cannot disregard norms and juridical culture. Nevertheless, juridical realism implies a radical change in the way of conceiving the history of any law. The essential point of reference is no longer the norm, but human beings and their interpersonal relationships. This does not mean that legal history loses its specificity, diluting itself in general history or sociology. Justice and injustice represent a peculiar object of human knowledge, with a historical dimension. The norms and culture of rights and law certainly contribute to determining the strictly juridical sphere, as they are instruments of that justice. However, the history of rights and law cannot be limited to that of legal texts, because what is right is understood primarily in the context of the life of real people and actual societies. Therefore, the general history, as well as all the specializations (economics, labor, art, etc.) and the other related disciplines (sociology, geography, etc.) are indispensable for a knowledge of the history of law understood in a realistic sense.

These considerations are fully applicable to canon law. It is impossible to develop its history on the margins of Church history, since intra-ecclesial justice is an intrinsic dimension of the very life of the People of God throughout the centuries. All aspects of ecclesiastical history, from the history of theology and spirituality to the history of its economic organization and its relations with temporal authorities, must be considered in order to understand the evolution of the relationships of justice in the Church. The contribution of sociology and of the other human sciences is certainly relevant,[2] but one must never forget the self-understanding of faith proper to the Church itself. In that self-understanding lies the true key to understanding its history, including its juridical history. Indeed, only in the faith can one find the reasons for what is specifically just or unjust in the Church.

This does not take away any relevance to the canonical texts (norms and other ecclesiastical acts with juridical effects, or manifestations of the culture of canonists): on the contrary, it allows the framing of them and the understanding of them in their juridical-canonical specificity. Precisely because they are specialized texts—that is, specifically connected with the dimension of justice in the Church—these texts occupy a place of special importance in the history of canon law. Nonetheless, this cannot let us lose sight of the priority of life, which in any event is never perfectly reflected in texts. Indeed, in some cases, lived experience follows alternative or independent paths. It is necessary, therefore, to have knowledge of other sources, not specifically juridical, that can show how juridical relationships have really been lived out in practice.

The history of canon law is usually divided into three parts or aspects: *the history of sources, the history of the science, and the history of institutions.* One thinks, respectively, of the following: First, we consider the canonical sources; that is, those causes that have contributed to the configuration of ecclesial rights and law. This would include not only the divine law inherent in the foundation of the Church, but also the norms of human law issued by ecclesiastical authority (or by the faithful within the sphere of their own competence), the various agreements between the Church and other social bodies, the singular administrative and judicial acts, etc. Canonical sources also include documents through which these causes are known (especially the so-called canonical collections). Second, we consider canonical science; that is, the works of those experts who cultivated the science and of those universities and research institutions where the science was developed. Third, we think of juridical-canonical institutions, understood as the main components of the ecclesial juridical order (e.g. the clergy, marriage, etc.). If the history of canon law is seen from the perspective of justice, the need to put these three aspects together becomes even more evident. If they are treated in isolation, however, the history of canon law cannot be adequately understood.

The history of canon law as a specialized discipline has developed over the past two centuries with growing scientific rigor.[3] A great deal of work remains to be done, however, both in terms of the editing of the sources (many are unpublished, and others—including those integrating the *Corpus Iuris Canonici*—lack a truly critical edition), and in terms of the study of institutions and the juridical-canonical life in all of its dimensions.

On the other hand, an even greater challenge is to recover the effective link between the study of the current law and that of history. Although the Code of 1917 positioned itself as being in close relationship with ancient law (*ius vetus*: see its canon 6), in point of fact, as indeed happened with civil codes, a substantial rupture in this relationship nevertheless occurred. With a few exceptions, canonists gradually felt less and less the need for a recourse to history, and this phenomenon was linked to a practically positivistic understanding of the canons. This perspective was effectively caricatured in the saying unveiled after the first codification: "*quod non est in Codice, non est in mundo.*" The damage deriving from this concept also impacts the historical knowledge of canon law itself, which owing to its separation from existing law may risk becoming mere erudition, thus losing its own juridical nature as well as its specific object.

This chapter offers a global panorama, focused (except in the part on origins) on the history of sources and of the science (seen together, given their inseparability), and with some indispensable references to the context of the history of the Church and its relationships with civil society.

## B. HISTORICAL PANORAMIC IN THE HISTORY OF THE CHURCH

### 1. Rights and law at the origins of the Church[4]

**22.** *In the Church of Christ there is an intrinsically juridical dimension from the beginning.* This affirmation is much easier to understand if a realistic conception of right is adopted as "that which is just." According to this concept, the juridical nature of the Church consists of the series of interpersonal relationships created in the new and definitive economy of salvation that has been established by Christ. If, on the other hand, we think of the juridical domain as a set of norms or as an object of a specialized science, we must recognize that the juridical-canonical system has developed slowly. Moreover, in this there is a human constant, perfectly respected in the divine foundation of the Church: life must precede human norms. Consequently, at the time of the Apostles and then during the time of the Fathers of the Church, the juridical dimension was seen and implemented in close symbiosis with the other dimensions of ecclesial life—i.e., the pastoral, moral, liturgical, etc.

*Ecclesial rights and law participate in the radical novelty of the order of Christian salvation*, and therefore cannot be conceived from the perspective of the law of the Old Covenant with the People of Israel. As St. Paul says, "when the fullness of time had come, God sent his Son, born of a woman, born under the law, to ransom those under the law, so that we might receive adoption" (Galatians 4:4–5). Certainly, among the many aspects of the history of salvation before Christ that are preserved and brought to their fullness, there is the same law of Moses in its properly moral aspects (above all the Decalogue): "Do not think that I have come to abolish the law or the prophets. I have come not to abolish but to fulfill" (Matthew 5:17). However, already from apostolic times it is clarified that the ritual and juridical-temporal structure of the Old Testament is transitory. In ecclesial law, that structure will be kept in mind, but only as an immediate institutional antecedent of the new Israel which is the Church,[5] and as a source of inspiration for certain juridical solutions.[6] The novelty—and the difficulty—in understanding ecclesial law comes precisely from the fact that it is a law of a salvific reality which is not primarily juridical, but one of grace. In the Pauline doctrine on justification by faith, there emerges in a forceful manner the notion of liberation from the precepts of the ancient law (such as circumcision), the significance of which was fulfilled with the arrival of Christ and his new Law (see Romans 7; Galatians 3).

Such liberation, however, is perfectly compatible with the existence of a juridical dimension in the Church of Christ itself. Obviously, at the beginning of the Church, the cultural and technical development and specialization of the juridical aspects in the People of God were lacking; the theses about the "non-existence" of the law at the origins of the Church often suffer from the current reduction of the notion of the law to its technical dimension. It is nevertheless possible to find an intrinsic dimension of justice in ecclesial interpersonal relationships. This dimension constitutes the substance of ecclesial law at all times.

The main source for knowing the essential juridical dimension of the Church is the *New Testament*. To search for rights and the law, it is necessary to broaden the investigation beyond simply explicit regulatory precepts.[7] In the *Church's mission itself* and in the way in which it gives rise to new relationships between men, the permanent foundations of canon law can instead be discovered.[8]

"All power in heaven and on earth has been given to me. Go, therefore, and make disciples of all nations, baptizing them in the name of the Father, and of the Son, and of the holy Spirit, teaching them to observe all that I have commanded you. And behold, I am with you always, until the end of the age" (Matthew 28:18–20). Jesus' mission passes to the Apostles and to the whole Church. The essential characteristics of this mission are the cornerstones of justice inherent in the definitive economy of salvation established in Christ.

The mission extends to all nations; it is *universal*. This implies an essential equality between men: "There is neither Jew nor Greek, there is neither slave nor free person, there is not male and female; for you are all one in Christ Jesus" (Galatians 3:28). The most important juridical question of the early Church concerns precisely the extent of this openness of the Church to the Gentiles. Saint Paul, the great instrument of the missionary expansion of Christians in the civilization of his time, united thanks to the Roman Empire, fought passionately to defend the freedom of Christians from the legal prescriptions of the Mosaic law, starting with circumcision. The first disciplinary intervention of the Church is the decision of the Council of Jerusalem around the years 49–50, which sanctioned that freedom, determining decisively the effective universality of the Church: "It is the decision of the holy Spirit and of us not to place on you any burden beyond these necessities, namely, to abstain from meat sacrificed to idols, from blood, from meats of strangled animals, and from unlawful marriage" (Acts 15:28–29). These exceptions were intended to avoid scandal on the part of the Jews.

To whom does the fulfillment of the mission entrusted by Christ belong? First of all, to the eleven *Apostles* who remained faithful, as well as to Matthias who replaced Judas the traitor (see Acts 1:15–25). In this substitution we can see the institutional nature of the Twelve, which is moreover evident from the moment of their special election by Jesus (see Matthew 10:1–4ff.). The Apostles have special powers in view of the ecclesial mission, first of all for the celebration of the Eucharist (see Luke 22:19; 1 Corinthians 11:24–25), for forgiving sins (see John 20: 22–23), to teach in the name of Jesus (see Luke 10:16), and to bind and dissolve; that is, by carrying out acts of government in the Church (see Matthew 18:18). Among the Apostles there is one, Peter, to whom belongs a unique mission, which gives him an effective primacy in the Church and in the Apostolic College (see especially Matthew 16:18–19; Luke 22:33; John 21:15–17). The Apostles will be joined by collaborators and successors, and at the same time the hierarchical structure of each local Church would be configured relatively early, with a Successor Bishop of the Apostles, assisted by priests and deacons. Peter's unique mission is linked to his ultimate seat in Rome, and therefore passes to the Roman Bishops.

Nevertheless, and in a manner that is completely harmonious with this special mission of the Apostles, equality between Christians as such is also reflected in the *participation of all the baptized in the mission of Christ and the Church*. In the first proclamation of the Gospel made by Peter as head of the Church, he quotes the words of the prophet Joel who thus describe the messianic era: "I will pour out my Spirit upon all flesh. Your sons and daughters will prophesy, your old men will dream dreams, your young men will see visions. Even upon your male and female servants, in those days, I will pour out my spirit" (Joel 3:1–2). This outpouring cannot be limited to extraordinary charisms, so important to the early days of the Church (see especially 1 Corinthians 12), but extends to the ordinary existence of Christians. One thinks, for example, of Paul's testimony regarding the family roots of the faith of his disciple Timothy: "I recall your sincere faith that first lived in your grandmother Lois and in your mother Eunice and that I am confident lives also in you" (2 Timothy 1:5).

The mission has a visible and social dimension, present in the three aspects indicated by Jesus in Matthew 28:18–20: *the teaching of the divine word, baptism (and other sacraments), and observance of the commandments of the Lord.* The word of faith appears as a "deposit" to be kept (see 1 Timothy 6:20; 2 Timothy 1:13–14). With this image taken from the juridical-contractual sphere, it is emphasized, on the one hand, that the good of the Word was given by Christ to his Church and, on the other, that it must be faithfully guarded, with the one in charge of the deposit not having any power whatsoever to change or alter the object entrusted to him. Similarly, baptism and the other sacraments have an essential configuration based on their institution by the same Christ. Therefore, for example, baptism must make explicit its Trinitarian reference (see Matthew 28:19), and the signs and words of Christ at the Last Supper become an indispensable reference point for every Eucharist: "Do *this* in memory of me" (Luke 22:19).

As for the commandments of the Lord, they certainly are, above all, those of Gospel morality, the essence of which is found in the Sermon on the Mount (Matthew 5–7; Luke 6:17–49). But there are also commandments concerning ecclesial life and discipline, such as those touching the same mission that we have just considered, as well as those in defense of the Church against those brothers whose behavior threatens the good of others (see Matthew 18:15–17). The Apostles then intervened effectively in this sense: "I urge you, brothers, to watch out for those who create dissensions and obstacles, in opposition to the teaching that you learned; avoid them" (Romans 16:17). Such efforts, however, are nevertheless always linked to the effort to obtain the salvation of the rebellious brothers themselves (see 1 Corinthians 5:5; 2 Thessalonians 3:15).

In order to adequately understand the commandments, the priority *of the freedom of the children of God,* reiterated by St. Paul in relation to the law of Moses (see Romans 6–8; Galatians 3–5), cannot be forgotten. Salvation in Christ entails a new freedom, as it does not consist in fulfilling certain prescriptions, but in living according to the Spirit. This obviously does not mean in any way eliminating the objective distinction between good and evil: "Shall we sin because we are not under the law but under grace? Of course not!" (Romans 6:15). Indeed, "the law of the spirit of life in Christ Jesus has freed you from the law of sin and death" (Romans 8:2). Consequently, in the new Covenant, the commandments concerning ecclesial life are reduced to the bare minimum, but continue to exist as expressions of the objective needs of an authentic freedom that loves the good of fidelity to Christ and his Church.

## 2. Canon Law in the first millennium

**23**. Beyond the many differences and changes over the first thousand years of the Church's existence (or, more precisely, the first eleven centuries), what unites it, from the juridical perspective, is the *rather embryonic state of both legal culture and legal technique* throughout that long period.[9] The *Decretals* of Gratian, however, written around 1140, mark the beginning of a new era. This era, in which we still find ourselves, is characterized by the existence of a specific scientific discipline and specialized practical operations in the field of ecclesial law. It must not be forgotten, though, that these long centuries represent a preparation for what, starting from Gratian, will come to fruition and maturity.

Different divisions can be made within the first millennium, depending on the stages of the general history of the Church or in accordance with the state of the canonical sources. In our exposition we will distinguish between Christian Antiquity (1st–5th centuries) and the Early Middle Ages (6th–11th centuries).

### 2.1. Canon Law of Christian antiquity (1st–5th centuries)

#### 2.1.1. The Church persecuted by the Empire (1st–3rd centuries)

**24.** In the first three centuries of the Christian era, the Church was not only unrecognized by the Roman Empire, but was periodically subjected to persecution by imperial power. However, there is a law within the Church itself, which, starting from the *apostolic tradition*, develops and consolidates with institutions certain norms and practices—more or less unitary or diversified—for each geographical area. If *custom* has always played an important role in ecclesial law, there is no doubt that in this initial stage it assumed a very particular importance. As with every juridical sphere, the institutions, norms, and practices of the Church derive from the life of the People of God: as a rule, only later are they subject to formalization through normative texts.[10] This also serves as an aid to understanding why at that time the main sources for the discipline of the Church are found in the texts of the New Testament as well as in those of the Fathers of the Church and other ecclesiastical writers. Certainly, there are some of those texts that contain aspects of a more directly disciplinary nature: in addition to the pastoral letters of St. Paul, we see also the first letter of St. Clement of Rome to the Corinthians (at the end of the first century) or the letters of St. Ignatius of Antioch (written about 100 A.D.). But it is the whole of *scriptural and patristic texts* that show the life of the Church, and therefore also its law, in its close connection with Christian doctrine.

The necessity to gather the traditions received as well as the perceived need to appeal to the apostolic authority in order to resolve questions explains a peculiar type of juridical source in these first centuries—namely, *the collections attributed to the Apostles*. Dealing mainly with disciplinary matters—as well as with other issues of a moral or liturgical nature—these collections certainly gathered a living tradition. From the point of view of fidelity, however, they must be critically examined, for there are aspects attributable to the (mostly unknown) compilers, and are at times even attempts to justify certain heresy on the basis of the apostolic tradition.

This phenomenon had particular importance in the Christian East. The oldest work of this type is the *Didaché* or the *Doctrine of the Twelve Apostles*, written in Greek, probably toward the end of the first century, within a Syrian or Palestinian Christian community. The *Didaché* influenced most of the subsequent collections, among which include the *Didascalia Apostolorum*, from the end of the third century, in Syria; the *Traditio Apostolica*, which arose in the West in the early third century, often attributed to St. Hippolytus of Rome, and especially relevant in liturgical matters; and the *85 Canones Apostolici*, dating back to the end of the fourth century, in Syria, and which already have a normative form similar to that of the canons of the Councils. These *Canones Apostolici*, together with the other mentioned collections (with some modifications), are found in the *Constitutiones Apostolicae*, a collection datable toward the end of the fourth century, and especially significant precisely because it brings together into an organic whole the most important previous collections. The *Constitutiones Apostolicae* enjoyed great authority in the East until the Second Council in Trullo (691), which refused them on suspicion of heresy, retaining only the 85 Apostolic Canons. In the West, although these *Canones* were considered apocryphal by a decree attributed to Pope St. Gelasio I (492–496), seventeen of them were included in the *Decretum* of Gratian.

From the fact that the interventions of the bishops of Rome were relatively scarce in those centuries, and although the ecclesial awareness of their primacy over the whole Church was clearly expressed, it could be deduced that each local community had its own independent juridical system. Such a view forgets that rights and the law of the Church are derived first of all from the very essence of the Church, which is known through its tradition. On the other hand, the Church has always had awareness of its *Catholic unity*, perfectly compatible with *legitimate regional diversity*: already in its embryonic realization in Jerusalem, the Church had the same potential universality that then would gradually manifest itself in time and space. Studies on *communio* in the early centuries show that it was lived as a reality with respect to the universal Church, and that it was both spiritual and juridical-institutional.[11] For example, the *litterae communionis* system was a tangible manifestation of the unity of communion. The traveling Christian had to provide a letter from his bishop and show it to the church where he was going; in the latter there was a list of the 'sees' with which it was in communion. The fact of having a letter of communion sent from one of the main sees, and especially from Rome, was a sign of being in communion with the whole Church.

*2.1.2. The accommodation of the Church within the Roman Empire (4th–5th centuries)*

**25.** The Church's relations with the Roman Empire changed radically starting from the recognition of religious freedom by Constantine (313) and from the proclamation of Christianity as the official religion by Theodosius in 380. Freedom, peace, and public support allowed a remarkable development of the Church and its institutions. The fourth and fifth centuries witnessed a great flowering of councils; that is, meetings of bishops that issued doctrinal, disciplinary, or judicial decisions. These decisions were given the name "canons," a term of Greek origin, still used today to designate the law of the Church. Some of these councils enjoyed universal authority, and are therefore called "ecumenical," the first being that of Nicea (325).[12] There were many other particular councils, especially provincial. Some of them—in the East, Africa, Gaul, and Spain—have a peculiar value, as their canons were not only recognized in the territory where they were born, but were received and observed in other, even distant, parts of the Church. This reveals that their authority was perceived not solely in relation to the power of those who issued them, but was understood as an expression of juridical needs common to all of the local Churches that were part of the one church of Christ. Similarly, the writings of the Church Fathers were used to support canonical solutions.[13]

Alongside the conciliar canons, the other juridical source of great relevance at this stage are the *decrees (or decretal letters) of the bishop of Rome*, manifestations of the increasingly frequent exercise of his primacy of jurisdiction. The decisions represented in the decrees were made in response to local requests (generally from the bishops), but could also be the result of the initiative of the Bishop of Rome himself. Originally the decisions concerned only concrete cases, but they eventually acquired a universal value in themselves, by virtue of the unique authority recognized in the See of Rome. In this way the legislative activity of the papacy began to develop, linked to the problems arising out of the lived experience of the whole Church, and which tended to forge a common discipline. Particularly numerous and significant in these centuries were the decretals of Innocent I (401–417) and especially those of St. Leo the Great (440–461).

The canons of the councils and the decrees of the Roman Pontiffs were collected in *canonical collections*, according to a predominantly chronological order. This not only facilitated the conservation and diffusion of those sources, but also expressed their consideration from the point of view of an authority transcending both time and, as we have seen with regard to the particular Councils, space. Among the various collections of this period we see that of the East, known as the *Syntagma canonum*, made in Antioch in the fourth century. Constituted of decisions from a series of particular eastern councils, others were added, especially those of the ecumenical councils and African councils. This is a collection of great importance in the Byzantine Church and throughout the Christian East, in which a very special authority has always been attributed to the sacred conciliar canons. In the West we know of collections of councils from Africa, Gaul, and Italy. The African and Gallic ones gathered the flourishing conciliar activity of those regions, the latter also adding some canons of other regions, especially from the East. The received Italic collections, meanwhile, contained Latin translations of Eastern councils.

In addition to these sources of an ecclesial character, *the influence of Roman law* on the juridical order of the Church must be considered.[14] Even before the Constantinian peace, Christians, like all the inhabitants of the Empire, lived under Roman law, but tried to make it compatible with the principles of their faith (e.g., in matrimonial matters). Even then, the Church, obviously without appearing as such (as it was not recognized and, indeed, considered illegal), sought formulas of Roman law with which it could solve problems of a patrimonial or an organizational nature. With its freedom and, then, with the official character it eventually assumed in the Empire, the contribution of Roman law increased considerably. A great deal of terminology came from Roman law, some of it also having a strong theological significance, as is shown in the writings of Saint Cyprian († 258) and especially Tertullian (c. 155–220): e.g., *ordo, potestas, sacramentum, decretum, constitutio, dioecesis,* etc. Moreover, many institutions had their roots in Roman law, especially in the formal configuration of government activity (council meetings, pontifical legislation, procedures, etc.) and in the context of matters of more civil importance, such as property matters. (This trend will happen with even greater intensity in the Middle Ages: see number 30, *infra*). It was natural for the Church to borrow such concepts from the juridical culture of the time, which was, however, already highly developed. Despite this, however, it remains certain that the substance and therefore the specificity of canon law does not come from Roman juridical institutions, but is instead based on the same apostolic tradition as well as on the initiatives inspired by the Holy Spirit in service of the fulfillment of the mission of the Church in every historical moment. Notwithstanding all of its importance, the contribution of Roman law remains at a rather technical and instrumental level, and helps in the understanding of the legal dimension common to both the civil and ecclesial spheres.

The influence of the Empire proved more problematic, however, at the level of political power. The Christian emperors, although obviously lacking the prerogatives belonging to the ancient divine cult, claimed their jurisdiction in the affairs of the new religion of the Empire. An example of such a mixture of power was the convening of the councils by the emperors. In the West this influence of the Emperors ceased with the fall of the Empire in 476. But in the Empire of the East, such influence, known as *Caesaropapism*, remained in existence until 1453. There was thus a continuous intervention of imperial power in Church matters, combined with the insertion of ecclesiastics into the sphere of temporal power. This created a singular mixture of politics and religion, linked to a more radical intertwining of cultural identity and religious identity, which still represents one of the most complex ecumenical problems for the return to Catholic unity of the Eastern Churches separated from Rome.

*2.2. Canon Law of the High Middle Ages (6th–11th centuries)*

*2.2.1. The Church in the East*

**26.** At the beginning of this period, in Constantinople, there was a moment of decisive importance for the entire history of law: the great legislative compilation promoted by the Emperor Justinian (527–565). An attempt was made to gather and order all of the material of Roman law that had accumulated up to that moment that is a systematic ordering of the judgments of the main jurists (Papinian, Paulus, Ulpian, Modestinus, etc.) (referred to as the *Digest* or *Pandectae*), imperial norms (known as the *Codex* and *Novellae Constitutiones*), to which was added a manual that assumed the rank of law (*Institutiones*). Although it was a cultural enterprise with a political purpose to restore unity and splendor to the Empire (which then included western regions), in reality this work, made possible by the presence of Roman juridical culture in the East, was in practice poorly implemented initially. In fact, it corresponded neither to the law as it then existed in the East, nor did it have much importance in the West of that era, which was increasingly dominated by Germanic invaders. Its historical destiny, rather, was to preserve the legacy of Roman law, where the true juridical art first developed. The compilation did this with the limits inherent in its moment of composition, i.e., not as a jurisprudence of rights, like the classical Roman one, but rather with a more legislative character. In later history, the medieval rediscovery of the *Corpus Iuris Civilis*, as the Justinian compilation was called, would prove to be instrumental in the revival of juridical science. In this way, its influence on canon law also proved to be profoundly significant (see number 30, *infra*).[15]

In these centuries there was a progressive and ever deeper distance between the Christian West and the Christian East, which eventually resulted in the schism of 1054 and is even today still unresolved. Despite the marked theological, spiritual, and cultural differences between the two spheres, the

ecumenical councils held in the East in these centuries still expressed the
unity of the universal Church, but were mainly concerned with matters of
a doctrinal nature. In disciplinary and pastoral matters, however, there was
diversity between the four patriarchies (Constantinople, Antioch, Alexan-
dria, and Jerusalem), each of which was endowed with great autonomy. To
this was added the separation of quite a few Churches because of the Chris-
tological heresies (Nestorianism and Monophysitism), which commingled
political issues regarding the independence from the Byzantine Empire.
There was no influence of coordination and unity in disciplinary matters
similar to that which came from the popes in the West. The pontifical decretals had little effect in the East: having been written in Latin, they were
sometimes not translated, or the Greek translations were not faithful. Instead, some writings of the main Eastern Fathers were used, which were divided into canons. In addition, the role of the Eastern emperors in the
ecclesiastical sphere was also keenly felt.

Thus Justinian II convened and supported the Council in Trullo (or
the "Quinisext Council")[16] in 691, in which, in addition to elaborating
102 disciplinary canons, it was determined what were the common canonical sources of the eastern discipline, which were added to those of the *Syntagma canonum*.[17] This led to the *Syntagma adauctum*, a fundamental point
of reference for the common canonical discipline in the East. There were
also imperial laws that dealt with ecclesiastical matters. These laws were inserted into a new type of collection, exclusive to the East: the *Nomocanoni*,
in which the imperial laws (*nomói* in Greek) and the canons concerning
the same matter are presented systematically—either entirely as an integral
whole, or, more often, by listing them.

### 2.2.2. The Church in the West in the sixth and seventh centuries

**27.** The invasions by the Germanic peoples and the weakening of the
Roman Empire in the West until its fall in 476 determined a new political
and cultural framework. There was a strong missionary expansion of the
Church, along with the conversion of many European peoples. Monasti-
cism, too, had a decisive impulse with St. Benedict (480–547). At the same
time, the tendency toward particularism was felt, even in the ecclesiastical
sphere: canon law was influenced by Germanic law, the law of custom and
oral transmission, proper to each people. The Germanic mentality favored

the decentralization and privatization of law, even in religious matters. Thus the churches submitted to the owners who had built them, and an intricate network of ecclesiastical entities (parishes, monasteries, etc.) was gradually created. Christian princes intervened more or less incisively with their authority in the affairs of the Church, exercising a *ministerium regis erga Ecclesiam*.

Knowledge of previous canonical sources and of ancient juridical culture assumed particular importance in these circumstances. In the years between the end of the fifth century and the first decades of the sixth century, a flurry of activity of great technical quality occurred in Rome. Directly promoted by the Roman pontiffs,[18] this activity gave rise to various collections, among which the *Collectio Dionysiana* stands out by far. It takes its name from its author, Dionysius the Humble, an Eastern monk who came to Rome and who first prepared a collection of conciliar canons (called the *Liber Canonum*)—of which there are three versions—as well as a collection of decretal letters (known as the *Liber Decretalium*). These two books were later unified as the *Collectio Dionysiana*. Dionysius' work marked significant advancement in the history of canonical sources. In fact, in his work the canons are clearly distinguished from the decretals, and an attempt is made to ascertain the authenticity of the texts, disregarding those deemed spurious. Thanks to the knowledge of Greek and Latin that Dionysius possessed, there is a much more faithful and accurate Latin translation of the canons in Greek. In the collection of decretals, he proceeds with a universalistic criterion—that is, collecting those sources that are of value for the entire Church. There is also a tendency to choose only the texts of a purely juridical nature, regardless of the doctrinal, historical, or other relevance. There are other signs of technical-formal improvement to facilitate consultation, such as indexes or some use of systematic criteria within a collection that remains essentially chronological. The *Dionysiana* became for a long time the quasi-official collection of the Church of Rome, and exercised a wide influence in Italy and throughout the entire Western Church, serving as the basis for several other collections, including some that we will see later (*Hispana, Dionysio-Hadriana*). As a result of the confluence of reasons regarding both their technical perfection and their subsequent authority—derived from their recognition and use by the Roman pontiffs—the importance of the *Dionysiana* collection is clear.

Many other collections of these centuries, on the other hand, are rather local in nature and of poor technical quality, since they tend to be more disordered accumulation of texts (as happened especially in various collections of Merovingian Gaul). Another type of canonical source also appears, which was also an expression of marked particularism and is fairly basic in nature: *the penitential books.* Emerging in the sixth century in Ireland and then in Scotland and emanating from the monasteries, an institution so central to the ecclesiastical life of the islands of that era, these books were also present in continental Europe from the seventh century onward. They testify to the practice of private confession, and contain lists of sins with an indication for each of the respective penance that the priest was to impose on the penitent. There is therefore talk of "tariffed penance," in which a penance imposed was proportional to the gravity of the sin confessed. By their nature, these books are closer to what would later be known as "manuals" for confessors rather than to what are, properly speaking, canonical collections.

Next to the *Dionysiana,* the other important collection of these centuries is the *Hispana,* composed during the seventh century in the context of Visigothic Spain. This collection reflects an ecclesial situation in which the preservation of the universal canonical sources of the past is combined with the typical elements of Germanic juridical particularism. *Hispana* collects with singular breadth and authenticity both universal and particular law, including that of Visigothic Spain itself contained in the famous and long series of the Councils of Toledo in the seventh century. Some attribute the first review of this collection to St. Isidore of Seville (560–636), author of the famous *Etymologiae,* a true encyclopedia destined to have a significant influence throughout the Middle Ages, even for its juridical aspects, as well as concretely for its doctrine about laws. As early as between 675 and 681 the *Hispana Systematica* was developed, arranging the 1630 canons of the original *Hispana* (which was chronological), according to the order of the previously composed *Excerpta,* as a systematic index along with summaries of the canons. The further spread and influence of the *Hispana* collection, especially in Gaul, was both extensive and enduring. It should be widely recognized that to both the *Dionysiana* and to the *Hispana* goes the merit of having transmitted the legacy of ancient canon law to posterity.

### 2.2.3. The Era around the Carolingian Reform (8th–9th centuries)

**28.** The Frankish kingdom reached considerable size in these centuries, including a large part of Europe. This was accompanied by the missionary extension, coming above all from the island church (present-day Great Britain and Ireland) and in which the figure of St. Boniface († 754), the apostle of Germany, stands out. An alliance was established between the Frankish dynasty and the papacy, which was thus protected from the Byzantines and above all from the Lombards. The papacy also received territories from the Franks, the initial components of what would later become the Papal States. The symbol of this union is *the restoration of the Roman Empire in the West*, which took place through the coronation of Charlemagne in St. Peter's in the Vatican on Christmas in year 800. In this way the model of medieval Christianity was launched, in which the spiritual power of the popes and the temporal power of the emperors, kings and other lords, merged into a reality which, while recognizing the distinction of powers, appeared endowed with profound unity. It is not the reappearance of an Eastern Caesaropapism, of a Church that is subject to emperors, but rather a mutual interpenetration by virtue of which the temporal power assumed certain functions in the service of the Church, and within which the spiritual power of the Roman Pontiff was attributed certain temporal power, precisely to protect the ultimate spiritual ends of *Christianity*. The application of this model during the entire Middle Ages will assume different forms, with much tension between the two powers.

The Carolingian Empire had a short and troubled existence. An emblematic moment remains, however, in which the two supreme authorities sought together the goals of the evangelization of new peoples, the reform of the Church, and a rebirth of culture. There was a great need for *reform of ecclesiastical life*, given that there reigned at that time a disciplinary anarchy alongside an obvious decadence in the moral lives and in the formation of the clergy. This was considered by the Carolingians as a problem also of a temporal nature: religious unity was decisive for political unity.

The collections of this era reflect the problem of ecclesiastical reform. For instance, efforts were made to eliminate the particularistic penitential books, or at least to replace them with new penitential books that were inspired by the genuine tradition of ancient law. Beyond that, this tradition was promoted through the use of large collections from the previous period. In this sense, the gesture of Pope Hadrian I is famous, who in 774 delivered to Charlemagne, king of the Franks, a new edition of the *Dionysiana*, which became known by the name of the *Hadriana* (or *Dionysio-Hadriana*). This collection became in fact very important for the Carolingian Reformation, as with it a firm link was established with the universal and authentic law of the Church, and with the see of Rome who guarded it in the *Dionysiana*. The *Hispana* collection also spread widely in Gaul, as a natural complement to the *Hadriana* collection (compared to the latter, the *Hispana* brought especially the conciliar canons of Spain and Gaul), up to the point that both were merged around 800 in the *Dacheriana* collection (so called by D'Achery, who published it in 1672).

The most peculiar phenomenon of this time in the field of canonical sources are the *falsifications*, carried out especially around the middle of the ninth century. The aim was the reform of the Church, but in a more radical way than the previous attempts. In fact, it was not only an effort to remedy the abuses existing in the Carolingian commingling of the temporal and spiritual spheres, but also a matter of increasing the independence and freedom of the Church with respect to temporal structures, in order to avoid the corruption of ecclesiastical discipline which resulted from it. Among other things, one sees a push to return ecclesiastical goods to the purposes desired by donors; to exempt clerics from secular jurisdiction; and to strengthen the power of the Bishops as well as the supreme power of the Roman Pontiff. This objective was sought by means of limiting the intermediate instance of the metropolitans, through which the temporal power often exerted greater interference in ecclesial affairs. The reformers also strove to favor the discipline of the clergy and of the Christian people. Given the fact, however, that both the imperial authority as well as the legislative activity of the Popes were weak at that time, those hoping for reform could not count on either emperor or pope for assistance in accomplishing their intentions. Furthermore, in the venerable ancient texts of the *Hadriana* and *Hispana* collections, there were no provisions directly related to these new problems. As a result, some hitherto unknown supporters of the reform decided to resort to various methods of falsification. It was not a new procedure, but it had never been carried out so systematically. Not only were authentic texts altered through interpolations and changes in the attributions, but entirely new apocrypha were created, giving them the appearance of legitimacy by means of the authority of ancient texts.

The falsifications concerned both canonical and civil texts, and were gathered in collections that mixed authentic texts with spurious ones. The most famous of these collections is called the *Decretales Pseudo-Isidorianae*,[19] composed between 847 and 852, which was widespread: many of its texts were used in later collections, including the *Decretum* of Gratian. The falsification became evident in the fifteenth century, and at the time of the Protestant Reformation, the affirmation of papal primacy was attributed to the influence of these forgeries. In reality, however, the pseudo-Isidorian collection presupposed this primacy, which was already clear in previous sources, and sought to give foundation to practical innovations, which prepared the way for the Gregorian Reform. The modern mentality takes for granted that these methods contrary to the truth are to be strongly disapproved. In any event, while certainly not admitting of any objective justification, it should not be forgotten that falsehood was seen as the only tool available for intentions that appeared, and were, very just for the protection of the freedom of the Church and of upright discipline. The falsification also concerned civil texts, such as the imperial "capitularies," presented in a way that favored ecclesiastical reform: this is the case of the *Capitularies of Benedict Levita* of Mainz (towards the middle of the ninth century), so called by the name of the alleged author.

### 2.2.4. The era around the Gregorian Reform (10th–11th centuries)

**29.** Although with the conversion of the Slavic and Hungarian peoples the process of expansion of the Church in Europe continued, the Roman pontificate endured a very difficult period in the tenth century. The authority of the Holy See was anemic: first it was in the hands of the factions of the Roman aristocracy, and then, after the renewal of the Empire with the coronation in Rome of Otto in 962, the German emperors intervened decisively in matters of the see of Rome. Until the middle of the century, they are the ones who carried out the reformist intentions of the Church. This subjection to the civil power, especially in Germany, occurred at all levels, so that the investiture of ecclesiastical offices (bishops, abbots, pastors, etc.) was carried out by temporal lords, based on the link of these offices to their respective benefices (i.e., the patrimony tied to the sustenance of the ecclesial office). The consequences of such a commixture of the discipline, especially of the clergy, were very negative: the fragmentation of the Church, the frequent practice of the buying and selling of ecclesiastical offices (simony), the relaxation of the law of celibacy, etc.

Against this deplorable state of affairs, a reformist movement arose in the beginning of the eleventh century. Echoing the defense of the *libertas Ecclesiae* in continuity with the Carolingian Reform already seen, it reached its zenith in the Gregorian Reform. The latter takes its name from Pope St. Gregory VII (1073–1085), whose pontificate represents the peak of the eponymous reform. Several factors helped this revitalization, including the strong spiritual movement dating back to the Benedictine Abbey of Cluny in southern France. To achieve its goals of the freedom of the Church and the morality of the clergy, the decisive element was the exercise of the universal power of the Roman Pontiff. All ecclesiastical offices and, therefore, their respective patrimonial benefits, were to be connected to him as the ultimate summit. The struggle between the Empire and the papacy, known as the "investiture controversy," ended with the Concordat of Worms (1122), which marked the substantial recognition of the freedom of the Church in its own sphere.

In the pre-Gregorian era, a collection of books of canon law known as the *Decretum of Burchard* stands out. Shortly after the year 1000, Burchard, the Bishop of Worms, compiled a very large and systematic collection, albeit rather disordered. The work was very influential until Gratian, inasmuch as it collected sources from many previous collections and presented itself as a universal collection. In his basic inspiration, Burchard places himself in the spirit of the reform of the Church, and seeks to favor the autonomy of the latter. While acknowledging the primacy of the Roman Pontiff, however, he rather insists on the power of the bishops, and to a certain extent admits functions that are specific to civil power in the ecclesiastical sphere.

The collections of the Gregorian Reform reflect the prevalence of a new aspect, resting decisively on papal primacy for the work of reform, and turning to the civil authority in order to obtain from it the recognition and protection of the autonomy of the Church. More than through legislative activity—which however is not lacking—the reform is promoted through new canonical collections, composed directly with the intent of advancing reform. Given the desire to return to the true ancient discipline, there is a clear concern for the elimination of apocryphal texts and the search for authentic pre-existing documents. Nevertheless, the *Pseudo-Isidorianae* falsifications were not noticed. The main Gregorian collections were these: the *Collection of 74 Titles* (around 1076), dedicated almost exclusively to explaining and illustrating the pope's supreme power, and which—after the *Dionysiana* collection—constituted an almost official collection of the Church of Rome; the *Collection of Anselm of Lucca* (shortly after 1081), which, being composed by a faithful follower of Pope Gregory VII, best reflects the spirit of the reform; and the *Collection of Cardinal Deusdedit* (between 1083 and 1086), which, like that of Anselm, contains not only the affirmation of the privileges of the Roman Church, but also the concrete norms of reform (on themes such as simony, celibacy, etc.), with the penalties that were to be applied to offenders. Another very famous source that vigorously expresses the primacy of the Roman Pontiff is the *Dictatus Papae*, a collection of 27 propositions on papal powers attributed to Gregory VII himself (1075).

The rigor at the beginning of the Gregorian Reformation was followed by a period of greater mildness and gradualness, which is reflected in the canonical collections. Key among them is that of *Ivo of Chartres*, Bishop of this French diocese (109–1115/17), who, in some ways, returns to the approach seen in the *Decretum of Burchard*. Three collections are attributed to him: the *Tripartita* (because it was divided into three parts, in which the chronological order of the sources prevails), the *Decretum* (a large systematic collection, which generally follows the order of the *Decretum of Burchard*), and the *Panormia* (a sort of synthetic manual, developed on the basis of the Decretum). The *Panormia* was widely used because of its logical order, its helpful summaries, and its relative completeness, all of which made it very practical. Its prologue, *De consonantia canonum*, is particularly famous (sometimes also included in the *Decretum of Ivo*, or constituting a separate booklet), and deals with the method of resolving the contradictions between the various sources by considering the nature of the conflicting precepts; that is, trying to determine whether they were enacted according to the rigor of justice or according to the moderation of mercy. Ivo is certainly an important and immediate precursor of Gratian.[20]

# 3. Classical and postclassical canon law (1140–1563)

## 3.1. The historical premises

**30.** The classical age of canon law begins with the composition of the *Decretum* of Gratian, and ends with the Council of Trent. Generally, however, the classical era strictly speaking is narrowed to the two centuries immediately after the *Decretum*, with the next stage being called post-classical, reflecting a certain decadence with respect to the previous splendor.

In the examination of the second millennium we will limit ourselves to the Church in the West; that is, Latin law, given that since the occurrence of the schism in 1054, the vast majority of the Eastern Churches have lived separated from Rome.[21]

The classical era of canon law is characterized primarily by the fact that a new scientific discipline was born and that it reached its maximum vitality—namely, canonical science. Gratian unquestionably represents the father of the new science, which will later have numerous adherents, including some who practice it at a high scientific level. A juridical science cannot exist, however, on the margins of the social reality at whose service it places itself. Therefore, the extraordinary summit of ecclesial law in this period must be explained in the overall context of medieval European Christianity. The golden age of canon law finds multiple parallels in other great achievements of the Christian spirit at that time, on the level of religious, cultural, and artistic life, not to mention the economic-commercial progress and urban development of the era.

Three aspects are more directly connected with the pinnacle of canon law. First of all, *the constant and effective exercise of Papal jurisdiction* should be remembered. The Gregorian Reform had already been a prelude in this sense. From a juridical point of view, such primacy entails the effective existence of a decision-making power on issues that had arisen throughout the Church, by means of an enormous number of decretals (for a description of the concept of decretal, see number 44, *infra*). Even in the ecumenical councils of that time, then called "general," the role of the Roman Pontiff was absolutely paramount. The pope's task in medieval Christianity, by virtue of the same intertwining that had been established between the

73

spiritual order and the temporal order, had a decisive impact on the latter. This had clear repercussions in the field of canonical laws and processes, which included clearly secular aspects—ecclesiastical jurisdiction was justified by means of its connection to the salvific mission of the Church (*ratione peccati*, as it was defined). For example, Church courts accepted judicial actions based on juridical acts (such as contracts or wills) without the formalities required by civil law, thus protecting the will of the individual, especially when an oath was involved. The canonical sentences then had civil effects.

The second factual presupposition that was directly influential in the golden age of canon law was *the rebirth of juridical science, based on Roman law*. The various parts of Justinian's compilation (see number 26, *supra*) were not only rediscovered, but were also rearranged. As a result, the revered *Corpus Iuris Civilis* was put back into circulation, through many handwritten copies. A decisive role in the reorganization of the *Corpus* and the launch of scientific work on it belongs to Irnerius († c. 1130), who worked in Bologna, the city at the epicenter of the medieval rediscovery of the science and of the art of law. The interest in having available the genuine *Corpus* and its very wide diffusion can be explained according to the practical application of the law itself, not simply for historical or cultural reasons. Jurisprudence is thus reborn as "*iusti atque iniusti scientia*,"[22] and along with it the figure of the professional jurist; that is, the expert practitioner. The jurist can certainly be theoretical or practical, but even when he is theoretical, his knowledge is ultimately aimed at practical life. At the basis of the remarkable cultural development of the *scientia iuris* founded on the books of Justinian there was a deeply felt social need. For this reason, students from all over Christian Europe flocked to the other centers of the study of law that were then proliferating. This Roman law, as a refined and well-developed law, would significantly influence medieval canonical institutions, especially in the way in which the scientific and practical methodology of canonists was established.

Thus we come to the third premise of classical canon law: *the birth of the University*; that is, the environment of study within which the sciences are transmitted and developed. Two sciences intimately connected with canon law occupy a primordial place—namely, law and theology. Canon law, while retaining its links with theology deriving from its specific subject (which is particularly visible in some areas, such as that of the sacraments), would become the subject of a specialized juridical science, taught and cultivated alongside that of civil law. In this way both one and the other systems of law (*utrumque ius*)[23] will be considered in the Middle Ages—and even after—common law (*ius commune*); that is, the universal law which is the proper object of the science of jurists. This universal law, with its categories and its principles, informs all the doctrinal and practical activity of jurists, including the variegated proper law (*ius proprium*) of the time (royal law, municipal law, local customs, etc.).[24] The development of the science of canon law is especially tied to the city of Bologna, home to one of the most important medieval universities, especially famous because of its masters of civil law. Other university cities where one could graduate *in utroque iure* were Padua, Perugia, Paris, Montpellier, Toulouse, Orléans, Salamanca, Cologne, and Oxford, among others.

As a result, canonists began to adopt the scientific method of civil lawyers. The starting point was the oral explanations of the masters, who explained or interpreted the legal texts. These glosses were written down by the students (*reportatae*), or by the teachers themselves (*redactae*), in the text itself, both between the lines (interlinear glosses), and in the margins (marginal glosses). The glosses were initially closely related to individual words (*expositio verborum*), but eventually became more systematic (*apparatus*). In teaching, the method of organized debates was employed (*quaestiones disputatae*). Furthermore, literary genres began to arise (*summae, commentaria*) which tended toward a more systematic exposition, naturally always in connection with the fundamental legal texts to which they referred. The civil lawyers elucidated the books of Roman law in the *Corpus Iuris Civilis*; the canonists proceeded in a similar way with the canonical collections that eventually became known as the *Corpus Iuris Canonici*.

### 3.2. The Decretum of Gratian

**31.** The *Decretum Magistri Gratiani*, which was originally titled *Concordia discordantium canonum*, is a work of utmost importance in the history of canon law. The two names of the work correspond to the two aspects of Gratian's work: it is above all a *Concordia*—that is, a great scientific effort to harmonize the existing canons following a dialectical method. Compared to the previous ones in this sense (see number 28, *supra*), the *Concordia* constitutes both a quantitative and qualitative leap of such proportions that it justifies, without any reservation, the title of father and founder of canonical science that is usually attributed to the master Gratian. At the same time, the title of "Decretum," which although was not the original one was the one that was ultimately imposed in use, shows its continuity with previous collections, some of which bore that name. The Decretum is also a canonical collection, although it is that collection which managed to replace all the others. In fact, it collects and transcribes a wide amount of texts from the canonical tradition, making use of the previous canonical collections, especially some of the Gregorian Reformation. But its success can be explained precisely on the basis of its scientific character: an attempt is made to present the texts as an organized whole, in which Gratian traces the systematic, sets out the principles for each subject, indicates the issues to be examined, and applies rules of interpretation to resolve contradictions. As a result, the Decretum is composed not only of *dicta* by Gratian himself, but also *auctoritates* or *canones*[25]—that is, the juridical sources reproduced in the construction of the *Concordia*. The huge amount of material contained in the first millennium's canonical sources, which in the centuries to come were to be used almost exclusively through the Gratian collection, is seen as a whole with sense and internal unity.

Little is known about Gratian's life. It seems that he was a monk and belonged to the Camaldolese order. As *Magister divinae paginae* (i.e., of theology), he almost certainly taught in Bologna. The definitive drafting of the *Concordia*—from data internal to the text—is usually dated around 1140. He died before 1160.

The internal structure of the Decretum is somewhat complex, and its organization, despite the great quality of the work, is still somewhat imperfect. It is made up of three parts: the first is divided into 101 *distinctiones*, which deal, at the beginning of the work (1–20), with law, its divisions, and its sources, and then with various matters relating especially to clerics. The second part is divided into 36 *causae*—that is, juridical cases that give rise to various *quaestiones*. The arguments of this second part are extremely varied, and concern especially the criminal, procedural, patrimonial, and matrimonial areas.[26] The third part, entitled *De consecratione*, is divided up into 5 *distinctiones*, which concern the other sacraments and various questions on worship. The breadth and completeness of the subjects addressed is evident.[27] Gratian's Decretum marks a turning point in the history of canon law. With it the intense compilation activity of previous ages is finally completed, and the foundations of a new science are established, one that affirms its specificity through a determination of its own scope and methodology. Gratian has often been compared to Irnerius for civil law. Gratian's work, however, goes beyond that of Irnerius, in the sense that Gratian's efforts were not based on existing juridical books—those of the *Corpus Iuris Civilis*—but on the elaboration of a new juridical book, intended to be the first book of the work ultimately known as *Corpus Iuris Canonici*. The Decretum was born as the work of a private author, and has always remained so. The *auctoritates* collected in it were valid according to their respective origin (councils, popes, Fathers of the Church, ecclesiastical writers, etc.).[28] The *dicta* were seen as statements by Gratian, with no value as a juridical source. Nevertheless, the value of the Decretum went beyond these considerations: in its doctrinal authority one sees a synthesis of the canonical tradition, prepared by means of a science. This means recognizing the existence of a truth about what is permanent in the rights and law of the Church. We must be faithful to this truth, and this allows us to place ourselves also in the line of vital interpretation, correction, and integration of the Decretum itself, the human and perfectible character of which must not be forgotten.

*3.3. The collections of decretals and the formation of the Corpus Iuris Canonici*

**32.** The Decretum of Gratian represented the great beginning of the classical era of canon law. Far from limiting itself to the mere study and application of the Decretum, it ushered into being the largest and most profound scientific and legislative development—especially through papal decretals (about this notion, see number 25, *supra*)—that the Church had ever known, at least to that point in history. This development spanned almost two centuries—that is, until the beginning of the fourteenth century. The papacy enjoyed an authority of undisputed prestige during this time, and was closely linked to the best ecclesiastical science of that era. Canonical science was not only in harmony with this increased pontifical authority, but truly influential and, indeed, contributed to it. The close symbiosis between the Popes, their decretals, and canonistic science is highlighted, among other things, by the fact that among the same Roman Pontiffs of the time not only were there many excellent connoisseurs of canon law, but some of them also enjoyed particular fame as canonists. It is above all the case of Rolando Bandinelli, who as Pope took the name of Alexander III (1159–1181), and who during his long pontificate issued numerous decretals; and Sinibaldo dei Fieschi, who became pope Innocent IV (1243–1254). Meanwhile, collections of decretals drawn up by the Roman See with an authentic character were being promulgated by sending them to the legal schools of the universities at Bologna, Paris, and others.

In this period, Gratian's *Concordia* remained extremely influential, both in the academic and judicial forums—that is, in the legal practice of the courts. However, the decretals and their organization into collections (discussed below) caused the focus to shift to them, inasmuch as they contained the new law, which was more suited to the needs of the moment and which responded more to the progress of canonical science. Until the beginning of the twentieth century—before the codification of 1917—the phrase *Ius decretalium* is used to designate the compilation that constituted the law of the Church.

This was an extraordinarily fruitful period for the development of the foundation of the universal canonical discipline, which in many ways forged the tradition that still exists today in many fundamental aspects. From that intense and prolonged work some legal monuments have sprung up, which surely must be considered among all those in which Christian creativity has been exercised in matters regarding the institutions of rights and the law. One thinks of the doctrine on marriage, which seeks to translate the light of the Christian revelation on natural marriage into juridical categories, or the elaboration of the Roman-canonical process, inspired by the yearning to seek the objective truth and to protect the rights of the parties. In these and many other matters, canon law today continues that medieval heritage; even modern Western civil law would be incomprehensible without considering the influence of classical canon law.

With the appearance of the Decretum, a concern immediately arose regarding the collection of those *auctoritates* that were not included in the Decretum itself, called for this reason *extravagantes*. From the additions to the text of the Decretum (the so-called *paleae*) and the appendices to it, the formation of new collections began. These were composed largely of the papal decretals, although there were also other sources (conciliar canons, which at the time were so closely linked to the pope that they were presented as being issued by him "in Council"; texts of the Fathers of the Church; certain secular laws; etc.). The multiplicity of these collections triggered a desire to offer systematic compilations of an overall nature. The *Breviarium extravagantium* composed as a private work by Bernard of Pavia between 1188 and 1192 replaced the previous collections, in arranging the texts (especially of the decretals after Gratian's Decretum) in a systematic order that would be followed by larger future collections. Bernard's work is divided into five books, remembered by a traditional mnemotechnical verse: *iudex, iudicium, clerus, connubia, crimen*, corresponding respectively to the sources of law and the ecclesiastical hierarchy, the judicial process, the rights and law regarding individuals (clerics, religious, and lay people) and temporal goods, marriage, and penal law. The books are divided into titles, and in the titles the subject is arranged in chapters. The decretals are often abbreviated, especially in the narrative part, which sometimes creates problems in application, as the reader can easily forget the case that was at the origin of the rule, thus raising the risk that a rule might be extended to completely different cases. As the production of new decretals continued to intensify, after Bernardo's work the collections multiplied again. Among them, the *Quinque compilationes antiquae* (the *Five Ancient Compilations)* have a particular importance, of which the first is precisely the *Breviarium* of Bernard of Pavia, therefore also known as the *first ancient compilation*. The organization of the first determined also that of the other four compilations, which are added to the previous ones, without replacing them, given that they contained new material and do not simply reproduce the material of the others. They mainly comprised decretals of Innocent III (1198–1216) and Honorius III (1216–1227), as well as the disciplinary constitutions of the Fourth Lateran Council (1215). For the first time in history, the third and fourth compilations were promoted and promulgated by the Popes themselves, by Innocent III and Honorius III respectively, by means of sending them to the University of Bologna.

The foundations were thus in place for the arrival of the *Decretals of Gregory IX*, the most important collection of decretals in the history of canon law. Appearing in 1234, almost a century after the Decretum of Gratian, the two works constituted the fundamental part of the classical law of the Western Church. Precisely in relation to the Decretum, the collection known as the *Decretals* is also known under the name of the *Liber Extra*— that is, containing that which was outside the compilation of Gratian. Pope Gregory IX (1227–1241), a good jurist, entrusted the task of creating a new overall compilation, which would replace the previous ones, to St. Raymond of Penyafort, a Catalan Dominican, a famous canonist and moralist. In 1234 the work was promulgated through its transmission to the University of Bologna and probably to other universities. In promulgating the Bull *Rex Pacificus*, the pope ordered that the new authentic compilation be used as the exclusive one both in trials and in schools, and prohibited the production of other compilations without the authority of the Holy See. This centralization of the compilation activity responded to the need to introduce order and certainty into the law of the decretals. Furthermore, the reference to the schools and the judicial forums shows the existence of a living body of law, studied and at the same time enriched and brought into relief by the need to resolve concrete disputes according to principles of justice.

St. Raymond used the organizational structure of Bernard of Pavia, with the same division into five books, and small adjustments in the titles.[29] He collected almost all of the material from the five ancient compilations, to which he added many decretals by Gregory IX himself. It should also be noted that the *Liber Extra* was conceived and presented as a unitary legislative work, the parts of which had juridical value precisely because they were included in the compilation by virtue of papal power. This explains why entire decretals judged to be similar or contrary to others were omitted, or why parts deemed to be superfluous or uncertain were removed. Sometimes changes were made to the texts or decretals of Gregory IX himself were added so as to solve juridical problems. The aim was obviously not historical-critical, but legal-practical. This aim was fully achieved, given that this compilation remained in force for almost seven centuries—that is, until the Code of 1917. Individual provisions of the Decretals of Gregory IX were naturally abrogated and fell into disuse, but overall they continued to be in force. Indeed, compared to the subsequent collections of decretals that were added, the compilation of 1234 always retained its undisputed centrality, due to its size and to the intrinsic quality of its content.

In the meantime, the evolution of canon law continued to be very lively, both in improving the existing discipline (such as resolving doubts and filling gaps), and in confronting new situations (including, for example, the rise of the mendicant orders of the Franciscans and the Dominicans, the crusades, the relations between the Papacy and the Empire, etc.). Pope Innocent IV (1243–1254), the great canonist Sinibaldo dei Fieschi, used at the beginning of his papacy—though without practical success—the method of inserting the new decretals and the constitutions of the First Council of Lyons (1245) into the respective titles of the Decretals of Gregory IX. Blessed Gregory X (1271–1276) did the same with the Second Council of Lyons (1274), as did Nicholas III (1277–1280) with some of his decretals. For practical reasons, however, two methods were preferred: the new decretals were either inserted as appendices to the *Liber Extra*, or gathered to form new authentic or even private collections of *extravagantes* decretals with respect to the *Liber*. Another expert in law who became pope, Boniface VIII (1294–1303), asked three jurists to compile a new collection which, without replacing that of Gregory IX, would complete it for the whole period that had just passed. What the Pope himself called the *Liber Sextus* came out in 1298; that is, the sixth book, relative to the five books of the great compilation of Gregory IX.[30] This compilation of Boniface VIII is characterized by the greater degree of elaboration (abbreviations, modifications, derogations, additions, etc.) compared to the decretals on which it is based. It represents the most important complement of the *Liber Extra*.

Subsequently the collection known as the *Clementinae* was added, gathering almost exclusively decretals of Pope Clement V at the Council of Vienne (1311–1312). They were promulgated as an authentic collection by his successor, John XXII, in 1317.[31]

From this period the legislative production of the popes decreases. First, as we have seen, classical canon law had already been substantially elaborated by that point, a feat to which the papacy and canonists contributed decisively. Second, around this time in history, the exercise of papal primacy begins a phase of decline. The prestige of the papacy was severely tested by several factors: (i) the period of residence in Avignon (1305–1377) had left the impression that the papacy had placed itself in the orbit of power of the French monarchs, (ii) the great Western schism had divided the Church, with two and even three simultaneous claimants to the papacy (1378–

1417), and (iii) conciliarism—that is, the doctrine that a council could be above the pope. These two centuries, then, until the Council of Trent, fall into a period that no longer merited the title "classic," but rather "postclassical."

In 1500, two other, not particularly significant, canonical collections were privately published, by Giovanni Chappuis, containing *extravagantes* decretals compared to the aforementioned authentic compilations: the *Extravagantes Ioannis XXII* and the *Extravagantes Communes*.[32] This completes the *Corpus Iuris Canonici*, made up of the great collections of the classical era: the Decretum of Gratian, the Decretals of Gregory IX, the *Liber Sextus*, the *Clementinae* and the two *extravagante* collections. The denomination of *Corpus Iuris Canonici* gradually became established, and obviously was inspired by that of *Corpus Iuris Civilis* (see number 26, *supra*), with which a certain correspondence between the books was desired; namely, the Decretum with the *Digest*, the Decretals of Gregory IX with the *Codex*, and the other collections with the *Novellae*.[33]

### 3.4. Classical canonical science: decretists and decretalists

**33.** The Decretum of Gratian became the fundamental juridical text for the canonical science. The so-called *decretists* were first of all glossators on the Decretum (on glosses, see number 30, *supra*). Decretists employed literary genres similar to those already indicated with regard to civil law (see *ibidem*). One such type was a *system of glosses*; a work of this nature composed by Giovanni Teutonico around 1215 and reworked by Bartolomeo from Brescia after 1245 became the most commonly known gloss on the Decretum—that is, the one most generally accepted in teaching and in tribunals. When copied, it was usually copied together with the glossed text. The second literary form used is known as the *summae*, a type of commentary that is different than that of civil lawyers—because despite having systematic elements and presenting themselves independently from the Decretum itself, they are closely tied to the exegetical method of the gloss. There were also various other types of writings, including *quaestiones, casus*, etc. The school in Bologna, where both Gratian and Irnerius themselves taught, was undoubtedly the center of decretists (and maintained this central role in the subsequent period of decretalists). The Bolognese *summe* developed gradually from 1140 until about 1190, starting from the rather short ones of Paucapalea and Roland,[34] continuing with the longer ones of Rufinus, Stefano Tornacense and Giovanni da Faenza, up to that of Simone da Bisignano and especially *Uguccione*. This last one is notable not only for its size, but especially for the quality and creativity of its scientific elaborations. In the same period there are other *summe*, mostly anonymous, belonging to the Franco-Rhine area (such as the *Summa Parisiensis*, the *Summa Coloniensis*, the *Summa Monacensis*, that of Sicardo da Cremona, etc.) as well as to the Anglo-Norman area (such as the *Summa Lipsiensis*, the *Summa Honorii*, etc.).

Starting from the first ancient compilation of the decretals, toward the end of the twelfth century, medieval canonical science was increasingly centered on the decretals, therefore becoming above all *decretalistic* (we speak of *decretalists*), although the study of the Decretum remains central. The method of reading and explaining the text of the decretals in schools, and the literary genres adopted, are similar to those already seen for the Decretum itself: glosses, systems of glosses, *summae*. The so-called *Summae titulorum*, however, are more systematic—less exegetical—works than the *Summae* concerning the Decretum—that is, they are more in conformity with the concept of the "summa" in the context of civil law or theology. After the *Liber Extra*, in the most classical period of decretalists, the *Lecturae* or *Commentaria* appear, which, unlike the *Summae*, examine the juridical texts according to an exegetical method that follows the procedural rules of a scholastic nature: a literal exposition, divisions, practical cases, parallel places, connection with other issues, etc.

The teaching and works of the decretalists were connected with the compilations of the decretals, especially the ancient compilations. Bernard of Pavia wrote a *Summa* sometime before 1198 with reference to the first compilation he himself had elaborated. In the first two decades of the thirteenth century, Tancredo's system of glosses (the same that would later constitute the fifth compilation) was added to the three ancient compilations, becoming the *Glossae ordinariae*. St. Raymond of Penyafort, probably between 1222 and 1224, had prepared a *Summa de iure canonico*, about which we only have partial knowledge. Among the various other literary genres that were being developed, the *Summae* for confessors deserve special mention. These were canonical-moral works for the administration of the sacrament of penance, in which we note the practical intertwining of morality and law in the Church. The origin and use of this of type of writing is closely linked to the apostolate of the mendicant orders (especially at the beginning of the Dominicans). The *Summa de paenitentia* of St. Raymond was widespread. The *Ordines iudiciarii*, explaining the steps of a judicial process—which was very similar in both civil and ecclesiastical courts—is yet another type of specialized literature that appeared toward the end of the twelfth century.

Since the development of sources and that of science go hand in hand in the study of classical canon law, it is well understood that the high point in the development of decretalists is closely linked to the Decretals of Gregory IX and, to a lesser extent, to other subsequent authentic collections, especially the *Liber Sextus*. The *Glossa ordinaria* to the Decretals of Gregory IX was composed by Bernard of Parma as early as 1241 (although it reached its definitive form in 1263)—that is, shortly after the date of the same compilation of Gregorio IX (1234). This stands in stark contrast to what had occurred a century earlier, when the *Glossa ordinaria* to Gratian's Decretum appeared almost a century after the composition of the Decretum itself. This shows how canonical science had matured. Moreover, even after the *Glossa ordinaria*, the *Liber Extra* continued to be glossed upon. Among the *Summae titulorum* that make reference to the Decretals of Gregory IX, the *Summa Aurea* written by Enrico da Susa († 1271) stands out. Known also under the name of Ostiense (as he was Cardinal of Ostia), da Susa was one of the most famous medieval canonists. Written around 1253 in France, his *Summa Aurea* might be considered the most important work of decretalists. In it the author shows a masterful knowledge of both canon and Roman law, and in dealing with questions with a scholastic method he knows how to take into account the principle of *aequitas canonica*; i.e., of that equity which, as we have already mentioned (see number 15, *supra*), is defined as "justice tempered by the sweetness of mercy," a definition that Ostiense attributes to St. Cyprian.[35] Toward the end of his life, da Susa composed a *Lectura* to the *Liber Extra*, reflecting changes of opinion on some issues, as well as a further maturation of his thought. The other very famous *Lectura* of the same compilation belongs to *Sinibaldo dei Fieschi*, who finished it after having become pope under the name of Innocent IV (1243–1254); he too commented on his own decretals that were included in the respective titles of the Decretals of Gregory IX.

The following period was dominated by the figure of Giovanni d'Andrea (1270–1348), the last great classical canonist, a married lay man. To him are attributed *Glossae ordinariae* to both the *Liber Sextus* and the *Clementinae*; his extensive *Lectura* on the *Liber Extra*, completed in 1338, collects the opinions of previous authors and offers his own solutions; he also composed a widely spread *Lectura* on the *Liber Sextus*.

Other literary genres also continued to develop, including those already mentioned above: the *Ordines iudiciarii* and the *Summae* of the confessors. Among the first to enjoy great and well-deserved fame was the *Speculum iudiciale*, by Guglielmo Durante († 1296), a classic of medieval canon law, developed by those who combined both teaching and judicial experience. Dominicans and Franciscans published numerous *Summae* for confessors (many of which consisted of several volumes, and some of which were also released in abbreviated form).

In the postclassical era of canonical science, signs of some stagnation and decay began to emerge, similar to those that were observed in the canonical sources themselves and in theological science. Nonetheless, canonical culture continued to spread, with the creation of many new universities in Europe, in which the teaching of canon law was extremely important, especially for the formation of clerics. Meanwhile, decretalists remained active, particularly those who taught in Italian universities. The Decretals of Gregory IX, the *Liber Sextus*, the *Clementinae*, and sometimes also the Decretum of Gratian, continue to be commented on. Among the most renowned authors that can be mentioned stands Baldo degli Ubaldi († 1400), famous above all as a civil lawyer but also for having commented on the first three books of the Decretals. Also worthy of note are the following: Cardinal Francesco Zabarella (1335–1417); Anthony of Butrio (1338–1408), a lay person; and above all the Benedictine abbot Niccolò Tedeschi (1386–1445), archbishop of Palermo, often called *Panormitanus*, whose works show a considerable maturity. Many canonists took an active part and wrote works relating to the Western schism and to conciliarism, either in favor of the conciliarists or in order to defend the power of the pope. In addition to those already seen, other kinds of writings connected with canon law also appeared, including monographs on individual topics of particular practical interest, the first collections of jurisprudence of the Roman Rota, manuals relating to the criminal inquisitorial process (i.e., *ex officio*), which concerned not only heresy but especially the practices of magic or witchcraft, the *Regulae Cancellariae Apostolicae* established by individual popes at the beginning of their pontificate regarding the manner in which the granting of privileges, dispensations, benefits, etc., were to be administered. The publications of these works contributed decisively to the diffusion of the canonical collections of the *Corpus Iuris Canonici* as well as to the knowledge of the works of classical and postclassical canonical science.

### 3.5. Final considerations

**34.** *Classical canon law is historically inseparable from medieval Christianity.* Characteristic of the best of that civilization, there was reflected within the laws and the science of the canonists of medieval era a momentum toward truth, a belief in reason illuminated by faith, a love of justice and of equity, as well as a profound awareness of the unity of Church. At the same time, the intertwining of the spiritual and temporal orders within the unitary social reality of Christianity, combined with the recognition of the superiority of spiritual power, explains the emergence of a unique ecclesial juridical order. This order embraced many aspects of civil life, from political issues to disputes about the value of contracts and of wills; even the resolution of questions properly ecclesiastical had a strong impact on the civil social structure (the patrimonial question of benefices is just one example). Once these historical-social assumptions vanished—and their decline was already underway during the so-called post-classical era—it was inevitable that medieval canon law would gradually lose its vitality as well as its cultural and social impact.

The juridical world of the *Corpus Iuris Canonici* will always remain a *glory of the Church*, since it corresponds to the most successful Christian achievement thus far in the field of law. Canon law developed its own sources, and managed to harmonize respect for tradition with an appropriate creativity. Especially noteworthy is the interpenetration between the *ratio auctoritatis*—that is, fidelity to the laws of the legitimate authority of the Church—and the *auctoritas rationis*—that is, the authority of a reason and a science that remained in harmony with the faith and with the teaching of the Church. The lasting contribution to universal juridical culture is unquestionable.

It is, however, not a glory without limits. The very image of the rights and law of the Church remained too closely linked to a juridical order that was temporal and to issues consisting of political and economic-patrimonial considerations. There was, consequently, a danger that non-spiritual criteria would prevail over spiritual criteria, including the risk that serious problems might arise as a result of the secular authority prosecuting crimes, such as heresy or carrying out crusades. At the same time, the strong cultural connections that medieval civil lawyers had with Roman law tended to favor a vision in which canon law could appear simply as a mere technique in the service of ecclesiastical power. There was, therefore, the risk of forgetting how original and specifically ecclesial the medieval juridical-canonical experience was.

The challenge even today is to recover what is valid in that experience—a vibrant and scientifically elaborated ecclesial juridical system—and, at the same time, to move beyond what was then historically incomplete. In this way, intra-ecclesial justice might be an ever-present reality.

## 4. From the Council of Trent to the promulgation of the first Code of Canon Law (1563–1917)

### 4.1. The new situation of the Church

**35.** The dissolution of medieval Western Christianity occurred through a rather prolonged historical process, extending from the fourteenth century up until the sixteenth. The question of power, with the decline of papal influence and the emergence of national monarchies, is certainly very relevant for understanding this period of history. But the problem runs deeper, as it affected the entire social life, and especially the life of the Church. After such a profound mixture of the temporal and spiritual orders like that of the Middle Ages, it is understandable that its dissolution was neither easy nor without threats to Christianity. First of all, the intertwining of the two orders certainly favored the infiltration of the worldly mentality into ecclesiastical circles, with the consequent corruption of some sectors of the clergy and with the deterioration of Christian life in general—even though there was both a growing concern and multiple initiatives for *the reform of the Church* during the last period of the Middle Ages. Moreover, the tensions between spiritual and temporal power increasingly transformed into a contrast between two antagonistic cultures: the Christian and the secular. Obviously the first of the two cultures appeared to be linked to the past, so the passing of medieval Christianity might be confused with the end of the Catholic Church or even of Christianity itself.[36] At the same time, it was during this period that the pontifical States were consolidated, in which temporal power was exercised by the Roman Pontiffs in order to protect the independence of their spiritual power.

In this context the *Protestant Reformation* arose, intending to link itself to the perennial concern of the Church for a return to the purity and authenticity of its origins, eliminating corruption and abuses from ecclesial life. To this end, the great reformers (Luther, Calvin, Zwingli) started in the first half of the sixteenth century a deeply radical movement of ideas that challenged many cornerstones of the Catholic faith, including those concerning the hierarchical structure of the Church and especially the power of the pope. The result was a painful division of Christians in the West, adding to the one that had existed with respect to the Eastern Churches since the beginning of the millennium. The Protestant Reformation was the main historical manifestation of spiritualist anti-juridicism (see number 1, *supra*).

Protestantism gave rise to very favorable conditions for secular princes to seize power over ecclesiastical affairs. Luther himself favored this process, considering the power of the princes as a tool for consolidating the Reformation within a certain order. The schism of the Church of England was instead the work of Henry VIII's royal power. In the European nations that remained Catholic, the somewhat parallel phenomenon of *regalism* developed, with strong interventions by the sovereigns in questions of ecclesiastical life by virtue of the so-called right of patronage. In these latter cases, the attitude of the Church's hierarchy oscillated between one of consent or tolerance. At times the system entailed effective support for the mission of the Church, as happened in the evangelization of Latin America and the Philippines.[37] But the dangers of the system were equally clear, especially if civil authorities became less favorably disposed toward the Church.

The era also included very positive news for the Catholic Church. Even before the Protestant Reformation there had been a broad consensus on the need to improve the spiritual condition of the clergy and the Christian people. The Protestant Reformation indirectly gave a strong push to this *Catholic or Counter-Reformation movement*, which concerned the revitalization of ecclesial life and the attempts to make it more authentically spiritual. This process of reform, far from opposing the observance of ecclesiastical discipline, remained faithful to the need to implement an authentic Catholic reform. It is therefore a reform not only promoted by the hierarchy, but in fact centralized by papal authority, which found itself fostering and cooperating with the new charismatic realities that were then being born. Among these stands out not only the Society of Jesus, founded by St. Ignatius of Loyola, but also others such as the Order of Friars Minor Capuchin. Figures such as great innovating bishops, like St. Charles Borromeo in Milan, or of reformers of religious and mystical orders, like St. Teresa of Jesus and St. John of the Cross in Spain, or of priests of great apostolic fervor, like St. Philip Neri in Rome—and many other saints who might be mentioned—show the extraordinary supernatural fertility in Catholic circles of the period immediately following the Protestant Reformation. Although of course the external problems of relations with the civil authorities continued to be very significant, it can be said that the center of gravity of discipline and of ecclesiastical governance clearly appeared to be increasingly fixed internally. Efforts regarding the protection of the faith and of the sacraments, the formation of the clergy and of all the faithful, missionary expansion, etc. all flow from within the Church itself. A new phase of ecclesial life therefore began, the effects of which lasted almost until the end of the millennium.

The *Council of Trent* (1545–1563) was decisive in this process, which marked the life of the Church in the following centuries. In its numerous sessions, the council not only issued decrees of great dogmatic importance (some of which, moreover, had great relevance for canon law, such as those concerning the sacraments), but also adopted numerous disciplinary decisions, significantly called *de reformatione*—that is, regarding reform. Provisions on almost all the subjects of ecclesiastical discipline can be found: on the life of clerics and religious, on the government of dioceses, on particular councils and on diocesan synods, on worship, etc. Some Tridentine canonical innovations are especially important: the insistence on the Bishop's obligation to reside in his own diocese for the good of souls; the establishment of the diocesan seminary as a specific residential center for the formation of candidates for the priesthood; the introduction of the canonical form as a requirement for the validity of the celebration of marriage, along with the related concept of non-recognition of so-called clandestine marriages—that is, marriages without publicity. Closeness of the shepherds to their flocks, a more demanding and more complete formation, greater certainty about marriages between the faithful—these were the juridical-pastoral aims of such reforms.

Another very positive aspect of this era is the *expansion of the Church* to the newly discovered lands. While many peoples in Europe were separating from the Catholic Church, the Church found previously unknown geographical and human spaces in which to grow. Spanish and Portuguese America is the emblematic case of a new culture that arises from the encounter of European and indigenous cultures, in which the Catholic faith plays a central role, and in which the institutional presence and missionary activity of the Church is linked to the monarchic power that sustains and strongly influences it. Foreign missions promoted directly by the Holy See will develop at a later date, bearing much fruit in many African and Asian countries. The Catholic Church became ever more effectively a world reality, with all of the challenges inherent in this effort to foster unity within cultural diversity.

### 4.2. The canonical sources

**36.** The *Corpus Iuris Canonici*, and with it the great tradition of classical canon law, continued to be in force. Indeed, after the Council of Trent and therefore in the climate of the reform of ecclesiastical discipline, the Holy See promoted an official edition of the *Corpus Iuris Canonici*, elaborated by the so-called *correctores romani*, and published by Gregory XIII in 1582. The fundamental layout of canonical institutions remained unchanged.

Nonetheless, the panorama of canonical sources changed very significantly, as a consequence of changes in the overall situation of the Church. First, the *disciplinary decrees of the Council of Trent* represent a point of reference more immediately connected with the reforming impulse of the Church of that period. The practical implementation of the Tridentine provisions in various places consisted of a long process that took place especially thanks to the zeal of many bishops, such as the aforementioned St. Charles Borromeo in Milan or St. Turibius of Mogrovejo in Lima.

After Trent, the Holy See devoted many efforts to the practical implementation of the reform throughout the Church. Sixtus V in 1588 configured the *Roman Curia* as a group of administrative and judicial bodies (congregations, tribunals, etc.) to help the pope in his universal mission. This configuration remains essentially valid today. Since that time, the various bodies of the Roman Curia have produced abundant decisions and sentences, which have created a body of jurisprudence regarding a wide variety of topics, containing many adaptations and modifications with respect to classical canon law. Particularly significant is the juridical activity of the Sacred Congregation of the Council, which, as its name indicates, was created precisely for the interpretation and application of the Council of Trent.[38] The important jurisprudence of the Sacred Rota Romana should also be remembered. It should be noted as well that the Rotal jurisprudence of that period touched on many different matters (unlike today's Rota, which almost exclusively deals with matrimonial nullity).[39]

As part of the missionary activity of the Church, the special Sacred Congregation *De Propaganda Fide* was established, taking definitive form in 1622. As a result, a concept of *law proper to the missions* took shape, with a special character compared to that of common law.[40] The missions enjoyed a particularly close link with the Holy See owing to a form of government that was exercised on behalf of the Supreme Pontiff. In addition, because of the difficulties of communicating with Rome, there existed the need to equip the respective vicars with special faculties. These factors gave rise to legislation that was both unified in the fundamental aspects but also decentralized, especially regarding the granting of faculties otherwise reserved to the Apostolic See. The application of this body of law greatly influenced the further development of the universal law of the Latin Church, which can be seen in the effect that it had on the codification of 1917.

During this period, there was no new official canonical collection added to those of the *Corpus*—despite a few attempts to assemble one. Instead, in addition to the acts of the Curia, there were many acts of the Roman Pontiffs of juridical significance. The names of these acts are very varied (bulls, briefs, etc.), and their collections, almost all private, received the name of *Bullarium*, taken from the most solemn issued acts—that is, the papal bulls.[41]

Among the popes of these centuries there is a distinguished canonist, Prospero Lambertini, who became *Benedict XIV* (1740–1758). In addition to several scientific works (see number 37, *infra*), he is responsible for a very large and particularly incisive series of apostolic constitutions, with which he introduced lasting innovations in the disciplinary structure of the Church. His laws remain as examples of wisdom in the art of legislating, as they move from real problems encountered in the whole Church (with which he had become familiar given his many years of experience working in the Roman Curia), to the search for just and prudently operational legislative answers. His approach was also noteworthy for its clear explanations of the reasons for the decisions being taken (either when confirming or in reforming previous laws), thus aiding in an accurate interpretation of the whole. By way of example, regarding the marriage nullity process, Benedict XIV's contributions include the introduction of the defender of the bond—whose task is to present the arguments and evidence in favor of the validity of the union—and the need of a double conforming sentence *pro nullitate* in order that the sentence of nullity could be enforced.[42]

From these summary points it is easy to observe *the accumulation of canonical sources* that progressively occurred over the course of the centuries mentioned above. One also understands the growing difficulty of orienting oneself in this multiplicity of sources—that is, of knowing which rules were in force, and which ones were to be considered prevalent in case of opposition. The need for order, clarity, and certainty was felt throughout the Church.[43] Therefore, numerous bishops proposed at the First Vatican Council the beginnings of what would later become the first Code of Canon Law, promulgated in 1917.

*4.3. Canonical science*

**37.** The situation of canonical science after the Council of Trent reflected the changes that had taken place in the Church and in its law. This was obviously a complex process, differentiated according to political and cultural spheres, but a fundamental trend can be identified, one which endures even to the present day: Canonical science went from being a juridical science cultivated together with that of secular law in the university context, to a system of knowledge that more and more affected ecclesiastical circles almost exclusively. The transmission of canonical knowledge became increasingly linked to the formation of clergy in seminaries, which entailed accentuating the moral and pastoral importance of the laws of the Church.

At the same time, the reception of the Tridentine decrees—which Pius IV had promulgated in 1564, and to which he had forbidden any glossed editions or commentary in the style of the *lectura*—and of the abundant subsequent acts of government by the Holy See, was carried out in an atmosphere of necessary affirmation of unity and hierarchical obedience. Such circumstances certainly did not favor any in-depth work of interpretation and scientific criticism.[44]

Nonetheless, canonical science remained alive and well, producing at times remarkable fruits. First of all, there was a multiplication of manuals of *Institutiones*, written on the model of those of Justinian which were a part of the *Corpus Iuris Civilis*. This rather elementary literature was not relevant so much in terms of its content, but instead represented both a testimony to continuity with the past and a means of serving the growing need for clarity and simplicity in the essentials in the face of the almost unceasing proliferation of source material. This explains its editorial success. Paolo Lancelotti inaugurated this method with his *Institutiones iuris canonici* (1563). Despite failing in the attempt to have his work included in the *Corpus Iuris Canonici*, it spread widely. In his work Lancelotti followed the organizational scheme of the Justinian *Institutiones* themselves, a plan dating back to the Roman jurist Gaius: people, things, and actions (i.e., processes). This structure was followed in substance by the 1917 Code.

Meanwhile, the tradition of the great commentaries on the Decretals of Gregory IX had an important following in the sixteenth and seventeenth centuries. New, large-scale works were published, written within the context of the Tridentine reform and reflecting as well a greater historical-critical sense. Notable examples include the many works by the Portuguese Agostinho Barbosa (1589–1649), the *Commentaria perpetua in singulos textus quinque librorum Decretalium Gregorii IX* (1673) by the Spaniard Manuel González Téllez, professor in Salamanca, and *Ius Canonicum seu commentaria absolutissima in quinque libros Decretalium* (1661) by the Italian Prospero Fagnani, secretary of the Sacred Congregation of the Council. There are also authors who, confirming the proximity between the two disciplines, are dedicated both to canon law and moral theology. Martín de Azpilcueta (1493–1586), known as *Doctor Navarrus* on account of his homeland, and Paul Laymann (1574–1635) might be remembered in this sense.

A new scientific method subsequently prevailed. Although following the order of the books and titles of the Decretals of Gregory IX, this new method tended to ignore commenting on individual chapters, and instead integrated into the relevant places the content from the other collections of the *Corpus*, the decrees of Trent, and subsequent legislation. This implies a change in the way of teaching the law of the Church, no longer according to the various collections, but arranged according to the subject in a single course. The first to use this method was Ehrenreich Pihring (1606–1679). Anaklet Reiffenstuel (1641–1703) and Franz Schmalzgrueber (1663–1735) were among the others who followed this same path. The treatises of these two authors, often republished, enjoyed a great deal of authority, even in the Roman Curia. These works, following the example of Pihring himself, adopted the name *Ius canonicum universum* or *Ius Ecclesiasticum universum* (the two denominations are completely synonymous), and remain very useful for their extensive information on traditional canon law. In this sense we must also remember the *Prompta bibliotheca canonica, iuridica, moralis, theologica necnon ascetica, polemica, rubricistica, historica* (1746), an alphabetical index prepared by Lucio Ferraris and re-edited several times until the end of the nineteenth century.

Several monographic works deserve special mention, which have remained truly classic in canonical science up to the present day. This is especially the case for the *De sancto matrimonii sacramento* (1602), by Tomás Sánchez, one of the most distinguished matrimonialists in history; and the monumental treatises of Prospero Lambertini, *De servorum Dei beatificatione et beatorum canonizatione* (1734–1738), and *De synodo dioecesana* (1748), published when he had already become Pope under the name of Benedict XIV (see note 36, *supra*). These works demonstrate both the profound juridical sense and the vast knowledge of the authors, who dedicated themselves to solving contemporary juridical problems.

In addition to canonists, canon law was also made present in theological treatises on law, especially by the so-called "Second Scholastic" or the "School of Salamanca," flourishing in Spain during the sixteenth and early seventeenth centuries, with such famous names as the Dominicans Francisco de Vitoria and Domingo Soto, and the Jesuits Luis de Molina, Juan de Lugo, and Francisco Suárez. The study of the juridical at that time found its main center of gravity in the treatise of St. Thomas Aquinas on law,[45] with the juridical being understood as both a precept and as a moral faculty of demanding something, leaving somewhat in the shadows the concept of "right" (*ius*) as the object of justice, as is stated by Aquinas himself at the very beginning of his treatise on justice.[46] The famous and highly influential treatise *De legibus ac Deo Legislatore* (1612) by *Francisco Suárez* is connected with this line of thought, favoring a vision in which the juridical order appears more as a part of the moral order, and the juridical interpretation of the laws themselves being linked to the determination of the will of the legislator, in order to establish what constitutes a moral duty of obedience.

One easily perceives that these positions led in some way to a mixture of moral theology and canon law, especially regarding matters more closely related to ecclesial life, such as the sacraments or the observance of the precepts of the Church. In such a context, canon law, taught to future clerics alongside moral theology, appeared as a complex set of rules that the faithful are bound to observe in conscience, under the guidance of the priest, exercised above all within sacramental confession.

Another discipline closely connected with canonical science, but essentially different from it—owing to it being rather a form of apologetics of the Church—is the *Ius Publicum Ecclesiasticum*. We have already briefly touched on this subject (see note 2, *supra*).

In any event, it must be borne in mind that the predominant juridical culture gradually abandoned the classical tradition in which canon law was seen as part of the common law. Rationalistic *ius*-naturalism, with its intent to elaborate a theory of law in the light of reason alone, leaves aside the canonical elaborations—although in point of fact, in many aspects the influences of Christian origin are nevertheless still felt. This represents an impoverishment of juridical culture. The ideal of codification of the law, which sees a triumph with the Civil Code of Napoleon (1804), certainly presents obvious technical advantages: it aims at facilitating both the knowledge and the application of the norms; it brings together all the norms in a unitary body that is clearly organized; it is composed of general principles set forth with completeness and with every possible clarification. But the idea of a Code conveys equally obvious cultural assumptions: juridical norms are configured according to a rationalistic model, and therefore tend to be seen as rules among which there is a logical-deductive coherence, fixed in an abstract way that takes into account neither historical changes nor the necessary exceptions demanded by the realities of the human experience. As a result, this philosophical model is easily linked to a positivist conception of the law—that is, one based solely on knowledge that is "positive" or empirical. As a result, the law is seen as product of social power, and is then identified with the rule of a State that necessarily enjoys a monopoly in all related matters. Legal regulation of religious matters pertaining to individuals and their religious affiliations is thus seen as falling under the exclusive competence of state laws (see number 9, *supra*).

*The historical school of law*, taking inspiration from the figure of Friedrich Carl von Savigny (1779–1861), developed in Germany in the nineteenth century. In some ways this school of thought represented an exception to the separation of canon law from general juridical culture. Attention to the living law, rooted in the "spirit of the people," meant that canon law, a very unique product of legal history, fell within the interest of these authors. It is therefore understood that the most important fruit of their work is historical in nature. Although illustrious predecessors are not lacking, such as Antonio Agustín (1517–1586)—traditionally considered the founder of the science of the history of canon law—with the German historical school this discipline is definitely launched and there is an important movement toward publishing canonical sources according to stricter criteria and with a more solid historical treatment of many issues.[47] Yet there were also extensive systematic treatises on current law viewed in light of historical precedents. The historical school was not aligned with any particular religious denomination, so both Catholic and Protestant authors were inspired by it, applying themselves to the examination of the different systems of ecclesial law, whether Catholic or Protestant, and regardless of whether the norms were of ecclesiastical or civil origin. For the first time, canon law was studied according to a method that tended to consider it as a simply human system of law, susceptible to a historical-systematic treatment independent of an adherence to the principles of the Catholic faith and of a vital union with the Church. In applying their systematic criteria, these authors were completely innovative with respect to the tradition of the order of the Decretals or the *Institutiones*.[48]

In the second half of the nineteenth century that is, on the eve of the first canonical codification ecclesiastical canonical science showed many signs of vitality. The first specialized scientific journals arose: the oldest, and still in print today, is the *Archiv für katholisches Kirchenrecht* (1857). The acceptance of the idea of codification among the canonists—perceived as a technical approach, considered separable from its positivistic background—was reflected toward the end of the nineteenth and the early twentieth centuries in the multiplication of private attempts in this regard, concerning either the entire body of laws of the Church or a specific sector (procedural, criminal, etc.). In this context there are several prominent names, among which the Jesuit Franz Xaver Wernz (1842–1914) and the future Cardinal Pietro Gasparri (1852–1934) deserve special mention. Wernz taught in Rome at the Gregorian University, and published his extensive *Ius Decretalium* (1898–1914), in which he sought a synthesis between German culture linked to the historical school and traditional Roman canonical science connected to the Curia. Gasparri, who was a professor at the *Institut Catholique* in Paris, published works of high quality such as his famous *Tractatus canonicus de marriage* (1891 and the second edition appeared in 1932 after the Code of 1917), and the *Tractatus canonicus de sacra ordinatione* (1893–1894). Wernz had considerable influence in the 1917 Code, Gasparri was truly its main architect.

## 5. From the Code of Canon Law of 1917 To the Present

### 5.1. The era of the first Code of the Latin Church

**38.** The pontificate of St. Pius X began in August 1904. After only a few months, following the wishes and proposals we have mentioned earlier (see number 36, *supra*), work began on the preparation of a Code of Canon Law for the Church of the Latin rite. It was certainly a demanding process, and was concluded by Benedict XV with the promulgation—on May 27, 1917—of the *Codex iuris canonici*, which entered into force on May 19, 1918. It is generally referred to as the Code of 1917 (or sometimes "Pio-Benedictine," from the names of those two Popes). Before examining the characteristics of the *Codex*, it is worth briefly sketching the historical climate in which the first codification was situated as well as the validity of that body of law.

Certainly the first half of the twentieth century was not a placid time, either for the Church or for the world. The greatest challenge was probably the cultural one, given the profound hostility toward the Christian faith that was spreading in various forms. The apparent affirmation of man, of his scientific reason as a source of progress, and the diffusion of various ideologies of a liberal or socialist bent claiming to offer solutions to all the problems of humanity, were often accompanied by a more or less open rejection of God and especially of a religion revealed by Christ and guarded by the Church. Complex challenges arose for Catholic doctrine itself, which was forced to confront new problems. At the same time, and precisely in order to be able to offer a response to these questions, the Church had to reject the perennial temptation to mix Christian faith and morals with incompatible elements considered more in keeping with modernity.

With regard to institutional relations between the Church with the world during this period, it must be noted that liberal regimes strongly opposed ecclesiastical activity. In addition, totalitarian regimes—whether communist or Nazi in orientation—would soon arrive, along with a period of atrocious persecution and many Christian martyrs. Two world wars then brought tragedies without precedent in the history of humanity. In such a turbulent world, one also increasingly interdependent thanks to improved means of communication, the voice of the Church, and above all that of the popes, took on an increasingly decisive role. The loss of the Papal States in 1870 marked the beginning of a new era of growing prestige for the See of Rome, often seen even by non-Catholics as a point of reference for the great common values of humanity. Meanwhile, it must not be forgotten that it was in that same year that the First Vatican Council proclaimed the dogmas of the infallibility of *ex cathedra* papal declarations as well as the primacy of jurisdiction of the Roman Pontiff.

These brief observations serve to better contextualize a clearly evident phenomenon during this period: *the substantial peace and internal cohesion enjoyed by the Church.* The sense of tradition and authority—primarily papal—supported the Catholic identity of the Church. While there was clearly no lack of disciplinary or doctrinal problems, they did not affect the common underlying coherence and solidity of the Church, and the interventions of ecclesiastical authority when resolving such problems were welcomed in a spirit of obedience. This was made evident with the energetic condemnation of modernism by St. Pius X. While certainly not resolving immediately the myriad of issues posed by modernity—philosophical, biblical, etc.—it was nevertheless emphasized that such problems had to be addressed in a spirit of fidelity to the traditional doctrine of the Church. The unity of the Church and union with the sacred Pastors, and especially with the Roman Pontiff as the definitive point of reference for visible unity, produced abundant pastoral and missionary fruits. Important new local churches, such as those of the United States in North America, matured in such a climate. In addition, the growth of local churches in Latin America meant that the majority of Catholics worldwide were now speakers of either Spanish or Portuguese—the celebration of a Latin American plenary council in Rome in 1899 was particularly significant in this regard. The Church also expanded to other continents, especially in Africa. At the same time, there were many fronts on which significant developments occurred: the biblical and liturgical movements, the apostolate of the laity, the social doctrine of the Church and its effective influence, etc. Even in this climate of substantial peace, however, there were obviously unresolved problems and tensions; these would surface in the period following the Second Vatican Council. Nevertheless, throughout this time there predominated the reality of a Church with a high degree of internal consistency in faith and action.

This historical context allows us to understand how it was possible to introduce the first *Codex Iuris Canonici* and the way in which it was effectively implemented in the Church. New legislation promulgated by the pope and in harmony with the great canonical tradition did not pose problems for the Church at the time; indeed, it was seen as a *most welcome technical innovation in the service of that same tradition and the unity of the Church*. With the Code there emerged clearly, as the fruit of a prolonged evolution, an understanding of canon law as the *internal order of the Church, and especially of its hierarchical component*. This conception was certainly in continuity with the classical tradition, but was no longer the law of Christianity as in the Middle Ages.

The Pio-Benedictine codification was an operation of expert legal technique, bringing together an extremely lengthy canonical tradition, contained in a vast and rather chaotic mass of sources, into a unitary, perfectly organized text, expressed in clear and precise language, which aimed to contain fully the legislation of the Church. As a result, all general laws of human origin that were not explicitly or implicitly accepted by the Code itself were abrogated (cf. canon 6, 6º). Consequently, what happened privately with the Decretum of Gratian took place in an official way for the first time; namely—that the new legislative collection became exclusive and eliminated all the previous ones, including those of the *Corpus Iuris Canonici*, which would from then on have only an interpretative value as part of the *ius vetus* accepted in the majority of cases by the Code (see the same canon 6).[49]

With respect to its content, the 1917 Code was intended to remain faithful to the discipline in force at the time, although that very determination sometimes required choices to be made. While certainly taking into account the classical juridical experience of the Church, this process also took into account in a very significant way what had developed in the activity of the Apostolic See, starting from the Council of Trent. With respect to its method, the 1917 Code followed the model of modern secular codes[50] —that is, the technique of simply compiling the laws was abandoned. Traditionally, texts could have been selected, abbreviated, sorted, or modified, but the collection itself was presented—at least materially[51]—as a set of previously existing documents. With the modern approach, however, new texts were composed. Called canons (instead of articles)—in accordance with the ecclesial tradition—these new texts condensed, clarified, and at times even represented innovations in canonical discipline.[52]

The drafting of the Code was entrusted to a Pontifical Commission made up of cardinals, who made use of the work of many canonists—with both academic and practical experience—as consultors. For the first time in the history of legislative bodies established by the Holy See, the worldwide episcopate was consulted twice, first to obtain proposals and then to receive observations on the nearly finished project. The soul and principle of unity for all of the work, however, was *Cardinal Pietro Gasparri*, who combined his scientific competence (see number 37, *supra*) with an extraordinary ability to work as well as manifest gifts of governance (he would later become Secretary of State).[53]

The 1917 Code, consisting of 2,414 canons, was divided into five books: (I) general norms, (II) on persons (including the canons on clerics—part of the hierarchical constitution of the Church—religious, and a few on the laity, almost exclusively limited to associations of the lay faithful), (III) on things (where the sacraments and worship were treated, along with magisterial teaching, as well as the norms regarding the patrimony of the Church), (IV) on trials, and (V) on crimes and penalties. This organizational system was inspired by that of the *Institutiones*, introduced by Lancelotti into Church law (see note 37, *supra*). It is obvious that the formulations (especially the generic one of *res*, or "things") were not specific to canon law; but it should not be forgotten that it was nothing more than a mere systematic ordering.

The Code was very well received, both in the Church in general and among canonists and other interested jurists (even non-Catholics). Certainly it marked an important and exceptional stage in the history of modern codifications. It garnered praise especially for its technical perfection, with the text being elaborated by canonists who were eminently faithful to the canonical tradition (sharing the same system of sources essentially required this). Equally clear was the Code's attempt to advance canon law through the use of precise concepts and terms.

The Code achieved its objectives of facilitating a wider knowledge of canon law, even by non-experts.[54] Indeed, in becoming the essential focus of canonical teaching[55] and practice, the knowledge of canonical tradition gradually became less familiar to those who dealt with current law[56] and the almost exclusive domain of specialists in history. The new quantum of legislation had been composed in such a rational and orderly manner—in the model of a modern Code—that it can be seen almost as a didactic exhibition. As a result, ecclesiastical canonism returned to an almost exclusive use of the exegetical method, conforming itself to the order of the laws themselves and taking into particular account the words of the canons (as had been done for centuries with the Decretals of Gregory IX). At the same time, the close link between canonical science and moral theology continued to exist, and there was no shortage of authors dedicated to both disciplines.[57] Meanwhile, canonical jurisprudence increasingly became limited to issues regarding marriage, especially with respect to nullity, with a resulting dearth of interest and activity in other sectors. The lack of a stimulus for norms and for research on the judicial resolution of disputes, led instead in practice to the resolution of such disputes only through the intervention of the ecclesiastical administrative authority.

All these factors explain *a certain isolation of the canonical science of the 1917 Code from general juridical science*. It was a scientific world made up of clerics and religious, who mainly used ecclesiastical Latin as their oral and written means of scientific communication (except in some linguistic areas, such as Germany or North America). It was also an atmosphere which was generally satisfied with the prevailing situation vis-à-vis canonical legislation and the science of the moment, without feeling the need for changes or openings to other theological or juridical disciplines. The so-called Italian secular canonical science that had developed in state universities was the only alternative line to this ecclesiastical canonical science of an exegetical style. Despite the merit of a reintegration of canon law into the secular juridical sciences and its fruitful use of the systematic method for the understanding and exposition of canonical concepts and institutions, the Italian lay school remained influenced by the then prevailing juridical positivism (see number 9, *supra*), and often placed itself in a rather foreign perspective to ecclesial life, as if it were looking at canonical problems from outside the Church, and concerning itself mainly with issues of a general nature or those more connected with civil society (Church-State relations, marriage, etc.).

The most appreciable scientific results of the ecclesiastical canonical science of 1917 came from authors who were in some way able to animate their work with the effective contribution of other cultural perspectives. In this sense, the Belgian Capuchin Gommarus Michiels made use especially of the juridical-philosophical doctrine of the treatise *De legibus ac de Deo Legislatore* by Francisco Suárez (see number 37, *supra*) to elaborate broad and well-grounded comments on Book I (on general norms), on much of Book II (on persons), and on Book V (on criminal law). The subsequent editions of these works, released over a period ranging from the late 1920s to the early 1960s, met with unanimous appreciation for their seriousness and completeness. The same reception was received by the commentary to Book I of the Code (published in the years 1920–30) by another Belgian author, Alois Van Hove, professor in Leuven, who knew how to apply his extensive historical knowledge in order to better elucidate the understanding of the current text. Especially famous is the volume of the *Prolegomena* (the second edition of which was expanded in 1945), in which Van Hove offers very erudite information on both sources and on canonical literature. The third example that we would like to cite is that of Francesco Roberti, later cardinal, who published his *De processibus* in 1926 (the fourth edition was released in 1959), in which he successfully incorporated modern Italian procedural doctrine, especially that of Chiovenda. The treatise received broad acclaim, even among civil lawyers.

### 5.2. The Second Vatican Council and the Code of 1983

**39.** On January 25, 1959, St. John XXIII announced the convening of an Ecumenical Council, Vatican II. Although he would open it in 1962, the council would take place almost entirely under the pontificate of his successor, St. Paul VI, until 1965. On that same date in 1959, the pope also expressed his decision to undertake the work of updating the Code of Canon Law. In so doing, he not only directly linked the work of the future council with the updating of the Code as its fruit and crowing glory, but presented this goal as something that had been a pre-existing and long anticipated objective. The fact is, however, that with the decision to celebrate a council, St. John XXIII started a process of change in the Church, the scale of which is still difficult to measure even today. The relationship between the Council and the revision of the Code was in fact realized, but the conciliar novelty that led to the new Code went well beyond the reform that could have been envisaged in 1959: the reform involved not only (or even primarily) technical innovations, but its very content, concerning even fundamental aspects of ecclesial law.

The purpose of Vatican II, according to the mind of John XXIII, was to bring the perennial vitality of the Gospel into contact with the contemporary world, marked by a profound moral and religious crisis. He wanted a decidedly pastoral council because, in his eyes, the Church, freed from rather defensive attitudes of the past, now seemed sufficiently mature to face the challenge of evangelizing a world so spiritually indigent with more incisiveness and openness. Already in the first conciliar session, the only one held under John XXIII, it was felt that the issues to be addressed—concerning all areas of the life of the Church—required far-reaching theological insights. The subsequent sessions were therefore quite troubled, but under the guidance of St. Paul VI, a body of documents was assembled that still remains, and will probably remain for a long time into the future, a main point of reference for the whole Church. The conciliar teachings concern almost all fields of ecclesial life.[58] The dogmatic constitution on the Church, *Lumen Gentium*, whose ecclesiological doctrine is of extraordinary importance for canon law, undoubtedly lies at the center (see number 14, *supra*). But it is the entire set of conciliar documents that constitute a patrimony from which the whole Church, and the sacred sciences in particular, continue to draw today. It is clear that the council was one of profound doctrinal and vital significance, and it is obvious that modern canonical science often resorts to the constitutions, decrees, and declarations of Vatican II.

On the occasion of the renewal promoted by the council, problems emerged that previously were more or less latent within the Church itself, unfortunately producing a great deal of confusion as well as many deviations in thought and practice, defections of priests and religious, the diminution of Catholic institutions, a decline in the overall vitality of the Church in some countries, etc. This situation raised the risk that the meaning and the profundity of the authentic conciliar teachings would be forgotten. In this sense, the greater external participation of all in the liturgy, especially through the use of vernacular languages, seemed to be linked to ideas and practices contrary to the nucleus of the sacred nature—both sacrificial and sacramental—of liturgical actions. The fundamental equality between all the members of the People of God was mistaken for a denial of the hierarchical constitution of the Church, often through conceptions of forms of democratic government that were incompatible with this constitution. Ecumenism and interreligious dialogue were often misunderstood as the relativization of Catholic identity itself. The dialogue with the world and the consequent pastoral concern of bringing Christ to modern man in his concrete circumstances was accompanied, in some sectors, by several misunderstandings: instead of Christianizing the world, Christianity was sometimes secularized in order to make it seemingly more attractive and closer to the men of our time. Secularistic projects of social action, influenced by Marxist ideas of a materialistic nature and of class struggle, as well as intra-ecclesial conflict and dissent on many essential points of Christian doctrine in the field of family morals and life, constituted two manifestations of the danger of such secularization. As a result, the true heart of the council—that is, its ecclesiological and spiritual doctrine on the universal call of all the faithful to holiness—has sometimes been left in the shadows.

Although Vatican II did not develop its own magisterium on canon law (among other things because there was no consolidated scientific *corpus* on which such an effort could be based), the council did offer the ecclesiological principles for a renewed vision of canon law, in accord with the principle of renewal in continuity with tradition. There has never been such a debate between canonists about the foundations of canon law than in the wake of the Second Vatican Council. Never in the years after the council has there been a lack of debate on the part of canonists about how to reflect on rights and law in the Church according to the bases laid down by the council. We have previously discussed this subject in the previous chapter (see number 4, *supra*).

At the same time, however, it was evident that canon law participated with singular intensity in the post-conciliar crisis. It was not a problem concerning only specialists. It was, rather, a generalized phenomenon. Some disputed the existence of canon law itself, pure and simple, as it was linked to obedience to the Hierarchy and the observance of a traditional discipline. Adherents to this position believed that the idea of laws, of legal obligations, of punishments, etc., was outdated in the Church. At the same time, they believed in an exaltation of the rights of the faithful, of their charisms, and of their freedom. In this view, there was no sense of a need for the juridical aspect—that is, of justice—which would have entailed recognizing in some way restrictions on these rights, limits linked to ecclesial communion.

Others, however, reasoning on the basis of the known identification between canon law and the Code, believed that there was no longer any reason for a law of the Church. It is true that the 1917 Code had not been abrogated, but as early as 1959 it was known that it had to be reformed. The actual course of the council showed that issues such as the rights of the faithful, their freedom and their charisms, episcopal collegiality, the legitimate autonomy of the particular Churches, etc., had to be taken into account. These phenomena certainly represented novelties that moved away from the model provided by the first Code. There had also been produced a growing number of various types of post-conciliar juridical documents (especially the kind known as "directories"), which regulated different subjects in a new way with respect to the Code, but often with little technical rigor and with a clear tendency to resort to exhortations instead of imperative norms. The widespread sensation of anomie—that is, the absence of norms, was also keenly felt at the time. To counter it, both St. Paul VI and St. John Paul II reaffirmed and even deepened, in various ways, the theological and pastoral value of canon law. The Sacred Congregation for Catholic Education even had to reiterate the need and the importance of teaching canon law to candidates for the priesthood in the period between the two Codes.[59]

In the meantime, the new Code was being drafted, in a long process that lasted for some twenty years.[60] The Revision Commission, created by St. John XXIII in 1963, decided to start formal work after the conclusion of the Council, which occurred in 1965. This decision shows *the profound nexus between the council and the new Code.* Many cardinals and bishops participated in the work as members of the commission, as well as a large number of consultors not only residing in Rome but coming from all over the world. In drafting the canons, different orientations and criteria were reflected, and although there was careful coordination of the work, the codification of the second Code obviously did not enjoy the basic unity of the first. As we have seen (see number 38, *supra*), the 1917 Code was received within the same canonical tradition from which it came, and even though Gasparri was not its sole author, he contributed in a significant way to the introduction of the entire work.

In 1967, ten principles for the new codification were approved by the Synod of Bishops, the pope's advisory body born at the time of the celebration of Vatican II. These ten principles indicated how the future Code was then viewed.[61] The schemas for the individual parts that were produced in the 1970s were sent to all the bishops—who had already been asked in 1966 to submit suggestions for revision as well as the names of possible consultors—and to other ecclesial bodies (the Roman Curia, universities, to the Union of Superiors General of religious institutes). The first overall schema appeared in 1980; it was the subject of a detailed examination by the members of the Commission, who met in a final plenary session in 1981. A *Schema novissimum* came out in 1982, which was personally examined by St. John Paul II, with the help of some close collaborators. The promulgation took place on January 25, 1983, and the Code entered into force on November 27, 1983.[62]

In the apostolic constitution *Sacrae disciplinae leges* with which he promulgated the 1983 Code, the Roman Pontiff emphasized its connection both with the canonical tradition of the Church and with the doctrine of Vatican Council II: "In a certain sense, this new Code could be understood as a great effort to translate this same doctrine, that is, the conciliar eccle-siology, into canonistic language," and "if the Second Vatican Council has drawn from the treasury of Tradition elements both old and new... then it is clear that the Code also should reflect the same note of fidelity in newness and of newness in fidelity."[63]

The decision of St. John Paul II regarding the promulgation of the Code,[64] made in agreement with the common sentiment of the bishops and responding to a very long period of expectation in the Church, con-tributed decisively to reinvigorating the ecclesial conscience about the need and the importance of rights and law in the Church. In a sense, one might have weighed the advantages of adopting anew the codical technique, with the attendant risk of identifying "the law" too closely with "the Code" alone, at the expense of canonical tradition, of particular law, and indeed of the very reality of the juridical dimension of the Church, which cannot be re-duced to positive standards. It would have also been possible to hypothesize the possible benefits of elaborating differentiated legal bodies according to the diversity of the cultural areas in which the Latin rite churches live. How-ever, in the historical circumstances present at the end of the twentieth cen-tury, the alternative choices appear unrealistic, if only because the abandonment of the codical instrument at such a time could easily have been interpreted at least as a weakening of the relevance of canon law and its unity in the essential disciplinary elements common to the whole Church.

In any event, the promulgation of the Latin Code in 1983—and then the Eastern Code in 1990 (see number 40, *infra*)—was part of the larger context of what the long pontificate of St. John Paul II represented for the Church, which began in 1978. In fact, this Pope, in the wake of the efforts of St. Paul VI, far exceeded the immediately post-conciliar dialectic between traditionalist integrism and progressiveness responding to the needs of the times, showing how the council could not be tethered to either of these two conflicting poles of thought. Although the path to rediscover a com-plete intra-ecclesial peace remains a long one and certainly will not be with-out its difficulties, there are, especially in the younger generations, attitudes regarding the certainty of faith, an awareness of the primacy of holiness, and a sense of the need for proper apostolic action that now transcend the aforementioned dialectic. As a result, there are signs pointing to a greater understanding of the richness and the future possibilities of the true teachings of Vatican II.[65]

The 1983 Code is somewhat shorter than the previous one; it consists of 1752 canons. An attempt was made to leave more room for the particular legislation of the Episcopal Conferences[66] and of individual bishops; even if, in our opinion, the text should have contained more specific rules in various subjects.[67] The text has already undergone some important changes,[68] and several pontifical laws have also been promulgated which touch on subjects not covered in the Code; in particular the apostolic constitution *Pastor Bonus* regarding the Roman Curia.[69]

The Code is divided into seven books: general norms (Book I); the People of God (Book II), which is divided into three parts (the faithful, the hierarchical constitution of the Church, and the institutes of consecrated life and societies of apostolic life); the teaching function (*munus docendi*) of the Church (III); the function of sanctifying (*munus sanctificandi*) of the Church (IV), which is also divided into three parts (the sacraments, the other acts of divine worship, and sacred places and times); the temporal goods of the Church (V); sanctions in the Church (VI), with two parts (crimes and sanctions in general, and then sanctions for individual crimes) and processes (VII). This last book consists of five parts: judgments in general, contentious trials, certain special trials, criminal trials, and the way to proceed in administrative recourse and in the removal and transfer of parish priests. Abandoning the organization scheme of Gaius, instead of the 1917 Code's book II on persons, the second book of the 1983 Code includes a juridical treatment on the People of God that is rooted much more in ecclesiology. Similarly, instead of the generic consideration of "things" contained in the 1917 Code, recourse was made to the theological distinction used by Vatican II among the *munera Ecclesiae*, so that new books appear on the *munus docendi* and on the *munus sanctificandi* (in addition to the one on temporal goods). The *munus regendi*, concerning the *potestas regiminis*, is the main subject of title VIII of Book I, but obviously the entire Code contains a type of self-regulation of the Church regarding the exercise of this function.

The central books of the Code, those dedicated to the People of God and to the function of teaching and of sanctifying, pertain to the specific nucleus of ecclesial rights and law, and therefore highlight the theological nature of such a concept. The first book, on the other hand—as well as the last three books—are more connected with the human operation of the configuration, the implementation, and the protection of rights and law in the Church. As a result, these books reflect more of a manifestly technical-legal nature. Nevertheless, it would be misleading to transform this distinction into some sort of contrast, as if the books of the first type had no juridical relevance, or that the others were devoid of theological importance.

The canonical science that followed the 1983 Code largely followed the basic guidelines that had emerged after the Council (see numbers 17–20, *supra*). There was, however, a waning of interest in questions of a fundamental nature, a phenomenon that is easily understood in light of the growing attention to matters regarding the interpretation and the application of the new Code.[70] It is precisely this latter task that sets forth once again the vitality of fundamental questions. Attention to these crucial concerns avoids the risk of a positivistic and merely instrumental exegesis of the Code; such an interpretive technique would not only remove the work of exegesis from its connection with the reality of ecclesial justice, but would also separate it from the canonical tradition and other sources of current law. Moreover, mindfulness of such basic issues helps us not to forget the specificity of rights and law and their characteristic methodology and practical operation, thus avoiding the misunderstandings caused by a so-called "theological" or "pastoral" reading that effectively ignores or obscures the juridical dimension of the Church.

### 5.3. The law of the Eastern Churches and its codification

**40.** In the course of our historical summary, beginning with the Great Schism of the East (1054), we have limited ourselves to dealing with the canon law of the West—that is, of the Latin Church[71]—because in the second Christian millennium most of the Eastern Churches were not in full communion with the Catholic Church.[72] In the East, however, there were some Churches that never separated from Rome (such as the Maronites in Lebanon). Moreover, over the years, other Churches (or at least a part of them) resumed union with Rome. Despite attempts at global reunification, especially during the Middle Ages, the separation persisted, resulting in serious damage to the entire Church. The Second Vatican Council dedicated a special document to the Eastern Catholic Churches[73]—namely, the decree *Orientalium Ecclesiarum*—and, at the same time, in promoting the unity of Christians through ecumenism, first of all took into consideration union with the non-Catholic Eastern Churches, in which all the sacraments (including sacred orders) exist and the proximity of the faith is relatively at its closest (see the decree on ecumenism, *Unitatis Redintegratio*, nn. 14–18). The council reaffirmed the great esteem for the institutions, liturgical rites, ecclesiastical traditions and the discipline of the Christian life of the Eastern Churches (see *Orientalis Ecclesiarum*, n. 1), and declared that "the Churches of the East, while remembering the necessary unity of the whole Church, have the power to govern themselves according to the disciplines proper to them, since these are better suited to the character of their faithful, and more for the good of their souls" (*Unitatis Redintegratio*, n. 16).

Already in the nineteenth century, before and during the First Vatican Council, the Holy See and the eastern hierarchy united in Rome felt the need to restore the discipline of their respective Churches, first of all by researching and publishing their own canonical sources. Subsequently, several particular synods were celebrated, revising the canonical discipline of the churches concerned. After the promulgation of the Latin Code of 1917, the opinion prevailed that another body had to be prepared with the laws common to all the Churches of the East, obviously respecting the variety of the discipline proper to each. Pius XI, in 1929, created a preparatory commission, and in 1935 he created another for the work of drafting a Code. The fruit of this work, in which many people from the East participated, was presented to Pius XII in 1948. The pope decided to proceed with a gradual publication, starting with those titles[74] deemed most urgent, concerning marriage and judgments.[75] Then the titles about monks and other religious were promulgated, along with those regarding the temporal goods of the Church and the significance of certain words.[76] Titles concerning the oriental rites and persons were also published.[77] In this way, 1571 canons were promulgated out of the total of 2,666 that had been prepared.

With the convocation of Vatican II and the prospect of a consequent revision of the entire discipline of the Church, this process stopped. It was reactivated in 1972 by St. Paul VI with the creation of a new commission for the revision of the Eastern Code, which was made up of Patriarchs and

other prelates of the Eastern Churches, in addition to cardinals of the dicasteries of the Roman Curia with competence over them. The consultors
were mostly Eastern, and some observers were invited from Churches not
in full communion. The revision was intended to take place under *a match-
ing and inseparable fidelity to the Second Vatican Council and to the genuine
Eastern tradition.* The principles for the revision were approved in the first
plenary assembly of the commission in 1974.[78] The systematic division into
titles was preserved, unlike the Latin Code's division into books and parts
of books.[79] In the early 1980s the partial schemas were sent to the Eastern
bishops and to other bodies for their consultation. With their observations
and after an effort at coordination, an overall schema was completed in
1986. Further work by the commission led to a final schema, already bearing the name that it would ultimately become definitive: the *Codex
canonum Ecclesiarum orientalium* (without the use of the word *ius*, considered to be not sufficiently in line with the Eastern tradition)—which was
approved by the plenary assembly of the same commission in 1988. St.
John Paul II, after a personal examination with the help of some experts,
promulgated the new Code through the apostolic constitution *Sacri
canones*[80] on October 18, 1990; the Code entered into force on October 1,
1991.

The Constitution *Sacri canones* underlines the very special importance
of the sacred canons of the first Christian millennium, a patrimony shared
by all of the Eastern Churches, Catholic or otherwise. Faced with possible
doubts about the benefits of the new Code from the point of view of ecumenism, taking into account the difficult relations between the Eastern
Churches united with Rome and those separated from it, St. John Paul II
affirmed, on the contrary, *the ecumenical intent of the Code*: its canons, necessary now for the orderly vitality of the Eastern Catholic Churches, will
remain in force "until abrogated or changed by the supreme authority of
the Church for a just cause, of which the full communion of all of the Eastern Churches with the Catholic Church is indeed the most serious, besides
being especially in accord with the desire of Our Savior Jesus Christ himself."[81] On the other hand, the Eastern Code has certainly contributed to
ensure that the other lung with which the Church must breathe, that of
the East (to use a comparison dear to St. John Paul II), is more present in
the Latin Church, especially with respect to canonical science.

Studies in Eastern Catholic law have experienced considerable develop-ment since the Code. In addition to the specialized centers (in the Pontifical Oriental Institute in Rome, and in the Oriental Institute "Dharmaram Col-lege" in Bangalore, India), chairs of Latin law have been instituted in the faculties of Eastern law. Furthermore, the recognized technical quality of the language and juridical solutions of the Eastern Code, that was able to im-prove upon the Latin Code in several aspects, makes this new legal *corpus* even more interesting for canonists: not only as a way of knowing the com-mon Eastern discipline, but also as a point of supplementary or alternative reference for general juridical problems in the entire Church.[82]

**41.** Bibliography

In addition to the works of Church history and general history neces-sary for the indispensable knowledge of the overall context, for more on the history of canon law and for a wider bibliography one can consult these manuals:

a) History of the sources:

A.M. Stickler, *Historia iuris canonici latini. I. Historia fontium*, PAS-Verlag, Taurini 1950 (rist. Romae, 1985)

J. Gaudemet, *Les sources du droit de L'Église en Occident du II<sup>e</sup> au VII<sup>e</sup> siècle*, Cerf—C.N.R.S., Paris, 1985I

ID., *Les sources du droit canonique. VIII<sup>e</sup>-XX<sup>e</sup> siècle*, Cerf, Paris, 1993.

B.E. Ferme, *Introduction to the History of the Sources of Canon Law*, Wilson & Lafleur, Montréal, 2007.

P. Erdö, *Storia delle fonti del diritto canonico*, Marcianum Press, Venice, 2008.

b) On the history of canon law as a science:

A. Van Hove, *Prolegomena ad Codicem Iuris Canonici*, 2a. ed., H. Dessain, Mechliniae—Romae, 1945, pars IV, pp. 408–612 (it is also very useful for information regarding the sources).

P. Lombardía, *Desarrollo histórico de la ciencia canónica*, in J. Hervada—P. Lombardía, *El Derecho del Pueblo de Dios*, vol. I, EUNSA, Pamplona 1970, pp. 189–225.

P. Erdö, *Storia della scienza del diritto canonico. Una introduzione*, Ed. Pont. Università Gregoriana, Rome, 1999.

c) history of the institutions:

B. Kurtscheid, *Historia iuris canonici: historia institutorum ab Ecclesiae fundatione usque ad Gratianum*, reimpr., Officium Libri Catholici, Romae 1951

*Histoire de Droit et des Institutions de l'Église en Occident*, edited by G. Le Bras and J. Gaudemet, Cujas—Sirey, Paris, 1955 ss.

W.M. Plöchl, *Geschichte des Kirchenrechts*, 3 vol., Herold, Vienna, 1960–1970.

A. García y García, *Historia del Derecho Canónico. I. El primer milenio*, Universidad Pontificia de Salamanca, Salamanca, 1967.

P. Lombardía, *Canon Law in History*, in *Exegetical commentary on the Code of Canon Law*, edited by E. Caparros, Wilson & Lafleur—Midwest Theological Forum, Montréal—Chicago (IL) 2004, vol. I, pp. 59–119.

H. E. Feine, *Kirchliche Rechtsgeschichte: die katholische Kirche*, 5ª ed., Böhlau, Cologne—Vienna 1972

C. Van de Wiel, *History of Canon Law*, Peeters, Louvain 1991 *History of Medieval Canon Law*, edited by W. Hartmann—K. Pennington, The Catholic University of America Press, Washington (DC), 1999 ss.

J. Gaudemet, *Église et Cité : histoire du droit canonique*, Cerf—Montchrestien, Paris, 1994

J. Orlandis, *Historia de las instituciones de la Iglesia Católica: cuestiones fundamentales*, EUNSA, Pamplona, 2003.

## Notes

1   The expression used is that of Pope St. John Paul II in his Bull of Indiction of the Great Jubilee of the Year 2000, *Incarnationis Mysterium*, 29 November

1998, n. 11, in AAS, 91 (1999), pp. 129–147. This purification includes different juridical-canonical aspects, among which, for example, are those linked to the means of protecting the purity and integrity of the faith.

2   Gabriel Le Bras, cultivator of religious sociology, has been able to enhance this contribution: *Prolégomènes*, Sirey, Paris, 1955, vol. I of the great *Histoire de Droit et des Institutions de l'Église en Occident*, edited by G. LeBras and J. Gaudemet.

3   This development dates back mainly to the German historical school of the 19th century (see number 37, *infra*). In the twentieth century, among the most important historians of canon law we can note the following: Paul Fournier (dating back to the end of the nineteenth century), Gabriel Le Bras and Jean Gaudemet (this French current gave birth, among other things, to the most important work in the history of institutions, still in the process of being published: see note number 2, *supra*); Stephan Kuttner, the founder of the Institute of Medieval Canon Law in the United States and the *Bulletin of Medieval Canon Law*, and a great promoter of the critical study of medieval manuscripts; Cardinal Alfons M. Stickler, who in addition to many other works, has written a now classic history of sources (see the bibliography at the end of this chapter); Rudolf Weigand, rigorous author of critical editions and historical monographs; etc.

4   See the classic work of J. Dauvillier, *Les temps apostoliques*, 1er siècle, Sirey, Paris 1970 (it is the second volume of the *Histoire de Droit et des Institutions de l'Église en Occident*, cit.). For a theological-biblical vision, see P. Grelot, *La tradition apostolique: règle de foi et de vie pour l'Église*, Cerf, Paris, 1995.

5   This aspect is highlighted by P. Erdö in *Teologia del diritto canonico. Un approccio storico-istituzionale*, Giappichelli, Turin, 1996, pp. 53–78.

6   One thinks, for example, of the tithes to meet the needs of the Church in relation to the tithes in favor of the Levites.

7   In general, the contributions in *L'enracinement du droit canonique dans l'Écriture*, in *L'Année Canonique*, 21 (1977), pp. 39–216 tend to focus on the law only in the perspective of the norm.

8   For a presentation according to this line of thought, in which special emphasis is placed on the notion of *communio*, see E. Tejero, "Mysterium salutis e la communio: valori fondanti dell'ordine giuridico dell'Antichità, in Il concetto di diritto canonico, edited by C.J. Errázuriz and L. Navarro, Giuffrè, Milan 2000, pp. 3–45.

9   It is therefore customary to treat this part as a whole, which then naturally requires subdivisions. See, e.g. B. Kurtscheid, *Historia iuris canonici: historia institutorum ab Ecclesiae fundatione usque ad Gratianum*, reimpr., Officium libri catholici, Romae, 1951; A. García y García, *Historia del derecho canónico. 1. El primer Milenio*, Universidad Pontificia de Salamanca, Salamanca, 1967.

10  On the importance of the oral transmission of law with specific reference to

the theme of the history of ecclesiastical celibacy, cf. A.M. Stickler, "Ecclesiastical celibacy. Its history and its theological foundations," in *Ius Ecclesiae*, 5 (1993), pp. 3–59, especially pp. 9–10.

11   See L. Hertling, *Communio, Chiesa e Papato nell'antichità cristiana*, Libreria Editrice Gregoriana, Rome, 1961; G. D'Ercole, *"Communio"–Collegialità–Primato e sollicitudo omnium ecclesiarum dai Vangeli a Costantino*, Herder, Rome, 1964; J. Liebart, *Communion Spirituelle et Institution dans l'Église avant IVᵉ siècle. Un Sondage*, in *L'Année Canonique*, 25 (1981), pp. 149–168.

12   The original texts of the Ecumenical Councils with English translations are easily accessible in *Decrees of the Ecumenical Councils*, edited by G. Alberigo and N.P. Tanner, Sheed and Ward—Georgetown University Press, London—Washington (DC) 1990.

13   As in many other fields, the figure of St. Augustine (354–430) stands out regarding the doctrine on the sacraments (on marriage in particular), and on communion itself. See A. Giacobbi, *La Chiesa di S. Agostino. I. Mistero di Comunione*, Città Nuova—Pontificia Università Lateranense, Rome, 1978.

14   *See* A. Gauthier, *Roman Law and its Contribution to the Development of Canon Law*, 2d ed., Saint Paul University, Ottawa, 1996.

15   In the shorter term, Justinian's collection inspired some oriental collections that took on the systematic technique of the *Digest*, the most important of which is the *Collectio L Titulorum*, compiled by Giovanni Scolastico in 550.

16   Convened and considered as ecumenical in the East, it has never been recognized as such by the Roman See, although individual provisions have been accepted.

17   We have seen (see number 24, *supra*) how the *85 Canones Apostolici* were recognized by Trullan II. They were at the top of the list, which also included conciliar canons and some from the popes. Following this list, the Trullana Collection was privately composed, containing the *Syntagma adauctum*.

18   G. Le Bras introduced the name "Gelasian renaissance" to designate this moment, which was also characterized by the intense legislative and governmental activity of the Popes of that time, in the period between Pope St. Gelasiius I (492–496) and Pope St. Hormisdas (514–523). Gelasius I is particularly well-known for his doctrine about the existence of two distinct powers; i.e., that of the Church and that of the king. Another pope of this time particularly relevant from a juridical point of view was St. Gregory the Great (590–604), well-adept in Roman juridical culture. Numerous letters of his are preserved, which enjoyed great authority in the Middle Ages. On his vision of the government of the Church with a view to justice, see J-Y., Pertin, *Justice et gouvernement dans l'Église d'après les Lettres de saint Grégoire le Grand*, L'Harmattan, Paris, 2015.

19   It contained canonical texts, both conciliar canons and decrees. Many of the latter are false, and some date back to the first century. The name of Isidore,

with which the author presents himself in the preface of the work, immediately evokes that of St. Isidore of Seville, so it is no wonder that the collection was known precisely as Isidorian, serving as a factor in favor of its authority and its success. The Donation of Constantine, a famous forgery according to which the Emperor had given Pope St. Sylvester I very extensive territories in the West, dates back to this period and appears in the Pseudo-Isidorian collection.

20  Other works of canonists of that time are known in this line of concordance, such as the *Liber de misericordia et iustitia* of Alger of Liege, composed between 1095 and 1121, whose originality lies not in the criterion used—in essence the same indicated in the Prologue by Ivo—but in the fact of having put it into practice in his book, in which he inserts not only the texts to be reconciled, but also his own comments. Other criteria of concordance were used: the authenticity of the texts, the time of issue, the circumstances of the act (the rationale, the recipients, whether they were of a temporary or a permanent nature, etc.), whether they were of the nature of a true law or simply advisory or exhortatory, the meaning of the words, the hierarchy between the authorities (the prevalence of Scripture, of the universal authority of the Church, etc.). In the Prologue of his work *Sic et non* (of which there are various reviews starting from the year 1115/17), the theologian Abelard sets out some of these principles of interpretation, and applies them to clarify texts concerning theological problems.

21  On the codification in the twentieth century of the discipline common to the Eastern Catholic churches, see number 40 *infra*.

22  *Digest*, 1, 1, 10.

23  The maxim *"legista sine canonibus parum valet, canonista sine legibus nihil"* (i.e., "a civil lawyer without a knowledge of canon law is worth little; a canon lawyer without a knowledge of civil law is worth nothing"), expresses the intimate connections between the two types of juridical knowledge.

24  On the common law, the work of F. Calasso, *Medioevo del diritto 1. Le fonti*, Giuffrè, Milan, 1954, is classic. A good panoramic view, focused on the role of science, is offered by M. Bellomo *The Common Legal Past of Europe, 1000–1800*, Catholic University of America Press, Washington, DC, 1995.

25  It should be noted that, in this context and in the future development of Church law, the term "canon" is not limited to the decisions of councils, but extends to any ecclesiastical rule. Today it is used to name the individual rules of the canonical codes, corresponding to the "articles" of the civil codes. Some canons of the Decretum are called *paleae*, and were introduced by others (it is customary to make the name of *Paucapalea*, disciple of Gratian) no later than around 1170.

26  *Quaestio* 3 of *Causa* 33, about penance, is in turn divided into 7 *distinctiones*.

27  The way of citing the various parts of the Decretum has changed over time.

In the Middle Ages, the canons were not numbered, so they were quoted according to the first words, a use that has remained for a long time among the canonists, and which still today serves to identify many conciliar and pontifical documents by means of the initial words (*incipit*): the constitution *Lumen Gentium*, the encyclical *Evangelium Vitae*, etc. Today only numbers are used for the Decretum. For the first part the number of the *distinctio* is written, followed by that of the canon: D. 23, c. 12; the second part consists of the number of the cause, then of the question, and finally of the canon: C. 23, q. 5, c. 25. For the treatment of penance and for the third part, we return to the system of the first part, as well as an indication of the subject: D. 1, c. 18, *de poen.*; D. 5, c. 26, *de cons.* In this way it is already clear which part of the Decretum is being referenced, without requiring any other explanation. The dicta are cited by indicating their positions (*ante* [a] or *post* [p]) in relation to the canons: D. 4, d.a.c. 1; C. 4, q. 3, d.p.c. 7.

28 The Decretum included most of the pseudo-Isidorian falsifications, which obviously did not thus acquire any new formal value.

29 The *Liber Extra* was cited by the word "extra," in full or—as is done today—abbreviated by the letter "X." The indication of the book, the title, and the chapter are then added. As with the Decretum, so also here the citation includes the words of the title heading or with the initial words of the chapter (most of the time corresponding to a decretal: e.g., Decretal *Quum tanto*) or simply a citation made up of numbers: X, 1, 4, 11.

30 Moreover, the same *Liber Sextus* was divided into the same five books as was the Decretals of Gregory IX, and is cited in the same way (see footnote 30, *supra*), using the acronym "in VI°." At the end of the *Liber Sextus*, 88 *regulae iuris* were collected as an appendix, coming from the scientific work of the canonists, based largely on Roman law, and intended for the interpretation, application, and teaching of canonical norms.

31 The *Clementinae* collection also retains the organizational scheme of Gregory IX's decretals. They are quoted with the abbreviation "in Clem."

32 These collections, abbreviated "in Extravag. Ioannis XXII" and "in Extravag. Com.," also followed the divisions of the Decretals of Gregory IX.

33 The edition of the *Corpus* usually used today is the one prepared by Emilio Friedberg, which appeared in 1879, and reproduced several times anastatically. To date there is no edition that can be called critical.

34 Current historiography no longer identifies him, as it once did, with Roland Bandinelli, the great canonist who would later become Pope Alexander III (1159–1181).

35 "Iustitia dulcore misericordiae temperata": Henricus de Segusio, *Summa*, Scientia, Lugduni 1537/Aalen 1962, Lib. V, *de dispensationibus*, 1, p. 289r.

36 The existence of a Christian-style secularism, however, which tends toward a de-clericalization of society, should not be forgotten. In this regard, see M.

Fazio, *Due rivoluzionari: F. de Vitoria and J.J. Rousseau*, Armando Ed., Rome, 1998, pp. 17–19.

37  As a result, in those lands the norms of royal law have been very important for the life of the Church; one observes, for example, the *Leyes de Indias* developed by the Spanish Crown. See A. de la Hera, *El gobierno de la Iglesia indiana*, in I. Sánchez Bella, A. de la Hera, C. Díaz Rementería, *Historia del derecho indiano*, Mapfre, Madrid, 1992, pp. 253–294.

38  Among the various other private collections of the acts of this Congregation, one with an official character stands out: the *Thesaurus Resolutionum S. Congregationis Concilii*, including decisions between 1718 and 1908, collected in 167 volumes. See *La Sacra congregazione del concilio: quarto centenario della Fondazione: 1564–1964: studi e ricerche*, Vatican City, 1964.

39  Among the various collections published, the most famous is the one started by Prospero Farinacio, entitled *Sacrae Rotae Romanae Decisiones Recentiores* (1697–1703) in 25 volumes that contain decisions between the years 1558 and 1684. Added to it were the *Decisiones Nuperrimae* (1751–1763), in 10 volumes covering the years 1684 up to 1706. The activity of the Holy Roman Rota was suspended in 1870 with the loss of the papal states, and resumed in 1908 when St. Pius X reorganized the Roman Curia. Beginning with those of 1909 and continuing until the present, the *Decisiones seu Sententiae* have been officially published each year. Since 1983, volumes of the *Decreta* have been added.

40  Among the various collections of the documents of missionary law, the principal one was edited by the Congregation itself, bearing the name of *Collectanea S. Congregationis de Propaganda Fide*. The two editions, one volume in 1893 (in systematic order) and two volumes in 1907 (in chronological order), were designed to serve the needs of the missionaries themselves.

41  Among the most important of the *Bullaria* is the *Magnum Bullarium Romanum*, which was started in the sixteenth century by Cherubini in Rome, and enriched in the eighteenth century by two other publishers, also in Rome, Maindardi and Cocquelines. There are 32 volumes which include pontifical acts from 440 until 1758. This collection was updated until 1834. Particularly with regard to the oldest acts, these collections are not very reliable in either their authenticity or their integrity. From 1865 an unofficial periodical publication began, entitled *Acta Sanctae Sedis*, which in 1909 gave way to the current *Acta Apostolicae Sedis*, which is official.

42  For an overall study of this, see T. Bertone, *Il governo della Chiesa nel pensiero di Benedetto XIV, 1740–1758*, LAS, Rome, 1977.

43  This does not imply, however, that there was in any way a situation of anarchy in the Church; in the concreteness of daily life there was a strong sense of unity and hierarchical obedience. It was precisely for this reason that the Holy

See's responses to the many questions that were constantly being asked were so important.

44  See G. Fransen, "L'application des décrets du Concile de Trente. Les débuts d'un nominalisme canonique, in L'Année Canonique," 27 (1983), pp. 5–16.

45  *Summa Theologiae*, I-II, qq. 90 ss.

46  *Ibidem*, II-II, q. 57.

47  One may also recall that the best edition of the *Corpus Iuris Canonici* in up until that time (although not properly a critical edition) was by Emil Friedberg (Leipzig 1879), an important figure in that school, who prepared it on the basis of another edition (Leipzig 1839) edited by another member of the same schook, Emil Ludwig Richter. In addition, the oldest journal specializing in the history of canon law began in 1911, as a section of Savigny's journal: *Zeitschrift der Savigny-Stiftung für Rechtsgeschichte, Kanonistische Abteilung.*

48  The *Kirchenrecht* (1845–1872) by the Catholic George Phillips adopted the division of the *tria munera* which will then be followed by Vatican II and the 1983 Code. The *Lehrbuch des katholischen und evangelischen Kirchenrechts* (1842), by Emil Ludwig Richter, introduced the division of matter into sources, Church-State relations, the constitutional law of the Church (hierarchical structure), and administrative law (the exercise of the power to teach, sanctify, and govern). This division was embraced by Wernz and had a considerable influence in the German area.

49  This intention of completeness was also manifested in Benedict XV's Motu proprio *Cum Iuris Canoni* (September 15, 1917, in *AAS*, 9, 1917, pp. 483–484). In fact, in the wake of what had been done with the Tridentine decrees, a commission of cardinals was established for the authentic interpretation of the canons of the Code (there were actually quite a few of these responses, formulated in a precise way so as to generate either an *affirmative* or *negative* answer to the proposed question). Moreover, the pope urged the Roman Congregations to refrain from issuing new general decrees, unless a serious need required it, and instead to resort to explanatory instructions of the Code. (The most famous of these instructions was *Provida Mater*, from the Sacred Congregation for the Discipline of the Sacraments, on August 15, 1936, regarding the processes of matrimonial nullity—in *AAS*, 28, 1936, pp. 313–361. This gave rise to problems of congruence with the codicial text.) It was expected that any new general decrees would be transformed by the aforementioned commission into new canons to replace the existing ones, or inserted as "bis" or "ter" without altering the original numbering (in reality, changes were very rarely made, and the system of inserting new canons was never in fact implemented).

In any event, after the Code of 1917 there was a great proliferation of legal documents of various kinds by the Holy See. The main collection is the one edited by J. Ochoa, *Leges Ecclesiae post Codicem iuris canonici editae*,

Commentarium pro religiosis—EDIURCLA, Romae, 1966, ss. It was continued after the 1983 Code, and the latest volumes are edited by D. Andrés. In the English language, the volumes of *Canon Law Digest* are very useful for knowing these legal documents.

50 Unlike secular codes of a State, the canonical code is not limited to just one sector of the system (civil, criminal, procedural, etc.), but embraces the entirety of the law of the Church.

51 Compilations often had a new formal value, resulting from the promulgation of the whole by the authority.

52 Cardinal Gasparri prepared an edition of the *Codex* with notes indicating the sources of each canon. These sources were collected by Gasparri himself and completed by J. Serédi in the nine volumes of the *Codicis Iuris Canonici Fontes*, Typis Polyglottis Vaticanis, Romae, 1926–1939. These publications are useful for a first approach to pre-code law.

53 There is autobiographical evidence of this; what appears especially interesting comes from what Gasparri said shortly before his death: P. Gasparri, *Storia della codificazione del diritto canonico per la Chiesa latina*, in AA.VV., *Acta congressus iuridici internationalis. VII saeculo a Decretalibus Gregorii IX et XIV a Codice Iustiniano promulgatis. Romae 12–17 Novembris 1934*, vol. 4, Pontificium Institutum Utriusque Iuris, Romae, 1937, pp. 1–10. In recent decades, research has intensified on the development of the first Code, especially on the basis of the Vatican Secret Archive. An exemplary fruit, with ample general information and a bibliography on the codification process is the book by J. Llobell—E. De León—J. Navarrete, *Il libro "de processibus" nella codificazione del 1917. Studi e documenti*, vol. I, Giuffrè, Milan, 1999. On the history of the codification of 1917, placed in a broad context, see the fundamental work of C. Fantappiè, *Chiesa romana e modernità giuridica. L'edificazione del sistema canonistico (1563–1903)*, Giuffrè, Milan, 2008.

54 One example of this is the excellent reception received by the Latin-Spanish edition with pedagogical comments, prepared by canonists of the University of Salamanca: L. Miguélez—S. Alonso—M. Cabreros de Anta, *Código de Derecho Canónico y Legislación Complementaria*, BAC, Madrid, 1945. It had 10 editions.

55 The decrees of the Sacred Congregation for Seminaries and Universities of August 7, 1917 (in *AAS*, 9, 1917, p. 439) and of October 31, 1918 (in *AAS*, 11, 1919, p. 19) sanctioned a virtual exclusivity of the Code as the material for the teaching of and examination in canon law exams in ecclesiastical centers of study. For a treatment of the canonical science in English during the period of the 1917 Code, see *The 1917 or Pio-Benedctine Code of Canon Law in English Translation and Extensive Scholarly Apparatus*, edited by E. N. Peters, Ignatius Press, San Francisco, 2001.

56 Different forms of connecting with tradition lasted a long time, however, due also to the continuity of canonical science itself. A typical phenomenon of the

transition to the codicial era were the manuals elaborated first by a canonist and later adapted by another (the books then bear both names: Wernz-Vidal, Lega-Bartocetti, Vlaming-Bender, etc.) or by the same author (Gasparri made the second edition in 1934 of his treatise on marriage, which was originally dated 1904).

57 For example, the canonical journal of the Gregorian University was called *Periodica de re morali, canonica, liturgica* between 1927 and 1990, the year in which it took the current name of *Periodica de re canonica* (although in fact for some time already it had been almost exclusively canonical).

58 In addition to the documents of Vatican II, many documents of the popes and of various departments of the Holy See can be found, in the original Latin and in different translations, on the official website of the Holy See itself: www.vatican.va. An overall presentation of the conciliar message—retaining all of the freshness and depth of a work that had been written for the faithful of his diocese—was written by the bishop of Krakow, a Conciliar Father, and the future Pope St. John Paul II: K. Wojtyla, *Sources of Renewal: The Implementation of the Second Vatican Council,* Harper and Raw, San Francisco, 1981.

59 Litterae circulares *Postremis hisce annis*, April 2, 1975, in *Communicationes*, 7 (1975), pp. 12–17.

60 In addition to the historical summary contained in the preface of the CIC, see the report recorded by one of the protagonists of the entire elaboration process, J. Herranz, "Genesis and Development of the New Code of Canon Law, in Exegetical commentary on the Code of Canon Law," edited by E. Caparros, Wilson & Lafleur—Midwest Theological Forum, Montréal—Chicago (IL), 2004, vol. I, pp. 121–168.

61 They can be found in the first issue of the Commission's magazine (currently published by the Pontifical Council for Legislative Texts) *Communicationes* (1, 1969, pp. 70–100), which, among other things, continues to publish material from the history of the second codification in Latin. See *I principi per la revisione del Codice di diritto canonico*, edited by J. Canosa, Giuffrè, Milan, 2000.

62 The Latin text, the only official one, is published in pars II of vol. 75 (1983) of *AAS*. An edition has been published with an indication of the sources of each canon and with an analytical index: Pontificia Commissio Codici Iuris Canonici Authentice Interpretando, *Codex Iuris Canonici, Fontium annotatione et indice analytico auctus*, Libreria Editrice Vaticana, Vatican City, 1989. There are translations in the main current languages. To reconstruct the drafting process of the canons, it is customary to use the Schemas and the *Relatio* with the comments of the members of the Commission to the 1980 Schema (these were documents printed by the Commission for their internal use, but they are now available in many libraries), to the aforementioned *Communicationes* magazine, and the volume that reports the plenary sessions of 1981, in which

several specific issues were discussed in greater detail: Id., *Congregatio plenaria. Diebus 20–29 octobris 1981 habita*, Typis Polyglottis Vaticanis, Vatican City, 1991. Useful for tracing the history of each individual canon is the volume of E.N. Peters, *Incrementa in Progressu 1983 Codicis Iuris Canonici*, Wilson & Lafleur, Montréal, 2005.

63 The original text is in *AAS*, 75 (1983), pars II, p. XI–XII.

64 The pope himself decided instead to stop *sine die* ( i.e., indefinitely) another legislative project that was being prepared simultaneously with that of the Code: a *Lex Ecclesiae fundamentalis* (LEF), destined to be a type of constitutional law; that is, superior to the Code itself and to all other ordinary laws, and common to the whole Church, both Latin and Eastern. In this way, the technique of modern constitutional law would have been introduced into the Church by means of the formalization of a text—something the States usually call a "Constitution"—the content of which would have prevailed over the rest of the set of norms. This would also have represented an advantage of an ecumenical nature, in that it would have clarified which was the fundamental discipline for all communities in full communion with the Catholic Church.

In the end, however, as we said, the idea was abandoned, at least for the time being. Nevertheless, several canons that had already prepared for the LEF (on the rights and duties of the faithful, on the supreme authority of the Church, etc.) were included in both Codes. The time was probably not yet ripe, as was amply demonstrated by the abundant misunderstandings that accompanied discussions surrounding the LEF project itself. To some, it seemed that a positivistic model of law was being adopted, as if instead of the divine law, known through the sources of Revelation, a positive human law was being formulated as the ultimate foundation of canonical juridicality. For others, the adoption of the constitutional technique necessarily entailed the acceptance of the liberal-democratic vision of modern constitutionalism in secular states, something that was incompatible with the hierarchical constitution of the Church.

On the history of the LEF project, see D. Cenalmor, *La ley fundamental de la Iglesia: historia y análisis de un proyecto legislativo*, EUNSA, Pamplona, 1991. Regarding doctrine, the most significant effort to elaborate a canonical constitutional law, even after the abandonment of the LEF—therefore basing itself only on the preponderance of material regarding juridically constitutional elements—was done together by Pedro Lombardía and Javier Hervada. On current canonical constitutional law, see M. del Pozzo, *Introduzione alla scienza del diritto costituzionale canonico*, EDUSC, Rome, 2015.

65 In this light, one can read the apostolic letter *Novo millennio ineunte*, written for the end of the Great Jubilee Year of 2000, by St. John Paul II on January 6, 2001, containing a program for the Church for the start of the third Christian millennium. In it the pontiff affirms that Vatican Council II is "*the great*

*grace bestowed on the Church in the twentieth century*: there we find a sure compass by which to take our bearings in the century now beginning" (n. 57).

66  For a collection and a comparative study, see J.T. Martín de Agar—L. Navarro, *Legislazione delle Conferenze Episcopali complementare al C.I.C.*, 2nd ed. updated, Coletti a San Pietro, Rome, 2009.

67  As one example, one can look to canons 807–814 on Catholic universities: to have a juridical definition of the same institution, that allows the confronting of existing problems, one must resort to the Apostolic Constitution *Ex corde Ecclesiae* of St. John Paul II, August 15, 1990, in *AAS*, 82 (1990), pp. 1475–1509.

68  A very significant one touches the duty of adherence to the magisterium *de fide tenenda* and the penal consequences of its non-observance: St. John Paul II's *motu proprio Ad tuendam fidem*, May 18, 1998, in *AAS*, 90 (1998), pp. 457–461. Another very significant integration of the legislation of the Code, although not formally presented as such, was implemented to specify the requirements for exercising the magisterium of the Episcopal Conferences: see the *motu proprio* of St. John Paul II *Apostolos suos*, May 21, 1998, in *AAS*, 90 (1998), pp. 641–658. In this sense, one might also consider the previously cited apostolic constitution *Ex corde Ecclesiae*. The most important reform was done by Pope Francis with the new legislation, replacing the previous canons, on the processes surrounding the declaration of nullity of marriage: see his *motu proprio Mitis Iudex,* August 15, 2015. At the time of this writing, there is currently underway an effort to reform Book VI of the 1983 Code, on sanctions in the Church.

69  June 28, 1988, in *AAS*, 80 (1988), pp. 841–930. Other laws of special importance concern military ordinariates, the causes of saints, the election of the Roman Pontiff, etc. At the time of this writing, work on a new constitution regarding the Roman Curia is underway.

70  There is now a fairly extensive and increasingly elaborate literature on the 1983 Code in different languages (Latin having almost completely disappeared as the language of canonical science). Meanwhile, the activity of canonical associations is growing, the number of students in faculties of canon law is increasing, new faculties are being created on the various continents, new periodical publications are appearing, etc. For information globally on the world of canon law, see the website www.iuscangreg.it, promoted by the Faculty of Canon Law of the Pontifical Gregorian University.

71  On the canonical discipline of the first millennium, see numbers 23–25 *supra*.

72  In addition to the Precalcedonese Churches, these are the Byzantine Orthodox Churches, among which historically the Patriarchate of Constantinople occupies the first place, and among which the Moscow Patriarchate, also of the Byzantine tradition (with more than 50 million faithful), currently stands out. In addition to Byzantine law, which is very influential in almost all of the Eastern Churches,

the law proper to each of those Churches must be taken into consideration. From a scientific point of view, it is interesting to note that even the greatest flowering of Byzantine canonical science occurred around the twelfth century; the name of Theodore Balsamone († after 1195) stands out. Similar to Gratian, Balsamone tried to reconcile conflicting canons, also taking into account those norms that had been issued by the emperors in ecclesiastical matters, a phenomenon of great import in the Church of Constantinople.

73 They make up a varied picture, including about 17 million faithful (the Orthodox exceed 200 million). Each Eastern Church *sui iuris* (on this notion, see number 183, *infra*) has its own rite; that is, a specific liturgical, theological, spiritual, and disciplinary heritage, closely tied to the culture and history of the respective people. The rites are grouped into different traditions, corresponding to the patriarchies of antiquity such as the Alexandrian, Antiochene, and Constantinopolitan traditions, as well as to other very ancient churches with a peculiar physiognomy, such as the Armenian and Chaldean traditions. On these notions, see canons 27–28 of the Oriental Code (CCEO). The most numerous Eastern Catholic Churches are these: the Maronite in Lebanon (of Antiochene tradition), the Syro-Malabar in India (of Chaldean tradition), and the Greek-Melkite, Ukrainian, and Romanian (of Constantinopolitan tradition). Emigrations, especially in America, have increased the presence of Eastern faithful in the diaspora; that is, outside the original territory of their own Churches, which entail various pastoral and juridical problems, in addition to in their relations with the respective local Latin rite churches.

74 That project, like the 1990 Code, was divided into titles, not books.

75 Regarding marriage, see the *motu proprio* of Pope Pius XII *Crebrae allatae sunt*, February 22, 1949, in *AAS*, 41 (1949), pp. 89–119; and on judgments, the *motu proprio* of the same pope *Sollicitudinem nostram*, January 6, 1950, in *AAS*, 42 (1950), pp. 5–120.

76 See the *motu proprio Postquam apostolicis litteris*, February 9, 1952, in *AAS*, 44 (1952), pp. 65–150.

77 See the *motu proprio Cleri sanctitati*, June 2, 1957, in *AAS*, 49 (1957), pp. 433–600.

78 One can consult the periodical of the Commssion *Nuntia*, n. 3, 1976, pp. 3–24.

79 This avoids having to elaborate a sort of legal architecture, which greatly reinforces the systematic nature of the Latin Code, also favoring a mentality that exaggerates the hermeneutic importance of codicial systematics. Furthermore, the titles can be arranged among themselves according to an order that best expresses their substantial priority. In this sense, the CCEO begins with Title I on the Christian faithful and all their rights and duties, leaving until the end Title XXIX on the law, customs, and administrative acts, in addition to Title XXX on the calculation of time.

80  In *AAS*, 82 (1990), pp. 1033–1044. The official text of the CCEO, preceded by a preface with a great deal of information on the history of Eastern codification, is found in pp. 1045–1363. There are already some translations, and an edition indicating the sources: Pontificium Consilium de Legum Textibus Interpretandis, *Codex Canonum Ecclesiarum Orientalium auctoritate Ioannis Pauli pp. II promulgatus, fontium annotatione auctus*, Libreria Editrice Vaticana, Vatican City, 1995.

81  *AAS*, 82 (1990), p. 1036.

82  The exposition of this book is limited to Latin law only. However, some particularly significant oriental peculiarities will be indicated, and also some points on which the CCEO in its general aspects may be interesting for the Latin canonist.

For an introduction to the current Eastern Catholic law, see D. Salachas, *Istituzioni di diritto canonico delle Chiese cattoliche orientali*, EDB, Bologna, 1993; R. Metz, *Le nouveau Droit des Églises orientales catholiques*, Cerf, Paris, 1997.

# Chapter III
## *THE CONFIGURATION OF RIGHTS AND THE LAW IN THE CHURCH*

### *1. Foreword*

**42.** *The configuration of canon law is that process by which what is just in the Church is established or modified.* To ascertain the *quid iuris?*—i.e., what is just—both in general principles and in a particular concrete situation, the canonist must always consider that process of configuration—that is, one must always determine *the canonical sources* that pertain to the respective matter or case. This metaphorical use of the term "source," very traditional in juridical science, alludes to the cause or origin of rights and the law, much like water emanating from its source. It is necessary, however, to avoid reducing such sources merely to human norms of a general nature (especially statutes or other types of laws), as this would lead to a disregard of the sources of divine law, as well as other sources of human law of a singular character (both of the ecclesiastical authority in its administrative and judicial functions and of the faithful as such).

The fundamental principle to be borne in mind in this area is that of the contemporary distinction and unity between divine law and human law, on which we have already focused (see number 13, *supra*). Now it is a question of exploring the various canonical sources, regarding both divine and human law, that need to be taken into consideration if one intends to study and to solve any canonical problem. Therefore, knowledge of this material, which is the subject of a large part of Book I of the Code, is a necessary prerequisite for the entire canonical enterprise.

These canonical sources give shape to the *juridical-canonical system* (see number 8, *supra*). In any juridical context, the knowledge, determination, and implementation of justice imply the progressive formation of a system which, within the inevitable human limits, declares, concretizes, and gives certainty and security to the realization of justice in this sphere. Even in ecclesial law, one cannot ignore the limits of human knowledge and of the human will, the historicity and mutability of man and his social relationships, the need to formalize that which is just in order to make it operational, the exigencies of "juridical security," which means that in a given situation justice is not always possible on this earth. It would be pure utopia to think about human relations of justice without such things as norms, judicial authorities, or in the absence of a scientific discussion on rights and the law. It is certainly true also in the Church; these requirements derived from her human dimension in history were neither avoided in the past nor can they be avoided in the future.

Thus, the canonical system can never be separated, whether in theory or in practice, from its purpose: to serve the realization of justice. The recurring temptation to identify the system itself with the juridical as such must be avoided, as if the latter were simply a tool. Yet it must not be forgotten that justice, even in the Church, cannot be implemented without the determinations and means of protection offered by the concrete system of law.

## 2. The configuration of divine law from the perspective of that which is intrinsically just in the Church

### 2.1 The essential juridical aspects of the Church

#### 2.1.1. Divine law as part of the revelation deposit entrusted to the Church

**43.** *Divine law, that is, the dimension of justice essentially belonging to the ecclesial reality* (on this notion, see number 13, *supra*), *has already been configured once and for all by Christ himself:* it participates in the definitiveness of the new and eternal covenant (see *Dei Verbum*, n. 4), and concerns the essential and immutable juridical aspects of the essence of the Church (positive divine law), as well as those inherent in human nature and therefore also valid in the intra-ecclesial sphere (natural divine law). Throughout history, it is up to the Church, moved by the Holy Spirit, to penetrate ever

127

more deeply into the Christian mystery implemented once and for all and revealed to men. Naturally, even with respect to the divine law there is a *process of growth in its theoretical and practical understanding*. This process, not without its own difficulties, must take place under the sign of fidelity: "So the Church, in her teaching, life, and worship, perpetuates and hands on to all generations all that she herself is, all that she believes" (*Dei Verbum*, n. 8a).

This *self-knowledge of the Church* constitutes in every historical moment the indispensable point of reference for ascertaining divine law, that is to say the demands of justice intrinsic to the ecclesial reality. To attune oneself to divine law it is necessary to place oneself within the Church, and therefore *in the light of the Catholic faith*. Outside of this supernatural horizon, divine law becomes a purely cultural category, inasmuch as it is not believed that it corresponds to the *juridical dimension of a living reality*, according to a divine plan to which man must absolutely adhere for the glory of God and of human salvation.

The knowledge of the Church concerning divine law logically refers to *divine revelation*, the definitive fullness of which is Christ himself. In the juridical field, these words of the dogmatic constitution *Dei Verbum* of the Second Vatican Council on divine revelation are particularly significant: "*This plan of revelation is realized by deeds and words having an inner unity*: the deeds wrought by God in the history of salvation manifest and confirm the teaching and realities signified by the words, while the words proclaim the deeds and clarify the mystery contained in them" (*Dei Verbum*, n. 2, italics supplied). It is enough to consider, in their essential configuration, the intra-ecclesial relations of justice concerning the sacraments, in order to understand their belonging to that intertwining of God's works and words that occurs in the economy of revelation. The institution of the sacraments, the election and the powers conferred on the Twelve and in particular on Peter, the universal missionary mandate and all the other foundational actions of the Church carried out by Christ, are inseparable from the whole teaching of Christ himself, and above all from his own life culminating in the paschal mystery of his passion, death, and resurrection. Divine law must be contemplated and lived as an aspect of Christian revelation, and is inconceivable and impracticable outside of this vital insertion.[1]

Divine law, like all of revelation, is contained in the inspired books of Sacred Scripture, and is also transmitted through Sacred Tradition.[2] *Scripture and Tradition, in their profound unity, are the primordial source of divine law.* Among the biblical texts, especially of the New Testament, and among the writings that reflect the Tradition (preaching, theology, liturgy, other documents, etc.) there are some of a juridical nature. This occurs not only when the text presents itself as formally juridical (as, for example, the decisions of the Council of Jerusalem: see Acts of the Apostles, chapter 5), but also when the text indicates a behavior deemed to be just or unjust in the Christian community. It is, however, necessary to discern in these texts that which shows essential and therefore invariable features of the Church, and those things which may be nothing more than a particular historical expression (even if very ancient). An example of this latter phenomenon would be the concrete rules for the exercise of the charisms, determined by Saint Paul for the Church of Corinth (see 1 Corinthians 14:26–40). On the other hand, there is no doubt that some determinations of the Apostles, moved by the Holy Spirit, are of such importance for the life and for the structure of the Church that they are to be received as definitive, inasmuch as they determine in fundamental points the same foundational configuration of the Church (as with, for example, the articulation of the ordination of bishops, priests, and deacons), or insofar as they give this configuration a concrete historical manifestation in basic aspects that were destined to perdure in the ecclesial tradition (for example, in the union between the ministry of the successors of Peter and the episcopal see of Rome).

*2.1.2. Divine law in the* sensus fidei *(sense of the faith) and in the Magisterium of the Church*

**44.** In order for divine law to be a juridically operative reality in the Church, it must be known with *certainty*. Otherwise, the question of what divine law consists would be an occasion for endless disagreements, which in fact can attack the unity of the Church itself, as has unfortunately happened throughout history. All the faithful, through the *supernatural sense of faith* (see *Lumen Gentium*, n. 12a, *Dei Verbum*, n. 10), participate in the knowledge of divine law: in their lives, especially in their common behaviors, constant and rooted in the convictions of faith they perceive the supernatural sense of justice in the Church, making up a part of the true sense of the faith. The same Holy Spirit who moves the faithful toward the truth taught by Christ, pushes them to adhere to what the sacred Pastors author-itatively teach as instructors of the faith. The *living Magisterium of the Church*, which is responsible for the authentic interpretation of the written or transmitted word of God (see *Dei Verbum,* n. 10b), is an external guide and guarantee of adherence to the deposit of faith. The magisterium is so connected to Scripture and Tradition that they cannot exist separately (see *Dei Verbum*, n. 10c). Without this magisterial function, made possible by the assistance of the Holy Spirit himself, it would be completely impossible to maintain the fidelity and unity of the Church around revelation and—particularly from a juridical point of view—around divine law.

It should be borne in mind that divine law includes natural law, the knowledge of which—though made more difficult by sin—is made easier by divine revelation and ecclesiastical teaching. Revelation contains moral norms knowable by natural reason, and these can be taught by the magis-terium, even in a definitive and infallible way.[3] Such moral norms obviously include those relating to the law and justice.

Sometimes magisterial documents are seen as extra-juridical; that is, as doctrinal texts without a disciplinary character.[4] The distinction between the two kinds of documents is clear, and it would not make sense to treat an encyclical as if it were a law, nor a law as if it were an encyclical. Their purpose is different: the texts of the magisterium intend to transmit and interpret Catholic doctrine, while disciplinary texts aim to regulate inter-personal juridical relationships in practice. Nevertheless, the magisterial documents, inasmuch they declare the doctrine about juridical aspects, have a juridical value in their very content.[5] Disciplinary texts, for their part, may contain, or at least presuppose, doctrinal aspects of a juridical nature.

In addition, the certainty that the Church needs in living divine law must sometimes (especially in the face of attacks on fundamental doctrines of discipline), require the maximum degree of *infallibility*; in other words, it is necessary to be able to discern *definitively* juridical questions linked to essential aspects of intra-ecclesial justice. The infallibility of the whole Church in this regard is made possible thanks to the existence of an infal-lible magisterium, which can include not only subjects proposed as divinely revealed, but also matters concerning faith and morals that are required to devoutly keep and faithfully expose the same deposit of faith. Infallibility can occur not only by means of a definition by an ecumenical council or by the Roman ontiff,[6] but also by means of a doctrine proposed by the ordinary and universal magisterium of the Church as definitive (on these two ways, see *Lumen Gentium*, n. 25b, c).[7] However, even non-infallible magisterium must always be kept in mind when solving juridical-canonical questions, especially when it comes from the pope and appears to have a particular relevance according to the mind and will of the pope himself, manifested primarily by the character of the documents, from the frequent repetition of the same doctrine, or from the manner in which he expresses himself (see *Lumen Gentium*, n. 25a).

### 2.1.3. The relevance of divine law in canonical questions

**45.** It may appear at first that matters pertaining to divine law are rather exceptional in the Church, so that most of the time practical solutions could be adopted without a formal pronouncement on divine law. There is some truth in this approach, given that the aspects of human law are of particular import in the configuration of the ecclesial juridical order. It would be misleading to suggest that problems open to varied historical solutions were solved only upon recourse to principles of divine law.[8] But neither is it possible to err in the other extreme, assigning a purely theoretical importance to divine law, tending to ignore it in practice, where "solutions" contrary to it are authorized for allegedly pastoral reasons.[9]

In reality, *the theme of divine law is present in some manner in any canonical problem.* In fact, there is always a dimension linked to the very essence of the Church itself and to the salvific goods entrusted to it by the Lord. This dimension is absolutely critical when configuring the human aspects of a problem, both generally and concretely. No juridical solution is purely and simply established by human persons, given that solutions always remain linked to the demands of justice intrinsically present in the human reality, and, inasmuch as such solutions concern canon law, they are also tied to the reality of the Church of Christ. Consequently, all sources of human law, which will be discussed later (see numbers 47–62, *infra*), aid in the knowledge and understanding of divine law as it manifests itself in the life of the Church and in its intimate intertwining with human law. Realizing this constant presence of divine law is not only indispensable when truly seeking justice, but for retaining a prudent and sufficiently critical sense of human law, which must always respect, protect, and favor divine law. Indeed, if this necessary reference to divine law is disregarded, human law would become both incomprehensible and easily manipulated for purposes contrary to justice in the Church. To take one example: if one forgets what marriage is as a natural and sacramental reality, the entire structure of canonical matrimonial law would become an instrument in the service of purely subjective interests, regardless of their conformity to justice. In fact, the essential objective reference would be lacking for the judgment of the validity or nullity of a given marriage, or when attempting to resolve any other juridical issue concerning marriage.

### 2.2 The concrete juridical-canonical situations

**46.** From a realistic viewpoint, *divine law refers to a concrete reality*: what is just in every ecclesial situation. Consequently, in order to know the configuration of divine law, in addition to the necessary consideration of essential principles of a permanent nature, it is necessary to take into account the individual facts present in each situation. These facts are not a kind of amorphous raw material, devoid of any kind of original juridical value, which become juridical merely because some rules of law are applied to them. Such a normativist scheme does not account for the truth of divine law (nor that of human law), which refers to an intrinsic dimension of real interpersonal relationships in the Church. To live according to divine law, one cannot be satisfied with a theoretical and inoperative observance of principles pronounced in declarations or general documents: it must be made effective in individual cases.

In this sense, the usual distinction between law and fact should be clarified (or, as one reads in judicial sentences, between *in iure* and *in facto*). The abstraction with which our intellect operates leads to distinguish between general principles and rules on the one hand, and, on the other, the individual circumstances of the case. It is not correct, however, to identify the juridical with merely general aspects: in reality, *concrete facts constitute the reality in which rights really exist*. Therefore, attention to such facts indicates one of the most important signs of an authentic juridical mentality. Even if a judge, in a given case, were to consider the principles and general rules in a careful manner, but failed to examine the factual details with equal care, the resulting decision could not be just. This is equally true for the application of divine law, which is properly itself in its reference to concreteness: for example, this person is a baptized person or an ordained person, and therefore is the holder of certain respective rights and duties; this action is either a Christian sacrament or it is not; this oral or written teaching either transmits the Word of God or contradicts it, etc.

The problems related to the *proving of facts* (i.e., the evaluation and interpretation of evidence) are extremely relevant in the context of trials because they decisively influence the ascertainment of rights and the law. At any point in the process of the configuration, the implementation, and the protection of the just thing in a given situation, the knowledge of the pertinent facts makes up an essential component of the juridical knowledge. Obviously, this affirmation also applies to divine law, the observance and protection of which requires an effective concern for the real life of the Church, for the concrete problems that require just answers in conformity with the foundational plan of Christ. Without due proof it would be unjust for ecclesiastical authorities, whether administrative or judicial, to exercise their jurisdiction in the Church.[10]

## 3. The configuration of human law from the perspective of that which is just as established by human persons

### 3.1 Preliminary considerations

**47.** The essential configuration of justice in the Church is of divine origin. Such a configuration, however, includes neither all the elements necessary to establish concrete relations of intra-ecclesial justice, nor the system for their protection and promotion. In entrusting the Church with the fulfillment of her mission, Christ conferred on it both the duty and the ability to determine those relationships of justice in the way required by the fulfillment of this same mission. A wide aperture was thus created for human law in the Church; that is, for *that which is just by means of the legitimate determination of the Hierarchy and of the faithful*, each within its sphere of ecclesial competence.

*Human law has its foundation and its limits in divine law.* The just thing of human origin can be just because the juridical force of the act that establishes it is derived, in the ultimate analysis, from the Church's own being.

An ecclesiastical law produces rights and duties for the faithful because there is hierarchical power in this regard, which is juridically binding in the context of the mission proper to the hierarchy for the common good of the Church. The marital covenant between two faithful gives rise to a reciprocal bond of justice in the Church because the reality of marriage between the baptized has been elevated to the condition of a sacrament.

*Any human decision, general or particular, contrary to divine law is devoid of any true juridical value*, even if it is draped with all kinds of formalities as a law, decree, sentence, etc. This statement of principle is always valid, and does not lose its value because in some circumstances it may be in fact impossible or inadvisable to modify the unjust effects of an act. The canonical legal system must work to avoid such cases, but it must take into account some structural limits deriving from being of the Church or from human nature. For example, the hierarchical constitution of the Church means that there can be no appeal against the supreme authority of the Church (i.e., the Roman Pontiff and the College of Bishops). The guarantees of justice then transcend the legal system, and ultimately come from the assistance of the Holy Spirit, who in making possible the indefectibility of the Church does not allow the conglomeration of injustices that might endanger it. At the same time, and without causing any damage to the permanent principles of divine law, human nature itself often requires that legal problems be put to an end, once normal means have been used to bring to light the just thing in a given circumstance (consider, for instance, the juridical principles of prescription and of *res judicata*). Allowing disputes to remain open perpetually would certainly be a much greater injustice, as legal problems prolonged without an end would be gravely damaging.

The *inevitable imperfection of all manifestations of human law* is a very different thing than injustice itself. Such imperfection derives from the fact that rules and actions put into place by men can never fully adapt to the complex, changing, and often unpredictable exigencies of the ecclesial reality. This requires a wise application of the rules, both through the concept of equity (see number 51, *infra*) as well as by means of other mechanisms of adaptation to the particular case such as dispensations, privileges, etc. (see numbers 58–60, *infra*). As a result, appropriate efforts may need to be made in order to modify rules that become obsolete or unsuitable. It is thus necessary to proceed in any case with realism and restraint, conscious of the fact that every human choice may entail certain disadvantages. Nevertheless, it is better to live observing certain imperfect rules, trying to limit as much as possible any imperfections in those moments when such rules are applied, than to pursue an absolutely perfect human law, which in this world is impossible, and in fact expresses a kind of contempt for human law that does truly exist.

Our presentation of the factors that shape human law will include both *general norms* and *singular acts*, given that both contribute to determining what is really just in concrete situations. General norms (laws, customs, and other norms issued by the authority or by the faithful) are certainly necessary, insofar as they declare aspects of divine law and introduce common determinations in juridical relationships and in the system that ensures their protection and promotion. The common good of the Church needs those declarations and determinations, without which it would be practically impossible to live ecclesial communion in its visible aspects. But the juridical is not identified with general norms, contrary to what is often thought. The juridical configuration must reach the individual situation and the individual subject. In this sense, singular acts of ecclesiastical authority or of the faithful as such are decisive in establishing what is just in the particular case.

We will focus only on properly canonical sources, those that originate from the juridical action of ecclesial subjects. Given that the Church lives in the world, other sources related to civil law (norms of international or state law, civil juridical acts, etc.) also affect its juridical structure. At times, canonical norms themselves refer to civil laws (see canon 22); and there are multiple agreements between the Church and the individual States (e.g., through concordats: see canon 3), which are discussed in the context of Church-State relations. The realistic view of right (*ius*) as the object of justice allows one to overcome any doubts about whether such intra-ecclesial obligations are binding: the essence of the juridical does not depend on the authority that issues a norm, but rather on its being something intrinsically just, issued in any case by those who have competence in the matter. It follows that every true right and law, including those concerning the civil dimension of the Church's action as an institution, must be recognized and respected within the Church.

*3.2. General canonical norms with the force of law*

*3.2.1. Ecclesiastical laws[11]*

   *a) Definition and relationship with law*

**48.** In canonical science, the definition of the law of St. Thomas Aquinas is traditionally cited: *"an ordinance of reason for the common good, promulgated by one who has responsibility for the care of a community."*[12] This definition captures the essence of every law, both divine and human, and can therefore perfectly apply to the laws of the Church. However, this concept of law is placed on the level of its fundamental nature, while in the canonical ambit—and in that of the civil—the expression "ecclesiastical law" has a precise technical meaning, concerning exclusively the *general written norms issued in the exercise of legislative power in the Church.*[13]

   The law is an *ordinatio rationis*,[14] which highlights its essential relationship with reason, with its *rationality* or its *reasonableness.*[15] Certainly no law can be promulgated if there is no act of will on the part of the legislator, and its legal value exists only within the social power of the respective legislator. Nonetheless, the Thomistic definition clearly shows that the essence of the law cannot be grasped in a simple imperative command: *the law has meaning and legitimacy according to the truth of what the common good demands.* This obviously occurs not only when the law simply declares the essential needs of the common good of the Church, but also when it prudently determines those needs that are necessary according to the reality of the historical circumstances of the community to which the law refers. Although this choice may suggest an act of mere will and power, there is in reality an essential aspect of reasonableness, of a prudential adjustment to the needs of the reality about which the law is concerned. *The irrational law is not law* because it does not introduce an order, but rather a disorder, and in so doing renders "legal" an option that is contrary to the needs of the social reality itself. Legislative arbitrariness must be rejected as a mere appearance of the law, particularly harmful to the common good precisely because, among other things, it damages the link with the social authority.

   Sometimes it is feared that this consideration of the rationality of the law may introduce insecurity in its observance, favoring a hypercritical mentality that is synonymous with disobedience. It should be noted in this regard that irrationality constitutes an extreme position, in clear and insuperable contrast to the norm in its generality with reality, such as to make the norm truly unjust. Obviously, it is not enough that, as often happens, the provision of the law is questionable, insufficient, or subject to improvement. On the other hand, in its interpretation and application, efforts must be made to ameliorate its possible limitations (e.g., by means of *epikeia* for individual cases that fall outside the *ratio legis*: see number 51, *infra*). At the same time, it must be reiterated that there is nothing safer than a confrontation with reality, beyond the consideration of mere will.

*Laws are juridical insofar as their provisions concern relationships of justice.* Legality is often thought of as the formal constituent of 'juridical quality' according to the logic of legalist normativism. In reality, the concept of law greatly transcends the realm of rights and the 'juridical law' (one thinks, for example, of the existence of laws that are moral, technical, etc.), so in order to determine what juridical laws are, it is necessary to ascertain in them a relation with that which is just. Ecclesiastical laws declare the rights and the duties of the faithful, introducing positive obligations and limits on liberty if the ecclesial common good so requires; they affect the institutional configuration of the Church and regulate the exercise hierarchical power; they establish the means of protection of the rights of the Church and of the faithful (through trials and sanctions), etc. All these functions are juridical in that they have to do with what is just among the People of God.

We must also not forget how much pedagogical importance and social cohesion is to be attributed to the laws: knowing what the right behavior is, and recognizing oneself united around the laws given by the pastors are two effects of legislation that highlight its intimate relationship with both personal and ecclesial life. This meta-juridical relevance of the laws explains the presence of moral norms in them,[16] and also of advice and exhortations which, without constituting a necessarily juridical obligation, signal to the faithful and to pastors alike those behaviors that are generally beneficial to fostering the development of ecclesial life.[17]

Beginning with codification, ecclesiastical laws became identified with an abstract, generally comprehensive and universal normative system, which as a result now enjoys a prominent place among the sources of the canonical system. Consideration of the history of canon law can be helpful in recovering the priority of the ecclesial reality itself, indispensable also when interpreting and applying the Codes. The absence of general written rules does not imply the non-existence of law: the life of the early Church was based above all on customs. The same pontifical legislation that had developed by means of decretals that responded to the concrete problems of ecclesial life—the solutions to which then were extended to similar cases—ultimately became general rules. The formation of Codes of Canon Law, then, presupposes a very long process of normative elaboration and adjustments of juridical institutions, the fruit of the combination of efforts by the faithful and the hierarchy with the contributions of canonical science. The Codes must then always be included in the totality of canonical sources: including law that is both divine and human, both universal and particular, and both general and singular.[18]

That being said, the phenomenon of the abatement of ecclesiastical law before civil laws (a phenomenon that is not unusual among legal systems), considered in general by canon 22 of the 1983 Code, also shows that what ultimately matters is not the formal source from which a given norm derives, but the fact that a solution reflecting justice is reached. There are cases in which the canonical system considers that the civil order is more suitable for regulating a specific question or matter, either because the relationship was born in the civil sphere (such as the adoption of a child: see canon 1094), or because the act is part of a legal transaction governed by common social criteria which are reflected in the respective civil order (think, for example, of property contracts: see canon 1290). The subordination configured by canon 22, also called "the canonization of the civil law," accepts civil law "with the same effects," meaning that the norm is taken not in isolation but in its actual operation in the respective legal system (therefore taking into account the set of regulatory, jurisprudential, and administrative factors that configure the norm at all times as an institutional solution of justice). Nevertheless, the canonical system always remains sovereign in its own sphere, so it can limit subordination according to what it deems appropriate for the intra-ecclesial sphere. For example, in the case of adoption, it is the canonical law (in canon 1094) that establishes those relationships that can constitute a canonical impediment for matrimony. In any event, as the same canon 22 states, there can be no such "canonization" of the civil law if the civil law is contrary to divine law.

## b) Legislative power in the Church

**49.** The power to legislate belongs in the Church to the sacred pastors who perform functions of a Head, both in the universal Church and in the dioceses and other hierarchical communities equivalent to the latter. At the universal level, the Roman Pontiff (see canon 331) and the College of Bishops (see canon 336) are legislators; at the particular level, the legislators are the diocesan bishops (see canons 381 and 391) and the other prelates who preside over communities similar to dioceses,[19] as well as—within the limits established by the canons—particular councils (see canon 445) and episcopal conferences (see canon 455).

Given that there is no division of powers in the Church, legislative activity does not take the form of a specialized body (such as the parliaments of countries), but rather an integral function of the unitary power of governance (*potestas regiminis* or *iurisdictionis*), which also includes the executive function (also called administrative) and the judicial (see canon 135 § 1). Nevertheless, there are those who participate in this function in a somewhat limited manner (vicars, delegates, etc.). Unlike the other functions, however, the legislative function is usually exercised by the same authority that possesses it. Indeed, "that which in the Church a legislator lower than the supreme authority has, cannot validly be delegated, unless the law explicitly provides otherwise" (canon 135 § 2). Wherever possible, the Code contemplates the delegation of legislative power only to those who enjoy executive power; this delegation must be expressly granted for particular cases, and the conditions established by the legislator in the act of granting it (see canon 30) must be observed.

By the very nature of the legislative function, which aims to introduce general norms with substantially stable solutions of justice for the life of the community, its institutional character is particularly evident. There is certainly a personal or collegial authority that legislates, but the law is not so much a momentary act as it is a permanent command, and thus not tied simply to the existence of the individual legislator who gave it life. Each law, then, is incorporated into the set of laws of the Church, with which it conforms in an organic unity, as a main part of the canonical legal system.

The legislation issued by the Roman Pontiff is usually universal in nature,[20] although it may also be particular (on the distinction between universal and particular laws, see number 52, *infra*), as his power extends immediately to the whole Church. Pontifical laws receive different names, mostly related to the form of the document (Code, apostolic constitution, *motu proprio*, etc.). The dicasteries of the Roman Curia "cannot issue laws or general decrees having the force of law or derogate from the prescriptions of current universal law, in force, unless in individual cases and with the specific approval of the Supreme Pontiff."[21] In this manner one avoids uncertainty about the value of the acts of the Holy See, distinguishing between those of an administrative nature—which cannot contradict laws enacted by the Pope—and those of a legal nature.

Thus, a formal hierarchy of sources is established, necessary so that laws with content of greater importance can actually prevail for the common good.

Throughout history, ecumenical councils have been a very relevant source for ecclesiastical legislation. One considers, for example, the canons of reform of the Council of Trent (see numbers 35–36, *supra*). Although the relevance of the Second Vatican Council with respect to canon law comes especially from its ecclesiological doctrine, its documents also contain many directives on juridical matters, made operative by post-conciliar legislation and then by the two Codes.[22]

Diocesan bishops, and those similar to them in the canonical order, can issue particular laws. Contrary to what is sometimes thought, the legislative competence of diocesan bishops, like the whole of their power of governance, is not reduced to those matters which universal legislation refers to diocesan legislation. On the contrary, their power is as wide as the exercise of their pastoral office (see *Lumen Gentium*, n. 27a; *Christus Dominus*, n. 8a), naturally respecting the competences of the higher authority (see canon 381 § 2). Therefore, "a lower legislator cannot validly make a law which is contrary to that of a higher legislator" (canon 135 § 2).[23] A very traditional way of diocesan legislation is constituted by diocesan synods, in which "the diocesan Bishop is the sole legislator," and the "other members of the synod have only a consultative vote" (canon 466).

The legislation of the particular councils makes up another very important source in the history of the Church. This possibility of laws pertaining to several particular Churches reflects the need for a common discipline. Today these laws are mostly brought into being through the episcopal conferences, which, however, enjoy legislative power only in matters for which they have received it—either by universal law or through a special mandate of the Apostolic See. Furthermore, as a requirement for validity, legislation from an episcopal conference must also receive approval by two-thirds of the votes of those prelates who belong to the conference with a deliberative vote, as well as the formal review (*recognitio*) by the Holy See (see canons 455 § 1–2 and 456). These limitations are to protect universal law, as well as the jurisdiction of individual bishops, so that when the Code refers to particular law without further specification (see, e.g., canon 279 § 2), it must be understood to mean diocesan law (or that which is comparable to diocesan law) and to that of particular councils. Such references cannot be read to mean the law of episcopal conferences, unless a special mandate of the Apostolic See has been granted (see canon 455 § 1), or each and every individual bishop has given his consent (see canon 455 § 4). In point of fact, however, in recent years the particular legislation that is the most relevant has tended to be that of the conferences, both because diocesan legislation has been rather scarce, and because the Code, despite a notable decrease in the number of matters that were entrusted to the episcopal conferences during the course of its preparation, has entrusted much more  competency to the decisions of the conferences.[24]

The exercise of legislative power is a delicate act of the pastoral prudence by one in a position of governance. The laws that result from such exercise must first of all be just; that is, they must be in conformity with divine law. But this is not enough. They need to adapt to the situation of the community, so that they actually favor the common good. In his classic enumeration on the qualities of the law,[25] Saint Isidore of Seville states not only the conditions of justice, but also those of benefit and opportunity, of clarity and precision. A wise law is the joint fruit of the prudence of the ruler and the sensitivity and technique of the jurist.

*c) The promulgation, reception, and validity of ecclesiastical law*

**50.** "A law comes into being when it is promulgated" (canon 7). In canon law,[26] *promulgation* means an official publication of the law, carried out in the manner provided by the same system, meaning that the legislative act is made manifest, at least potentially, to the entire recipient community. It therefore differs from factual disclosure, which can take place before or after.[27]

The promulgation of universal laws takes place through the publication in the *Acta Apostolicae Sedis*, the official publication of the Holy See, unless a different manner of publication is established for particular cases (see canon 8 § 1). With respect to particular laws (including those coming from the supreme authority), the choice of means by which they are promulgated is left to the legislator (see canon 8 § 2). Naturally, it is suitable that this choice involve a stable publication method, thus making the laws truly accessible to the recipients.

Insofar as the laws update the future behavior expected of the faithful as well as the structure of ecclesial institutions, it is normally appropriate to leave a period of time (a *vacatio legis*) dedicated to understanding the new provisions and preparing for their implementation. Therefore, universal laws enter into force only three months after the date of the corresponding number in the *Acta*, unless due to the nature of the case they immediately oblige,[28] or unless the law itself establishes a shorter (or longer) interval (see canon 8 § 1). The deadline set as a general rule for particular laws, also subject to exceptions, is one month after the day of promulgation (see canon 8 § 2).

The Code does not allude to the theme of *the reception of laws on the part of the community*, present in the canonical tradition[29] and re-emergent in the post-conciliar period, both regarding the magisterium and matters of ecclesial discipline.[30] This is an issue that goes beyond that of simple theoretical knowledge of magisterial or disciplinary acts, as it concerns rather the recognition itself of the value of such acts by the faithful.

Reception cannot represent a requirement for the validity of the hierarchical acts of the *munus docendi* or *munus regendi*: this would clearly imply conditioning the power of the hierarchy on the consent of the people, along the lines of democratic schemes that would deny the hierarchical principle proper to the Church. However, the need for a reception for hierarchical acts is something that derives not only from the exigencies of communication that are proper to human nature, but also from the active participation of all the baptized in ecclesial life. Therefore, the interventions of pastors must be rendered alive in the faithful (it is in this sense that we can speak of a true "inculturation" that needs to take place). The faithful must then implement an active and creative synergy in their lives along with their pastoral guides which will be influenced in turn by the attitudes of the faithful. There should be no illusions about solving ecclesial problems, including juridical ones, with documents that remain almost completely unknown or disregarded. Moreover, the reception on the part of the faithful can have a very important impact on magisterial or disciplinary development. In fact, the truth about faith and morals is better studied and clarified through the contribution of the sense of faith of the entire People of God. While it is certainly true that those who dedicate themselves to the sacred sciences can make a particular contribution in these areas, it is important not to limit ourselves here: the contribution of others, especially of the saints, is often even more significant. Finally, the behavior of the faithful often influences the very validity of the laws (as demonstrated, among other things, by the possibility of a custom *contra legem*, but also the other species of custom; i.e., *praeter and secundum legem*: see number 56, *infra*).

All this, however, does not mean introducing a sense of disobedience into the Church, given that any authentically ecclesial reception—which should be carefully distinguished from any illegitimate rebellion—must always be done in communion with the hierarchy, and enhancing in a spirit of faith the unique function of the Church's hierarchy. This finds its maximum manifestation in the case of definitive and infallible teachings of the magisterium, or when the ecclesiastical authority confirms a discipline, whether the authority teaches that it is matter of divine law, or if it is only a matter of human law, the authority intends to maintain that discipline and therefore condemn any contrary custom. Contrasting reception and obedience leads to nothing but a complete misunderstanding of the ecclesial sense of these realities.

"Laws concern matters of the future, not those of the past, unless provision is made in them for the latter by name" (canon 9). By their nature, *laws are usually for the future, so their retroactivity is exceptional.* In fact, as far as the configuration of human law is concerned, laws intend to introduce new regulations, normally leaving intact already consolidated juridical situations.[31] It is nonetheless possible, however, for a law to address something in the past: there are situations which, even though they may have already been consolidated, stand in need of a change in order to advance the common good. The Code prohibits this possible retroactive effect in the case of a law that authentically interprets another, when restricting it, extending it, or clarifying it because it is doubtful (see canon 16 § 2). In criminal matters, the canonical law itself contemplates a special retroactivity in favor of the offender (see canon 1313).

The law can *cease* in various ways: First, it could cease intrinsically owing to a change in the regulated social reality (e.g., if a law is issued for a transitory situation—such as a religious persecution—and this situation no longer exists). Second, a law could cease by operation of a custom *contra legem* meeting the requirements of canon 26. Third, a law could be repealed by the competent legislator. In addition to these express means of abrogation, there are two other forms: one based on direct opposition between respective provisions, and another deriving from a new overall order of the same subject matter, in which it is understood that there are not even aspects of the previous law that could be compatible with the new one, in light of the fact that the whole has changed (see canon 20).[32] The same canon 20 specifies that "the universal law, however, does not derogate from a particular or from a special law, unless the law expressly provides otherwise."[33]

Good legislative technique includes trying to clarify the consequences of the new law with respect to pre-existing laws and other sources. In the preliminary canons of the Codes of 1917 and 1983, one finds an example of such transitory norms. However, doubts often remain, which the canonical order resolves in the name of legislative continuity: "In doubt, the revocation of a previous law is not presumed; rather, later laws are to be related to the earlier ones and, as far as possible, harmonised with them" (canon 21). This continuity also manifests itself in another interpretative principle, sanctioned with regard to the relationship of the Code with ancient law, but which has a more general value: "To the extent that the canons of this Code reproduce the former law, they are to be assessed in the light also of canonical tradition" (canon 6 § 2). In this regard, it should not be forgotten that continuity concerns first and foremost the divine law, present in the laws, and then extends especially to those institutions and rules which have become so traditional that they constitute an ecclesial patrimony of wisdom and of right ecclesial order.

*d) The juridical and moral effects of ecclesiastical laws;* epikeia *as justice of the particular case*

**51.** Every juridical law, civil or canonical, has a double inseparable effect: the first and most immediate one is of a juridical nature, as it regulates an intersubjective relationship, determining rights and duties, and preparing the means for the protection and sanction of the right order; the other is of a moral nature, and comes from the fact that the law affects the area of justice and obedience, and these virtues with their acts are requirements for the entirely good behavior of people. The determination of juridical relationships and the rise of a moral duty are two inseparable aspects of the same reality: if the law determines what is just, obeying it is a duty simply because it is acting according to justice, not by virtue of a further injunction of the authority.[34]

The moral relevance of ecclesiastical law is particularly evident, given that it is primarily concerned with the salvific goods of communion (see number 11, *supra*). Furthermore, the duties of Catholics, beginning with those summarized in the precepts of the Church, are established not only for reasons of the common good. While this explains their juridical nature— as obligations of justice toward the whole Church—they also seek to foster the salvation of the faithful themselves: for example, by virtue of the obligation to attend Sunday Mass, to confess and receive holy communion, etc. (see number 15, *supra*). Therefore, there is a whole ecclesial tradition that underlines the obligation of ecclesiastical laws in one's conscience. The same holds for the obligatory nature of just civil laws. In laws in which there are declarative aspects of divine law, the Christian moral duty to observe them is nothing other than the very obligation to live according to the divine law. Regarding canonical laws of human origin that generally determine juridical relationships in the Church, such determinations must be respected in conscience by the faithful by virtue of their ecclesial legitimacy.

The general nature of such human legal determinations requires careful consideration, both juridical and moral, of the individual case. Thus we arrive at one of the classic meanings of *equity* (often referred to by the Greek term *epikeia*): *the justice of the particular case*. We have already seen how equity has functions that transcend the ambit of justice (see number 15, *supra*). Here, however, we are concerned with its operation with respect to human laws (and other human rules). Despite the exceptions and adaptations provided for by the same laws (the so-called *aequitas scripta*), these never manage to foresee all cases in contingent matters, given that laws proceed on the basis of generalizations, for which they establish rules valid in the great majority of cases (*ut in pluribus*). As a result, situations necessarily arise in which the general human norm proves to be inadequate.

To be exempt from a law requires more than a claim that the law is simply inopportune or that a rule is useless in an individual case; general rules exist precisely to ensure that degree of uniformity in the conduct of people that the competent authority considers appropriate for the common good, even if such uniformity may be unnecessary in a given situation (it is not easy, though, for an individual to judge this objectively).[35] There are situations when the law, while being just in general, becomes unjust in a particular case because it is contrary to the rights of individuals or communities. Only in such an instance does the *epikeia*, as an element of justice itself, move the person to the non-observance of the general rule, precisely to safeguard justice. Because this judgment, in practice, is not easy—especially when it concerns situations in which the subject has special interests—the faithful have traditionally been advised to resort to the competent authority for a corresponding dispensation from the law, which in such a case would be declarative. As we will later discuss (see number 60, *infra*), the dispensation in itself does not represent any kind of injustice, as it concerns an exemption from the observance of a law in cases where it is appropriate in light of the good of the faithful, in the judgment of the competent ecclesiastical authority.

*Epikeia* can be considered not only from a strictly legal point of view, but also from a moral point of view. Thus one hears of grave inconvenience, of moral impossibility, etc., as causes for which the faithful are no longer required to observe the law. These categories are valid above all for those positive legal obligations common to all the faithful—such as the aforementioned precepts of the Church—in which the corresponding right belongs to the whole Church, and whose fulfillment by an individual member of the faithful might be met with practical difficulties. Such problems must be resolved by the faithful with the formative help of those who can advise them in a given area (parish priest, confessor, etc.). Given that these obligations are usually free of legal sanctions, questions regarding the merits of a given self-granted exception do not arise in administrative or judicial matters, remaining generally within the scope of personal conscience.

The configuration of juridical relationships through laws can also extend to the requirements necessary to carry out juridical acts. In other words, positive law can introduce requirements (relating to capacity, form, etc.) not deriving from the nature of the act itself, but which are nevertheless required in order to better protect the ecclesial common good. Such requirements introduced by the legislator (unless they are only exhortations or advice) are obligatory for the recipient: according to the traditional expression, they arise *ad liceitatem*; that is, they are necessary for the juridical-canonical liceity[36] of the act. On the other hand, the canonical tradition has shown itself to be restrictive in the face of the other effect that can follow from demanding these requirements. Only in exceptional cases does canon law allow for *ad validitatem* efficacy; that is, preventing a given act from producing its own effects whenever a given requirement is not observed.[37] Therefore, canon 10 states: "Only those laws are to be considered invalidating or incapacitating which expressly prescribe that an act is null or that a person is incapable." It should be noted that invalidating or incapacitating laws, which establish requirements for liceity only, are not necessarily without their own legal effects. Given that by their nature they belong to the field of juridical relationships, non-compliance with such laws can lead to various penalties, not solely administrative but even criminal.[38]

### e) The recipients of the laws; universal laws and particular laws

**52.** Every human person is objectively connected with the Church, inasmuch as the Church is the universal sacrament of salvation. From a juridical point of view, this implies recognizing the right to be baptized if a person is well disposed. The *baptized*, having been incorporated into the Church, then enjoy certain juridical rights and duties. These duties include observing canonical discipline, including ecclesiastical laws.

A problem arises, however, regarding the obligation of obedience to the laws of the Church by baptized non-Catholics, who are not in full communion with the Catholic Church. The 1917 Code, as a general rule, applied to all the baptized (see its canon 12), although it exempted them from concrete obligations such as that of the canonical form (see its canon 1099). The 1983 Code, on the contrary, modified this general rule by prescribing in canon 11: "Merely ecclesiastical laws bind those *who were baptised in the Catholic Church or received into it…*" (italics added). This change, although not based directly on the texts of Vatican II, responded to the increased efforts in the field of ecumenism thanks to this same Council.[39] Any submission on the part of baptized non-Catholics to the legislative power of the Catholic Church seems meaningless, given that there would be no practical efficacy, either legally or morally, in such a theoretical affirmation. Its partial veracity can be traced back to the right and duty of all the baptized in order to embrace the fullness of communion, which can naturally be implemented to the extent that this fullness is manifest to them.

The Code does not, however, exempt from ecclesiastical laws Catholics who have broken the bond of communion. The baptized condition can never be lost, for the baptismal character is indelible. Similarly, the condition of being Catholic, the bond of belonging to the Catholic Church, is never considered canceled by the Church, even in the case of apostasy. With this, the Church certainly does not intend to unnecessarily complicate the lives of its members: so much so that, at least in our view, the Church should remove those canonical duties that could hinder the exercise of natural rights related to ecclesial rights, e.g., the right to marriage.[40] Nor does it appear to make much sense to imagine that a Catholic, who is separated in some way from the Church, would have an obligation with respect to individual laws over and above the persistence of the central one; i.e., his objective obligation to return to living in communion. The Catholic Church always remains his, without any readmission being necessary; it is enough that a person accept the demands of communion, including those of a disciplinary nature.

For the mandatory nature of purely ecclesiastical laws, two other related requirements must present to the faithful: the sufficient use of reason and, unless otherwise provided, to have completed seven years of age.[41]

To determine which laws concretely bind the faithful, it is necessary to take into consideration the scope of application of the respective law as well as the situation of the person with respect to such scope (for instance, if the person has a domicile or quasi-domicile in the pertinent area, or instead is just passing through). Regarding the scope of application, one must first distinguish between universal laws in the proper sense, i.e., laws prescribed for the whole Church, including the Eastern Churches,[42] and those laws applicable only within the Latin Church. Within this latter type, laws are classified by the Code into *universal and particular* (see canons 12–13). Universal laws are those addressed to all of the faithful of the Latin Church who find themselves in the situation foreseen by the respective legal norm. Universality is therefore not absolute, but relative to the faithful of the Latin rite, because Eastern Catholics follow the Eastern canons, both common and proper to each Church. Particular laws may come from the competent lower legislators, as well as from the supreme legislator. A classic legal issue, with a complex historical evolution, is that concerning the territoriality or the personality of the laws. In the current canonical order, particular laws are presumed to be *territorial*,[43] that is to say, according to the meaning specified by canon 12 § 3, applying to all of the faithful who have domicile or quasi-domicile in that territory and who currently live in it. They can sometimes be *personal*; that is, they follow the person wherever he may be if his transgression causes damage in his own territory or if the law is expressly personal (see canon 13 § 2, 1º). In matters relating to public order, or concerning the formalities of acts or immovable property located in the territory, everyone is required to respect the laws of the territory in which they are located (see canon 13 § 2, 2º).[44]

The *objective lack of certainty of the law* or the *subjective lack of knowledge of it* by the person also affects his or her obligation and the other legal effects (validity or scope). Traditional canonical doctrine, very close in this matter to the treatment of similar matters in moral theology, spoke of causes that excused one from law: doubt, ignorance, or error. They may be "of law," if they concern the actual existence of a law for a specific case, or "of fact," if they concern the existence (or not) of the concrete situation to which the law refers. The rules on *doubt* favor the good of the juridical freedom of the faithful. If the doubt concerns the law, even invalidating or incapacitating laws do not oblige (*lex dubia, lex nulla*), provided that no damage is done to third parties. If the doubt concerns a fact, an Ordinary is authorized to grant a dispensation, even when such dispensation is normally reserved to another authority, provided the latter usually grants it (see canon 14). On ignorance and error, the Code contains traditional rules of proof (*presumptio iuris tantum*; i.e., a rebuttable presumption, which requires evidence to the contrary) based on common sense: "Ignorance or error is not presumed about a law, a penalty, a fact concerning oneself, or a notorious fact concerning another. It is presumed about a fact concerning another which is not notorious, until the contrary is proved" (canon 15, § 2).

Regarding the effects of ignorance and error on rights and duties, the Code does not enunciate the general principle, of Romance origin and common in civil law systems (although now with less frequency and force, especially in criminal matters), according to which only ignorance of fact excuses, and not that of the law. In this view, laws are given for the common good, and it would therefore not be permissible to dispense with them for a lack of subjective knowledge. This approach is accepted, as a general rule subject to legal exceptions, only for the invalidating or incapacitating effect of laws: the act would in any case be invalid even though there was ignorance or error regarding the law (see c. 15 § 1). In the matters of penal law, however, *ignorantia iuris* is expressly taken into account, both of the law (the exempting circumstance of canon 1323, 2°) and of the penalty (the mitigating circumstance of canon 1324, 9°), provided that this ignorance is without fault.[45]

### f) The interpretation of ecclesiastical law

#### 1) The nature of juridical interpretation of the laws, as an aspect of juridical knowledge

**53.** Like any other human text, ecclesiastical law needs interpretation; that is, an intellectual effort to better understand it. This not only applies in cases in which the words of the law are obscure, but also in any case, given that no general human norm, however clear it may be, can be applied to individual cases without giving rise to problems that require clarifications to determine the true sense of the norm.

The art of interpretation or hermeneutics is an extremely important part of the work of a jurist, and, therefore, of the canonist. The solution to any juridical question requires a search of the laws and of other relevant sources, a comparison of them to establish their internal harmony (in the words of Gratian, the *concordia discordantium canonum*), and then the determination of the applicability of general solutions to particular cases, with the possible recourse to equity as an exception to the general human norm in order to meet the needs of justice in a concrete situation (see number 51, *supra*).

To grasp the specific nature of the juridical interpretation of the law, it is essential to connect it with the very reality of law, understood to be that which is just. The legal interpreter tries to penetrate the meaning of the norm with a very specific purpose: that of *knowing the just and the unjust*, both in general—in the field of juridical science—and in particular—in the field of juridical prudence. Juridical hermeneutics is not a philological or literary analysis, nor a process of historical reconstruction of the original sense of the norm, nor a study of its cultural, philosophical, theological contents, and so on. All these aspects can be very useful for the interpretative work of the jurist, but they acquire their proper juridical dimension only when they are connected with the search for "that which is just."

This means that the decisive point of reference for interpretation is always the practical, concrete reality of rights and the law. The scientific task of a general exegesis of norms and of an abstract systematic arrangement of them (in concepts, institutions, etc.) only makes sense to the extent that it serves the purpose of arriving at just solutions to the multiplicity of problems posed by life. A fundamental consequence derives from this: *juridical interpretation must always refer to the social reality to which the text refers, to the case in question, in its concrete being and in its circumstances.* If, on the other hand, we try to understand and systematize legal norms without that sense of realism—something that occurs all too often these days—we end up seeing legal norms as a sort of superstructure, extrinsic to the reality of persons and of their intersubjective relationships. The concept of the juridical as that which is just is thus confused with the legal system (see number 8, *supra*), thus rendering impossible the work of a true juridical interpretation. A theoretical world consisting of self-referential legal texts and legal sources takes its place, resulting in an arbitrariness in the resolution of concrete juridical problems. When trying to confront juridical questions in such a system, norms appear to be, above all else, merely tools to be used in the service of the subjective interests of the parties.

Juridical realism implies admitting that in human reality there is an intrinsic dimension of justice. Concretely, in intra-ecclesial relations of justice, this dimension comes first of all from the very being of the Church. This implies taking *divine law* into account in an effective way in juridical work, not as a mere limit or as a remote foundation, but as a constant hermeneutical horizon.[46] In order to be truly juridical, hermeneutics must overcome the patterns of positivism, which by limiting oneself only to positive norms prevent the true understanding of those same positive norms. Expecting, for example, to understand and to apply norms regarding parishes or canonical marriage without an adequate appreciation of the reality of parishes or marriage—both in their essential features and in their concrete historical realization—is to deprive oneself of the only way of ascertaining the meaning, the merits, and even the limitations of these norms. When this is not done, it means that the positivistic prejudice is at work, according to which the juridical order relies entirely on human norms. In such case, reality in itself would be considered to be non-juridical, capable of receiving any normative-positive juridical structure.

From a realistic perspective, the interpretation of the law necessarily fits into the broader context of *the body of knowledge that the jurist must have to resolve a question of justice*. The Code prescribes: "If on a particular matter there is not an express provision of either universal or particular law, nor a custom, then, provided it is not a penal matter, the question is to be decided by taking into account laws enacted in similar matters, the general principles of law observed with canonical equity, the jurisprudence and practice of the Roman Curia, and the common and constant opinion of learned authors" (canon 19). This is a rule expressed in view of a *lacuna in the law* (or custom), which must be filled through the use of sources of *supplementary law*. In reality, even when express provisions of law exist, one must resort to the other sources stated in the canon, not out of a spirit of opposition to the law, but precisely in order to be able to understand it more adequately. No law or other norm can be interpreted in isolation, as if it were sufficient in and of itself; the constitutive reference to the reality that is the subject of the norm presupposes the use of all factors that can illuminate the just or unjust reality.

In this sense, *laws given for similar cases* (or "parallel places," as canon 17 calls them) represent ways of access, through analogy, by which real similarities and differences in the solutions of justice can be found.[47] The *general juridical principles* refer to a patrimony of juridical wisdom, which cannot in any way be understood as a set of formulas to be applied mechanically, but rather as traditional expressions—collected in various ways in laws,[48] in other juridical sources, and in canonical doctrine—of a wisdom that arrived at such formulations through a realistic comparison of the fundamental demands of justice, both in general and specifically in the Church. The application of the principles of law "*with canonical equity,*" in referring to the various meanings of equity (the justice of the individual case, the benign and merciful moderation of strict justice within the possible limits and by those who are competent to do so: see numbers 51 and 15, respectively, *supra*), once again expresses the exigencies of human and Christian realism.

The reference to *the jurisprudence and practice of the Roman Curia* means the juridical solutions generally adopted by the bodies of the central organization of the Church, in its activities of both a judicial (jurisprudence) and administrative (practice) nature. In its own order, the same applies to every legitimate jurisprudence and canonical administrative practice, obviously in due subordination to the criteria of the Apostolic See as the final instance. It is worth reiterating that these never simply represent a mere application of general norms. In coming into contact with the reality of particular situations—naturally with the proper respect due to laws and customs as well as above all to divine law—the judgments of the courts and the acts of the administrative authority, especially when they reflect a common and stable orientation, facilitate an understanding of that which is just in the concreteness of life (obviously they can also reflect injustices, more or less entrenched, which must be removed).

*The common and constant opinion of learned authors*[49] is included in this list not because the canonical legislator is attributing to it a quasi-legal value, but because the consolidated consensus of the scientific community constitutes a privileged way to access the truth of the law in the Church, both in its divine and also in its human aspects. Moreover, from where do most of the institutions and solutions adopted by the legislator himself originate, if not from science and experience? Finally, the same Code, consistent with the canonical tradition, highlights the hermeneutic relationship between law and custom: "Custom is the best interpreter of laws" (canon 27). The law must come alive in social behavior; therefore, this vital realization, provided it conforms to the substance of the law,[50] is the best source for understanding the actual meaning of the law itself.

The realistic perspective in the interpretation of the laws also takes into account *the historical dimension of the law* (see numbers 38–39, *supra*). Calling attention to the historicity of human laws, including ecclesiastical ones, could appear at first sight to be a dangerous pretext to relativize the same laws and to favor non-compliance with them. In fact, this would be so only if the juridical consisted merely of human norms, which had to be constantly reworked (sometimes we hear of "evolutionary interpretation" or similar expressions) in an attempt to reach an ever-changing and pluriform social reality. In such a manner, we would yield to a historicist conception of the juridical, in which one denies the existence of the essential and permanent, thus losing any point of reference for the determination of what is changing and what is different. If, on the other hand, an adequate historical perspective is taken, the changes that have taken place in reality—along with their related juridical consequences—will certainly be highlighted. At the same time, and precisely as a *sine qua non* condition for the delicate hermeneutical process, both the divine but also the human elements of the juridical will be reaffirmed, constituting the basis on which new solutions required by ecclesial life can be elaborated. The reference to the canonical tradition, made explicit as an interpretative principle of the Code concerning the matter of continuity with ancient law (see canon 6, § 2), allows for the reaffirmation of the juridical value of canonical laws. This is true first of all in the measure in which they collect aspects of divine law, but also in those human aspects that reflect the historical experience of the Church, which, guided by the Holy Spirit, has incorporated into its life. Precisely because these human aspects are incorporated in the life and mind of the whole People of God—especially in connection with the respective principles of divine law—this lived experience cannot be ignored without proportionately serious reasons.

### 2) Authentic and private interpretation

**54.** The interpretation of ecclesiastical law can be *authentic* or *private*. It is authentic when it takes place within the context of an act of Church authority, whether legislative, judicial, or administrative. It is private when it comes from the behavior of the faithful or from the doctrine of jurists, especially those dedicated to canonical science (i.e., doctrinal or scientific interpretation).

An authentic interpretation presented in the manner of a law is nothing more than a new law, and therefore has the true force of law and must be promulgated as such. Like any law, as a rule it is not retroactive: usually a legal interpretation innovates the pre-existing regulation, by restricting or extending it, or at least clarifying it in cases of doubt. The Code establishes that "if it simply declares the sense of the words which are certain in themselves, it has retroactive force" (canon 16 § 2), but it is evident that in such a case the same previous legal text is invoked, corroborated by a merely declarative subsequent intervention.

Beginning with the disciplinary decrees of the Council of Trent (cf. n. 35), and then with the 1917 Code, the documents of the Second Vatican Council and the 1983 Code, the canonical system provided for authentic interpretations issued with a general character by an organ of the Holy See. Currently, the Pontifical Council for Legislative Texts has this competence: "With regard to the universal laws of the Church, the Council is competent to publish authentic interpretations confirmed by pontifical authority, after consulting the dicasteries concerned in questions of major importance" (*Pastor Bonus*, article 155).[51] In the early years of the 1983 Code there were some authentic interpretations of this type.[52]

Authentic interpretation through judicial sentences and administrative acts has formal value only in the particular case to which it refers (see canon 16 § 3). However, even in canon law the importance of consolidated precedents is recognized, as is shown in canon 19 when it includes the "jurisprudence and practice of the Roman Curia" among the supplementary sources that can be taken into account if there is a lacuna in the law. Furthermore, article 126 of *Pastor Bonus* states, with respect to the Tribunal of the Roman Rota: "The Roman Rota is a court of higher instance at the Apostolic See, usually at the appellate stage, with the purpose of safeguarding rights within the Church; it fosters unity of jurisprudence, and, by virtue of its own decisions, provides assistance to lower tribunals." Such juridical force of precedents is more material than formal, so it depends above all on the justice of the solutions adopted. If a jurisprudential orientation or an approach on the part of the ecclesiastical administration is consolidated—especially when it occurs at the level of the Holy See—it represents a very relevant interpretative indication for similar cases. The canonical system does not formalize this recourse to precedents, but like any order of justice it values them as an expression of justice, and also because such precedents can serve juridical certainty.

Jurisprudence in particular is of exceptional importance for the entire operation of rights and the law, as well as for the vitality of juridical science itself. Ultimately, administrative practice should also be subject to it by way of the system of contentious administrative recourse, which gives rise to a specific jurisprudence. But the traditional role of the work of the courts in the Church has been fading, and in fact current jurisprudence is today limited to causes of matrimonial nullity (the sentences of the Roman Rota, at the level of the Holy See), and to some matters pertaining to contentious administrative recourse (which is the exclusive competence of the Supreme Tribunal of the Apostolic Signatura), which as yet is having some difficulty developing. It is not easy to critically assess this situation. It seems to us that factors of a very different nature are contributing: on the one hand, a lack of organization, culture, and legal technique, as well as prejudices against the law, which should be overcome; and, on the other hand, peculiarities of the juridical-canonical goods (word of God, sacraments, etc.) whose practical implementation hardly takes place through a direct judicial route that is better suited for the possible application of canonical sanctions that protect the community.

Private interpretation makes a decisive and constant contribution to the configuration of juridical relationships. The same intersubjective behavior of people constitutes the most important part of such a contribution (see the aforementioned canon 27 on the relationship between laws and custom). The work of practical jurists, in their advice to the faithful and to institutions, in administrative and judicial disputes, creates a continuous flow between practical experience and the science of canon law. Theoretical science itself must be based on practical justice, tending to favor a wise application of laws in the context of the search for intra-ecclesial justice. The canonical tradition, which is echoed in canon 19 of the 1983 Code, *in fine*, enhances the unity of canonical science. Such unity certainly presupposes obedience to just laws, but this same obedience refers to a higher principle, that of fidelity to the Church, concretely in its dimension of justice. Pluralism of thought is good insofar as it reflects the richness of being, which never lets itself be completely grasped by a specific human system. However, true pluralism leads to dialogue, and the latter presupposes the possibility of knowing objective truth, which in ecclesial law is inseparable from the faith and the magisterium of the Church. Therefore, any juridical-canonical interpretation that claims to place itself outside of this hermeneutical framework cannot truly be considered to be an authentic effort to penetrate what is just in the Church, but rather a simple argumentative technique seeking to oppose canonical discipline in favor of interests not founded on truth.

### 3) Criteria and rules for interpreting the laws

"Ecclesiastical laws are to be understood according to the proper meaning of the words considered in their text and context. If the meaning remains doubtful or obscure, there must be recourse to parallel places, if there be any, to the purpose and circumstances of the law, and to the mind of the legislator" (canon 17).

Given that the law is a written norm, it is obvious that the first interpretative resource must always be that of the words used by the legislator. The criterion of the canon refers to the proper meaning of words: to ascertain what it is, it is necessary to take into account the text and the context. In fact, the terms used by the law, like any expression in any human discourse, are never comprehensible in isolation, as they acquire their concrete meaning in the context of the sentence, of the canon or the article, of the parts into which the law is divided, of the law as a whole, and then of the entire canonical system. This does not mean, however, that in order to interpret each word one must embark on an almost endless operation. Basically, the correct way of understanding words essentially depends on the realistic criterion with which the interpretation must be carried out (see number 53, *supra*). Classical canon law, with a phrase from St. Hilary, had formulated it effectively: "Not reality to the word, but the word subjected to reality."[53] Only with this basic realism is it possible to realize whether at a given moment a term is to be understood according to a technical meaning (of legal science, or even defined by the law itself[54]) or according to that of usual and customary language. Similarly, one must determine whether the insertion of a norm in a certain place of the organizational scheme of the law serves to clarify its meaning, or whether it is indifferent, or whether it must even be discarded as a factor that would only obscure the understanding of the precept, etc.

The same realism solves the problem of harmony between the spirit and letter of the legal precepts. Often these two elements are presented in a moment of tension, when the limits of the letter are highlighted, the spirit having to prevail. But this invocation of the spirit against the letter runs the risk of being arbitrary if there is no objective point of reference; i.e., the concrete justice that is to be achieved. Precisely in order to favor the real juridical justice of this world—and not the utopian ideals that often foment tyranny or anarchy—the letter of the positive law must always be taken into due consideration: it is necessary to obey the legitimate provisions of ecclesiastical authority, for the common good of the Church, which truly constitute obligations and rights based on the law. In fact, it is the spirit of the law that requires such obedience to the letter. Naturally, the letter must always be understood in relation to its spirit, as an expression of a solution of justice. In this way we avoid the danger of literalism, of a manipulation of the letter against the truth of its meaning; instead, we can ascertain the limitations of human texts, which in particular cases can demand the application of equity in order to arrive at a just solution (see number 51, *supra*).

The other criteria set out in canon 17 (parallel places, the purpose and the circumstances of the law, the *mens legislatoris*) appear in the canon as subsidiary means of interpretation, to be used when the words remain dubious and obscure. It is true that in simple cases there is no need for anything other than reading the text with the essential basic knowledge it presupposes. But the problems of interpretation are, so to speak, of ordinary administration. Therefore, all available hermeneutical resources must be used simultaneously. If this is not done, there is a real risk that the legal texts will be manipulated, based on mere quibbling, perhaps supported by some unfortunate expression chosen by the legislator or by some obvious error made in the drafting of the law. This literalism, typical of the smooth-talking swindler lawyer in Manzoni's novel *The Betrothed*, does not even deserve the name of interpretation.

In addition to parallel places (see number 53, *supra*), different aspects of the interpretive criteria of the law are listed in canon 17, which allow the law to be historically situated as a concrete order that presupposes a compelling purpose for its enactment (understood as the *finis operantis*; that is, as the purpose that drives the legislator to promulgating the norm), remote or proximate circumstances that influence the preparation and the elaboration of the law, and the mind or understanding of the legislator (*mens legislatoris*) as the soul of the text that explains its intrinsic purpose (*finis operis*) and its internal rationality. The legislative technique of codification makes these criteria less operative, as an attempt is made to formulate abstract and permanent norms, whose connection with a specific act of the legislator is much less significant in terms of the content of a given norm. In such a context, the process itself of an elaboration of a Code (see number 39, *supra*), which is often used in interpretative work, must be reduced. Such a review can certainly allow us to identify the reasons that led to some options, just as it can show us which other options that were not ultimately adopted. But it would not be sensible to expect that such motivations and choices give rise to a decisive criterion of interpretation, that could be in some way over and above what the text really says and the connections a particular text establishes with the rest of the system—let alone with the reality of relations of justice. To apply these criteria well, it is necessary to overcome a vision of the law that is too focused on the mandate of the will. Where, on the other hand, one appeals to the ordering of reason according to justice, certainly the historical aspects of legislation help us to understand it and possibly to ascertain its limits, but one immediately sees that, as is attested by the whole history of law, the true value of laws comes from their being socially institutionalized solutions of justice. Therefore, in our opinion, the expression *mens legislatoris* itself is not very convincing, because it easily leads us to place ourselves in a subjectivist perspective, extraneous to the objectivity with which the now promulgated law must be understood. Instead, the explanations contained in magisterial acts relating to the same subject are often very significant and helpful in juridical hermeneutics.

The extension of a law to similar situations is a consequence of the very nature of the law as a general solution to questions of justice. The criteria of the law, both those declaring divine law and those containing determinations of human law, are often taken into account in similar cases. Certain laws exist, however, to which this concept does not apply, given that such laws are strictly limited to the cases for which they were enacted, thus requiring them to be interpreted narrowly. "Laws which prescribe a penalty, or restrict the free exercise of rights, or contain an exception to the law, are to be interpreted strictly" (canon 18). Criminal law and its interpretation are the subject of criminal law. The strict interpretation of the laws that restrict the free exercise of rights is a consequence of the priority of the juridical good of freedom in canon law (see number 11, *supra*). As for laws that contain an exception to the law, it is logical that the exception is understood as an exception, avoiding transforming it, as sometimes happens, into a general rule that empties what the law itself established. Put another way, exceptions read too broadly can lead to a situation in which the "exception swallows the rule."

### 3.2.2. Canonical customs[55]

**56.** Canonical custom is an *unwritten general norm having the same force as ecclesiastical law*. It comes from the community of the faithful, both universal and particular, which introduces it through behavior that is both uniform and lasting. This normative source highlights in the most prominent

way the participation of the entire People of God in the general human configuration of intra-ecclesial juridical relations. Such participation constitutes
a mode, especially significant from the point of view of rights and the law, of
the exercise of the governing function (*munus regendi*) which is the responsibility of all the baptized. The configuration of a custom is not the result of a
mere factual coincidence of practices; it is rather the product of an intention
to introduce a rule of law (*cum animo iuris inducendi*), which then lasts over
time by means of the faithful adapting their conduct to this rule, which is
perceived precisely as a binding ecclesial rule of justice.

The current legal system of the Church, in the wake of the canonical
tradition, recognizes this source of law, and expressly attributes to it the
force of law as long as it meets certain requirements that are determined by
the law (see canons 23–28). The approval of the legislator, mentioned in
canon 23, should be understood just as the verification of those legal requirements. A traditional debate, still alive in recent years,[56] focuses on
what is the basis of the normative value of custom, whether it is the faithful
themselves who introduce the custom—with some declarative intervention
and control by the Hierarchy—or, whether it is the Hierarchy that is the
formal source of the norm, which then has only a material prerequisite in
the practice of the community. In our opinion, such a discussion becomes
less relevant the more one considers, in the first place, that the action of
the ecclesial community must always proceed in hierarchical communion
with the pastors, all the more so when it comes to introducing general
norms for the common good of Church. Secondly, the nature of custom
highlights the fact that its value as a source of law essentially depends on
the intrinsic justice of solutions brought about by custom, which includes
the very important social need to determine certain rules and practices. In
fact, the very formation of laws is normally linked to a process of experi-
mentation and verification of practices from lived experience.

Custom, like ecclesiastical law, must always be adapted to divine law
(see canon 24 § 1). The Code, collecting a requirement made explicit in
the era of classical law,[57] also requires that it be *rationabilis* (i.e., "rational,"
or perhaps, even better, "reasonable") (see canon 24 § 2). The same text
specifies that it cannot be rational if it is "expressly reprobated in the law."
Of course, even this reprobation by the legislator must be rational. This
requisite of *rationabilitas* shows that the legitimacy of norms requires not

only their adaptation to the essential principles of divine law, but also their congruence with the whole of the juridical-canonical system and above all with the needs deriving from the life of the Church.

In the regulation of custom, a classical distinction is used, concerning the relationship of custom with the law. In fact, custom can be *secundum legem*, when it follows the prescript of the law and therefore contributes to determining its meaning (see canon 27, about which we have already spoken in number 53, *supra*); *praeter legem*, when different juridical rules come from it but are not contrary to those in the law; and *contra legem*, when there is an opposition between custom and the legislative provision. In order for a custom *praeter* or *contra legem* to obtain the force of law, it must have been lawfully observed for thirty continuous and complete years; but against a canonical law that expressly prohibits future customs (as does, for example, canon 1076 in the matter of matrimonial impediments) only a centennial or immemorial custom can prevail (see canon 26).[58]

There is currently a paradox in this matter. On the one hand, the doctrine carefully considers custom in the context of the theological and juridical studies of a fundamental nature on law in the Church.[59] On the other hand, however, custom appears more as an object of interesting speculative debates rather than as a concrete juridical experience. In the end, the decisive question for a jurist always emerges: what are the customs really in force at present?

To resolve this paradox it may be useful to take into account a simple but often disregarded distinction. The code legislation on custom concerns that custom that has the force of law. Custom is always equated to the law, from the description in canon 23 up to the requirements of canon 25 (e.g., the community where it arises must be capable at least of receiving a law, and the intention of introducing a law is required) and the norms on cessation (see canon 28). The canonical tradition and the current Code have well-defined legal norms in mind, with precise consequences of rights and duties.[60] Today, however, we believe that it is problematic to find customs of this type, given that it is difficult to find the conditions for the establishment of customs such as those provided for by the Code: our legal culture is closely linked to writing, social behaviors change at increasing speed, globalization increasingly unites the practices of different communities, etc.

However, the custom that is so dear to canonists is rather that which, even without having the efficacy of law, reflects the effective juridical life of the People of God. Certainly, it must be reiterated that it cannot deviate from the requirements of communion, and that those customs reproved by ecclesiastical authority are those practices which undermine not only divine law but also the rationality of canonical discipline, in the sense explained above.[61] However, from the same regulation of custom by the Code, very important data emerge for issuing a considered judgment on customs that do not properly constitute a law. Although they are not sources of obligations and rights, they are legally relevant to the extent that behavior is based on them that can be considered lawful; that is, not contrary to any rights of others. In addition to the consideration of custom as an excellent interpreter of the law (see canon 27), those practices that are either *praeter* or *contra legem*—so long as they are not opposed to divine law and are endowed with reasonableness—must be considered a legitimate expression of the freedom of the ecclesial community. Even though they may not have perdured long enough to satisfy the requirements of the Code, provided they have not been reproved *a priori* or *a posteriori* by the legislator, they are still juridically relevant (we usually speak of an *inchoata* custom). In addition to protecting authentic diversity in the Church, and inseparable from the concept of unity in essential things, we see that the objective of any juridical system is not to impose uniform solutions by an authority, but to find reasonable solutions of justice well-rooted in particular times and places, a task to which the authority of the sacred pastors and the prudent decisions of all the faithful contribute harmoniously. These decisions acquire a special communal value when they promote the achievement of unity in disciplinary aspects, where unnecessary distinctions could easily degenerate into division. The discernment of the Hierarchy, which includes the reprobation of certain practices in view of the common good, always remains indispensable to ensure just unity and just diversity in the Church.

### 3.3. The effects of ecclesiastical administrative activity on the configuration of juridical-canonical relations[62]

#### 3.3.1. General administrative norms

**57.** *The distinction between the various functions integrating the power of governance* (see canon 135 § 1) was one of the main technical-juridical concerns of the new codification.[63] The acts of judicial power, especially judicial sentences, have always been well defined. Less familiar, perhaps, were the boundaries between the acts of legislative power and those of a general nature emanating from executive (or administrative) power, especially regarding general norms. The material difference between the two types of norms—legislative and administrative—is rather problematic, given that they concern the same matter of regulations of a general nature. The consideration of the specific nature of executive power, usually performed in a rather residual way (i.e., anything that is not legislative or judicial is administrative), does not throw too much light on the subject. Therefore, to ensure the *hierarchy* between the two types of norms (issued at the same level, whether that of the universal Church, diocese, etc.), and to guarantee one of the aspects of the *principle of legality* in the context of ecclesiastical administration,[64] it is decisive in practice that these norms are adequately formalized as either legal acts or as administrative acts. In this way, too, administrative norms contrary to the laws do not derogate from the law—and indeed are seen as invalid. Such normative formalization is even more important if we keep in mind that in the Church the capital offices—i.e., the pope at the universal level and the diocesan bishops at the level of the particular churches—are the holders of all the functions of power. This hierarchy between norms guarantees that legal provisions, of a more basic nature and pertaining to the fundamental determinations of the rights and duties of the faithful, are respected in the acts of executive power, including the general norms issued by it.

The Code of 1983 introduced a new title with respect to the 1917 Code, on general decrees and instructions (see canons 29–34). After specifying that the name of "general decrees" can be applied to laws (see canon 29), including those issued by holders of executive power following a delegation received from the competent legislator (see canon 30), two types of general administrative norms are regulated: *general executory decrees* (see canons 31–33) and *instructions* (see canon 34).[65]

General executory decrees define more precisely the manner of applying a law or urge the observance of laws. They are equivalent to those administrative norms which in secular law are normally called "regulations." Their recipients and the subjects who are bound to observe them are the same as those of the respective law (see canon 32), and therefore the same norms that apply for laws—i.e., those regarding promulgation and the intervals that apply before a norm comes into effect—apply to these general executory decrees as well (see canon 31 § 2). There is nothing to prevent general executory decrees from being issued at the particular level concerning the way in which a universal law may be observed, which would obviously be valid only in the respective sphere.

Instructions, on the other hand, are addressed not to all the recipients of the law, but to those who have the task of ensuring that the laws are carried out (with respect to the Church as an institution); they are therefore internal rules of the ecclesiastical administration. The instructions clarify the legal provisions or develop and determine the procedures in carrying them out. Given that they oblige only the representatives of the Church as institution, the instructions are not subject to the rules on promulgation and the *vacatio legis*.

Both general executory decrees and the instructions must conform to the laws; otherwise, they are devoid of any value (see canons 33 § 1 and 34 § 2). They are understood to be so closely linked to their respective law that they cease when the latter is no longer valid (see canons 33 § 2 and 34 § 3).

### 3.3.2. Singular administrative acts

#### a) General notions

**58.** The most characteristic activity of executive power is that concerning concrete situations. The daily governance of the Church at all levels requires *singular administrative acts*, through which the ecclesiastical organization is configured (erections of dioceses and parishes, establishment of offices, etc.), functions related to the Church as an institution are assigned (ecclesiastical appointments, grants of powers, administration of ecclesiastical goods, etc.), and actions are taken to implement the means of control by which ecclesiastical authority oversees the correct exercise of certain rights (e.g., by means of associations or publications). In some instances, graces are granted; that is, ecclesial goods to which the faithful do not have a right in the proper sense; from the point of view of the juridical content of the act, these are commonly referred to as dispensations or privileges. This description highlights the influence of singular administrative acts on the concrete configuration of juridical relations in the Church.

The Code dedicates Title IV of Book I to these acts. It reflects the legacy of the canonical tradition, which had already codified in 1917 in the canons on rescripts, privileges, and dispensations. There is also a common regulation of the administrative act inspired by modern secular administrative law, following, as already mentioned (see number 57, *supra*), the distinction between the functions of ecclesiastical government.

Administrative acts come from the holders of executive power, be it ordinary or delegated, within the limits of their competence (see canon 35). The legislator introduces some norms common to all administrative acts (see canons 35–47). The other chapters of the title are dedicated to certain kinds of administrative acts: *singular decrees* and *precepts* (see canons 48–58), *rescripts* (see canons 59–75), *privileges* (see canons 76–84), and *dispensations* (see canons 85–93). The classification of administrative acts into singular decrees (of which singular precepts are a subspecies, characterized by containing a command; see canon 49) and rescripts pertains to a formal element, concerning the relationship with the faithful concerned. In fact, the singular decree, by its nature, does not suppose a petition made by someone (see canon 48). A rescript, for its part, is essentially an act given at the request of someone (to this is added the material aspect of conveying the granting of a grace) (see canon 59 § 1). With regard to privileges and dispensations, these are categories based on the material content of the acts: privileges correspond to a grace (therefore not a right) of a stable and presumably perpetual nature (see canon 78 § 1), granted in favor of specific persons, physical or juridical (see canon 76 § 1).[66] Dispensations, meanwhile, consist of an exemption from the observance of a purely ecclesiastical law in a particular case (see canon 85).

From the perspective of the effects of singular administrative acts on juridical-canonical relations, and therefore on the rights and obligations of subjects, we will examine two questions: First, the relationship of these acts with ecclesiastical law, and, second, the notion and concept of a dispensation, taking special note of its practical aspect.

*b) The relationship of singular administrative acts with ecclesiastical law*

**59.** The Code establishes in unequivocal terms the application of the *principle of legality* to singular administrative acts: "An administrative act, even if there is question of a rescript given motu proprio,[67] has no effect in so far as it harms the acquired right of another, or is contrary to a law or approved custom, unless the competent authority has expressly added a derogatory clause" (canon 38). The reference to custom, to law in general (thus including not only human ecclesiastical law, but also divine law) and to acquired rights shows the broader configuration that is given to the principle of legality. In other words, the legality of singular administrative acts is not reduced to compliance with the written law alone, but is extended to all the requirements of justice, which cannot be modified by the executive power from which administrative acts originate (see canon 35).

Respect for the principle of legality in the activity of the ecclesiastical administration was certainly inspired by the development of secular administrative law over the last two centuries, as civil states attempted to ensure justice in the relations between the citizenry and the organs of administrative authority. But this principle, and the very distinction of functions (legislative and administrative) on which it rests, are a technical approach that formalizes a need for justice that is intrinsic to the reality of the Church. In effect, this means that the hierarchical authority must first of all, in the exercise of any of its functions, act in accordance with divine law; but then, in the specific function of the immediate governance of the Church, it must also follow the general norms and the concrete situations of justice of human origin, whether deriving from some action of the Hierarchy itself in the legislative function or from the action of other faithful (by means of custom, juridical acts, etc.). Performing the administrative function in opposition to these norms and legitimately established juridical situations must be considered to be an unjust act, in that it would infringe on the true rights of the faithful and other ecclesial subjects. The general change of these norms and juridical situations of human origin can only take place through acts suitable for these effects, that is—with regard to the Hierarchy—by acts of a legislative nature. If the Hierarchy in administering did not respect the legal norms set by the Hierarchy in its own legislation, the ecclesiastical laws would be seen as a mere expression of a power, not as rules of justice that also oblige the authority in its activity of administering.

However, in accepting the concept of the administrative act, the canonical system has not renounced a traditional way of conceiving legality which, although in itself congruent with any legal sphere, today contrasts with the current vision of the civil sphere. In fact, in the Church, juridical equality does not always imply equality before ecclesiastical laws. Aware of the intrinsic limits of the latter, due to their note of generality, the juridical-canonical system admits of the existence of *legitimate singular exceptions to the general precept of an ecclesiastical law, even when the same law in its general formulation has not provided for them.*[68] This *flexibility or elasticity of the canonical order* does not concern only those cases in which the application of the general rule becomes unjust (thus allowing for a claim of being free from the law itself),[69] but, on the contrary, extends to other situations in which the ecclesiastical authority may consider it reasonable to establish exceptions to general legal norms. Such exceptions cannot be based on motives of arbitrary favor, nor can they derive from an unjust connivance of persons or groups with the Hierarchy. Instead, we must deal with acts which conform to an objective cause, something which justifies an exception to a general human norm on the basis of a deeper equality, based on the reality of each situation. Such an approach postulates diversified solutions: common solutions for usual cases, and special solutions for intrinsically exceptional situations. The evaluation of the common good and the good of individuals, which the authority must perform for these purposes, is by its nature of a prudential, discretionary character (although there may be criteria based on law or custom that might need to be respected).[70]

An exception to a law can be seen as a granting of a special grace (a privilege) or as an exemption from purely human legal obligation (a dispensation, which in reality also constitutes a particular type of grace). Yet an exception could also involve the configuration of an obligation in a singular case not foreseen by human law: a singular precept. While mainly serving as a means of urging of the observance of an ecclesiastical law, a singular precept can sometimes lead to the birth of a new juridical obligation. And while certainly based on the requirements of divine law, it might not come immediately from it, but rather from the act of power which commands a specific behavior or omission (see canon 49).

After the codification of 1983, the doctrine questioned whether the acts of granting privileges and dispensations, and the issuing of precepts the content of which went beyond established ecclesiastical law, might be considered to be administrative acts (following the organization of the Code) or rather should be considered legislative acts[71] (falling into the category of singular norms).[72] Such acts are singular acts, not of a general nature as are legislative ones, yet their scope exceeds those of a typical administrative act, insofar as they renew a juridical situation that was determined by the law. In our opinion, this phenomenon—apart from its connection to the fact that there is no separation of powers in the Church—confirms that the distinction between the legislative function and the administrative function is not one of an essential nature; that is, the difference between the two functions is not so fundamental that every act must necessarily be legislative or administrative. Indeed, with acts such as privileges, dispensations, and precepts, we are dealing with acts that participate in some way in both functions. So the real legal question becomes this: What are the juridical consequences of configuring the acts as one or the other type of act under the Code? On the one hand, in certain cases it must be argued, both by explicit affirmation of the Code[73] and by an elementary principle of congruence,[74] that singular acts can only come from someone with legislative power. Furthermore, it cannot be denied that, to the extent that the act differs from the general norm, it deserves to be considered as a singular juridical norm, even when issued by a holder of executive power who is authorized to do so by the law itself. To hold otherwise would link the idea of generality of prescriptions with that of norms, which seems not only unrealistic, but even close to the legalist notion that rights and the law are constituted exclusively through general norms of law. On the other hand, bringing all these acts, even those issued by legislators, into the category of administrative acts, in accordance with the choice of the Code, has the practical effect of opening the door to the possibility of challenging such acts before the higher authority by means of the recourse formalized *ad hoc* by the same Code (see canons 1732–1739). If they were considered to be formally legislative acts, the current system would not contemplate any recourse against them.

*c) Special consideration of dispensations from ecclesiastical laws*[75]

**60.** The term dispensation is defined by the Code, with a phrase taken from the canonical tradition, as "*the relaxation (relaxatio) of a merely ecclesiastical law in a particular case*" (canon 85; emphasis added). Dispensation in the proper sense; i.e., as a grace and not as a right, exists when the duty to observe ecclesiastical law is present; that is, there are no reasons in equity (understood as justice in a particular case) which in themselves would authorize the faithful not to respect the law. Put another way, to the extent that the law has *not* become unjust in the individual case, and there is thus still an obligation on the part of the faithful to comply with the law, a dispensation may be granted as a matter of grace. If, however, reasons of equity *do* exist, a dispensation can be requested, but the nature of such a dispensation would be of a different nature. In such a case, it is no longer an exemption from an obligation of human law, but an authoritative declaration of the non-existence of this obligation. In this type of situation, which could be motivated either by juridical or purely moral reasons (i.e., for the peace of conscience of the faithful), there is a right to obtain the dispensation.

Such a right, however, does not exist in the case of a regular dispensation, which must be distributed according to the criteria of good governance; that is, after a careful consideration of the reasons for and against the requested exception. Therefore, the existence of a *cause for the dispensation* assumes capital importance in the institution of the dispensation. Such a cause must be just and reasonable, and therefore must derive from the contemporary and correlative consideration of the circumstances of the case and the gravity of the law from which one is being dispensed (see canon 90 § 1). In this regard, it is necessary to avoid a simplistic contrast between the common good and a personal good, as if the former always required the application of the general rule, and the latter automatically required a dispensation. In reality, there is an intrinsic interpenetration between the common good and the personal good, for which the personal good itself requires the habitual observance of the law, and dispensatory exceptions must be justified in relation to the common good. The dynamic between the general and the exceptional must exist; otherwise, if exceptions became the general rule, the law itself would have to be modified.

A dispensation granted without cause is unlawful, and even invalid, unless it was given by the legislator himself or by his superior (see canon 90 § 1). The principle of the validity of a causeless dispensation granted by the legislator or his superior may be useful for the security derived from the firmness of the act, but it is also a bit perplexing: it could appear to be a remnant of a voluntaristic conception of the law and of dispensations generally. Under such a view, the legislator, as master of his law, would always be seen as ordering dispensations validly, even if he did so arbitrarily.

In any case, dispensations without cause given by the legislator could also be the subject of an appeal by any interested parties seeking to challenge it. Neither should it be forgotten that this norm, as well as that according to which "a dispensation given in doubt about the sufficiency of its reason is valid and lawful" (canon 90 § 2), are intended to protect the position of the recipient of the dispensation. It should also be noted that if an apparent act of dispensation were to touch divine law, it would obviously be invalid. In such a situation there could never be a true dispensation, which can only be configured in relation to merely human laws.

*One can be dispensed only from purely ecclesiastical laws.* Divine laws are, by definition, non-dispensable, as their obligation comes from the very being of ecclesial juridical realities. The word "dispensation" is sometimes applied by law or by doctrine to other institutions of a nature different than that of dispensing from the law, including vows and cases of dissolution of marriage. The use of this same term for both realities could create confusion—if, for example, someone were to think that there are exceptions to the divine law regarding the indissolubility of marriage. In reality, the question consists of determining what is the sphere of the indissolubility of marriage, because once it is established that it exists as a reality of divine law, no human authority has the power to change what God himself has brought into being (see Matthew 19:6).

"In so far as laws define those elements which are essentially constitutive of institutes or of juridical acts, they are not subject to dispensation" (canon 86). This canon includes, first of all, aspects of divine law that are present in institutes or acts, but it also extends to those elements of human law that work together to constitute such institutes or acts. For example, the requirement that laws be promulgated cannot be dispensed with (see canon 7), nor can a parish be conceived without the faithful (see canon 515 § 1). A dispensation in such a case would imply an intrinsic contradiction, and therefore would be completely invalid, even if there were no positive norms in this regard.

*Who can dispense?* From the combined provisions of canons 85–90, these rules can be formulated:

1) *In general*, in addition to the legislator who issued the respective law and his superior, *the holders of executive power* at the level of government (universal or particular) in which the law was promulgated, and the other

subjects who have the power to dispense, either explicitly or implicitly, either by means of the law itself or by virtue of a legitimate delegation (see canons 85 and 90).

2) *From the laws promulgated by the supreme authority of the Church,* whether universal or particular, in addition to those with the power to dispense according to the aforementioned general rule, *the diocesan Bishop* can dispense, except in the case of procedural or criminal laws, or for those laws whose dispensation is reserved in a special way to the Apostolic See or to another authority (see canon 87 § 1). This discipline reverses that of the 1917 Code (see its canon 81), according to which the bishops could not dispense in ordinary cases from the general laws, unless they had received this power (which happened quite frequently and systematically for certain matters, and not only in mission territories). The new discipline is directly linked to the affirmations of the Second Vatican Council regarding the proper, ordinary, and immediate power of the bishops in their particular Churches (see *Lumen Gentium*, n. 27a and *Christus Dominus*, n. 8a),[76] and found a formulation expressed in the same Council (see *Christus Dominus*, n. 8b), which substantially coincides with that of canon 87 § 1.

"If recourse to the Holy See is difficult, and at the same time there is danger of grave harm in delay, any Ordinary can dispense from these laws, even if the dispensation is reserved to the Holy See, provided the dispensation is one which the Holy See customarily grants in the same circumstances, and without prejudice to canon 291"[77] (canon 87 § 2).

3) The Code clarifies in these terms the application of the general rule with respect to *particular laws issued at the local level*: "The local Ordinary can dispense from diocesan laws and, whenever he judges that it contributes to the spiritual welfare of the faithful, from laws made by a plenary or a provincial Council or by the Bishops' Conference" (canon 88).

4) In accordance with the same general rule, *sacred ministers not endowed with executive power*, that is, "parish priests and other priests or deacons cannot dispense from universal or particular law unless this power is expressly granted to them" (canon 89). The Code itself grants the parish priest the power to dispense from the obligation to observe a holy day or a day of penance, or to commute the obligation into some other pious works; an analogous faculty is attributed in its own sphere to the superior of a religious institute or a society of apostolic life, if they are clerical of pontifical

right (see canon 1245). In addition, special norms regarding dispensation from matrimonial impediments and the canonical form of marriage should be kept in mind.

*3.4. The effects of ecclesiastical judicial activity on the configuration of juridical-canonical relations*

**61.** Although the study of this question belongs to canonical procedural law, it is helpful to indicate here some basic ideas, in order to have an overall picture of the juridical-canonical system of sources.

The operation of every legal system, aiming to determine and to protect the law (that which is just) is essentially connected to its judicial moment. This does not mean that the law exists only when judges exercise their function and issue sentences to settle disputes. Law, understood in the sense of what is just, precedes the administration of justice, which aims to *declare the right in the concrete case* because it is contentious or because it needs the intervention of the judicial authority, through the instrument of the trial and taking into account all the factors of divine and human law that pertain to the case.

Such an operation, however, cannot be simplistically reduced to the mere application of positive norms to the situations to be judged. Reality is much richer: in solving real problems of justice, judicial sentences not only offer individuals (as subjects of law) the means to protect their violated or threatened rights with the force of public authority, but also contribute to determining what these rights are in the single case, often highlighting the inconsistencies and gaps in positive norms. Leaving aside other aspects of a constitutive nature present in the judges' resolutions (particularly those relating to compensation for damages, administrative and criminal sanctions, as well as other interventions that guarantee the rights entrusted by the law to the organs of justice, e.g., for the protection of minors), *the declarative nature of their interventions must essentially refer to the actual juridical relationships themselves*. To declare them, it is necessary to indicate the meaning of the rules of the system, including judicial precedents (especially when they constitute clear guidance, as with jurisprudence), but only as a means to be able to declare what is concretely just. This requires knowing how to interpret the rules of the system, ascertain their limits, and sometimes introduce a new equitable determination to the rights and duties of the parties, where they are uncertain and have not been peacefully determined by the parties in the areas in which they can legitimately configure their own rights.

Canon law in its long history has lived this judicial dimension intensely, and in fact having made many essential contributions to the development of procedural law in general. Nevertheless, at the present time it is clear that canonical processes are limited, in practice, almost exclusively to cases involving the nullity of marriage. To this one could add administrative-contentious processes (that challenge the administrative acts of the Dicasteries of the Roman Curia in front of the Apostolic Tribunal of the Apostolic Signatura) as well as some criminal trials. Except in these cases, the allusion in canon 19 to the jurisprudence of the Roman Curia as a supplementary criterion for settling a case, risks being inoperative; indeed, the formal resolution of a real judicial case is rarely seen in the Church today.

It is not easy to issue an assessment on this situation. There are probably some positive factors behind this, such as an increased awareness of the need to avoid trials *pro bono pacis* whenever possible. There may be less felicitous factors, though, linked to the same crisis of law in the Church, such as the lack of experiential knowledge of the way in which such processes should be carried out. There remains an essential need for the resolution of juridical questions by means of the procedural method that is essentially congruent with such rules: ensuring that the parties can intervene, and that they will have access to an impartial judicial hearing. This procedural method is appropriate for the resolution of issues relating to the validity of the marriage, not so much because the dispute between the parties requires it (a controversy may even be lacking, as when both are in agreement when requesting a declaration of nullity), but to be able to have the guarantees proportionate to a binding ecclesiastical declaration on the existence (or not) of a marriage (which among the baptized is a sacrament), especially given the fact that this matter is not, by its very nature, susceptible to compromises or renunciations by the interested parties. Apart from the civil recognition in some countries of canonical sentences of nullity of marriage, these canonical processes continue to be initiated by the faithful, who are fully aware of not only their juridical-ecclesial effects, but especially their moral effects. Such effects depend on the nature of their marriage situation; i.e., whether it is "regular" or not.

The other typical juridical problems in the Church that need judicial treatment concern mainly the situation of the faithful vis-à-vis the entire Church (in the criminal sphere) and the relations of the faithful with respect to ecclesiastical authorities (in the area of administrative litigation). The application of criminal sanctions through trials seems to be very congruent and desirable for the protection of a member of the faithful who has committed a crime, provided that the defense of ecclesial public order is ensured through timely precautionary measures. The contentious administrative process—that is, those processes by which acts of ecclesiastical executive power are challenged—could perhaps develop more in the future, in an ecclesial climate in which the dichotomy between the needs of communion and the rights of the faithful and other subjects is overcome. At present, such processes are often misconstrued, being seen as if they necessarily express a rejection of ecclesiastical authority. The further development of such processes would serve the effective protection of justice and of rights in the Church, and would certainly also benefit canonical science itself, as it would help it not to lose its essential reference to juridical practice.

### 3.5. The participation of the faithful in the configuration of human law

**62.** We have already studied custom, a general rule whose origin is a uniform behavior of the faithful (except in cases where the norm on customs concerns the exercise of ecclesiastical authority itself). But the participation of the faithful in the configuration of ecclesial human law is broader, and mainly concerns the sphere of juridical autonomy of the baptized in the Church; that is, the field in which the competence to make certain decisions having juridical-canonical effects belongs to the freedom of the same baptized (see numbers 81–82, *infra*). The conception of canon law as a set of rules issued by the power of jurisdiction prevents us from grasping the intrinsic juridical nature of the acts of the faithful. According to such a view, such acts would be juridical only insofar as they were the object of laws or other acts of sacred power. On the contrary, from the point of view of rights as the object of justice, it is understood that the creation, determination, modification, and extinction of rights—and the corresponding duties—is very closely linked to the exercise of the freedom by the faithful. The object of this liberty includes both (i) the birth of juridical relations with the Church as an institution and (ii) the configuration of relationships that are the result of the exercise of the autonomy of the faithful. Examples of the first include the reception of baptism, which presupposes the freedom of the adult (or that of the child's parents) or the many ways of participation in the particular structures of the Church as such (diocese, parishes, etc.). Examples of second include the celebration of marriage, the foundation or the membership of associations, etc.[78]

Even those who are not baptized, or those who are baptized non-Catholics, participate in the configuration of human law in the Church. Indeed, through their juridical acts, they can influence the relations of justice concerning ecclesial life. The classic example is that of a marriage celebrated by one of them with a Catholic. Yet this is also seen in the promotion of ecclesiastical activities with a human concern (works of charity, education, health, etc.) or in areas involving the patrimony of the Church, and in doing so they often make contact with the Christian faith.

The acts of the autonomy of the faithful can concern concrete situations, or have a general normative character. In the first case, we are talking about *juridical acts*; that is, human acts done with the intention of changing juridical relations.[79] In the second hypothesis, we are dealing with *juridical norms* that regulate juridical relations between the faithful within the scope of their intra-ecclesial autonomy (later we will talk about statutes and regulations, referred to in canons 94 and 95).

In canons 124–128, some legal provisions applicable to juridical acts in general are contained. Essentially, the fundamental requirements for the validity of an act are laid out. For an act to produce its juridical effects, there must exist all of the following: the capacity of the person, the essential elements of the act itself, and compliance with the formalities and other requirements required by the legal system for the validity of the act (see canon 124 § 1). Any invalidating effect (either invalidating the act or incapacitating the person) must be expressed in the law that establishes it (see canon 10; number 51, *supra*). Furthermore, the validity of the act is the subject of a general presumption, which is very relevant in any juridical system: "A juridical act which, as far as its external elements are concerned, is properly performed, is presumed to be valid" (canon 124 § 2). If, in addition to these external elements, the validity of an act were required to be established each and every time, any number of special reasons could be advanced in order to justify non-compliance with the obligations of justice.

Canons 125 and 126 determine some rules regarding the juridical significance of defects in legal acts. The act performed as a result of violence (*vis ab extrinseco*)—that is, physical force, that eliminates all external freedom, so that in reality there is no act of true will—is null. An act performed as a result of grave fear (*metus*) that is unjustly inflicted, or as a result of deceit (*dolus*) is valid, but can be rescinded by a sentence of the judge, at the request of a party or *ex officio* (see canon 125). Fear is moral violence; that is, something that does not deprive external freedom (unlike *vis*) but intends to influence the mind of a person, who makes a voluntary choice, but one that is compromised by the psychological pressure of fear. Deceit, on the other hand, is a deception produced by another person, which leads to act performed under the influence of an error deliberately induced by another so as to generate the act. The rescission or the annulment of an act in cases of fear and fraud implies a judicial sanction that eliminates the juridical effects of an act that was valid. Therefore, it is to be distinguished from nullity, which means the absence of such effects from the moment the act was performed (even a null act, however, usually produces some collateral effects, such as the right to be compensated for damages unjustly suffered). Regarding ignorance or error, an act is null if the ignorance or error concern the substance of the act or if they concern a *sine qua non* condition; in other cases, there is only a right to ask for rescission (see canon 126). The two canons provide that for some concrete acts the law has ordered nullity in case of fear, deceit, ignorance, or error. This is what happens in marriage, in which, moreover, it would be impossible to foresee an "annulment," as it is contradictory with the indissolubility of the bond. In practice, almost all of the canonical doctrine and jurisprudence in this matter concerns marriage.

Juridical acts can be unilateral, bilateral, or multilateral, depending on whether they are the result of the will of one, two, or more subjects. A *contract*, understood in a broad sense, is the typical bilateral juridical act. By means of the consent of both parties, new rights and duties are created between them. Strictly speaking, that which is the most common in both canonical and civil juridical science, the notion is restricted to those agreements whose effects arise within the autonomy of the parties and remain subject to their will. Generally, even in the canonical sphere, one thinks above all of property contracts (see canon 1290),[80] which despite their relevance in terms of providing the material means for carrying out the Church's mission, do not concern the substance of it. In fact, there are contracts in the Church (known also as "agreements" or other similar names) that pertain not only to the working activity of persons (see canon 231[81]), but also the relationship of the faithful with the structures of the Church as an institution (see canons 271,[82] 296[83]). Associations can also enter into agreements between themselves and with hierarchical communities, and these communities can do the same between them.[84] It requires an examination on a case-by-case basis whether there is a contract in the strict sense or whether there is only an agreement that gives life to a relationship transcending the will of the parties. The contract or agreement, therefore, is a concept well suited for formalizing ecclesial relations of various kinds; a reductive vision of its use in exclusively the area of Church property should be avoided.[85]

The faithful, in their own field, can also determine *general norms*. The most typical case is the statutes of associations and foundations created by the faithful. The *statutes* contain the fundamental norms regarding the purpose, the constitution, the governance, and the way in which the entity created by the faithful acts; the statutes oblige only the members of the association or those who govern the foundation. The faithful, within their sphere of autonomy, can also issue *regulations* on how to carry out the conferences they themselves freely call; these regulations are normative only for the participants (see canons 94–95[86]).

## *Bibliography*

**63.** In this matter, some works relating to *CIC*-1917 continue to be very useful:

A. Van Hove, *De legibus ecclesiasticis*, H. Dessain, Mechliniae—Romae, 1930.

Id., *De consuetudine. De temporis supputatione*, H. Dessain, Mechliniae—Romae, 1933.

G. Michiels, *Normae generales juris canonici: commentarius libri I codicis juris canonici*, 2nd ed., Typis Societatis S. Joannis Evangelistae, Parisiis—Tornaci—Romae 1949, 2 vol.

A. Cicognani—D. Staffa, *Commentarium ad librum primum Codicis iuris canonici*, 2 vol., apud custodiam librariam Pontifici Instituti Utriusque Iuris, Romae, 1939–1942.

M. Cabreros de Anta, in *Comentarios al Código de Derecho Canónico*, BAC, Madrid, 1963, vol. I, cc. 1–35.


Among the manuals after the CIC:

H. Heimerl—H. Pree, *Kirchenrecht: allgemeine Normen und Eherecht*, Springer, Vienna—New York, 1983, pp. 1–148.

P. Lombardía, *Lecciones de derecho canónico,* Tecnos, Madrid, 1984.

Javier Otaduy—E. Labandeira, *Normas y actos jurídicos,* in AA.VV., *Manual de Derecho Canónico,* edited by Instituto Martín de Azpilcueta, 2nd ed., EUNSA, Pamplona, 1991, pp. 281–343.

F.J. Urrutia, *Les normes générales. Commentaire des canons 1–203,* Tardy, Paris, 1994, pp. 1–163 and 199–210.

*Exegetical commentary on the Code of Canon Law,* edited by E. Caparros, Wilson & Lafleur—Midwest Theological Forum, Montréal—Chicago (IL), 2004, vol. I, canons 1–95.

A. Bunge, *Las claves del Código: el Libro I del Código de derecho canónico,* San Benito, Buenos Aires, 2006.

V. De Paolis—A. D'auria, *Le norme generali: commento al Codice di diritto canonico*, Urbaniana University Press, Vatican City, 2008.

Javier Otaduy, *Lezioni di Diritto Canonico, Parte generale*, Italian translation, Marcianum Press, Venice, 2011.

E. Baura, *Parte Generale del diritto canonico*, EDUSC, Rome, 2013.


In particular, on administrative norms and acts:

E. Labandeira, *Tratado de derecho administrativo canónico,* 2ª ed., EUNSA, Pamplona, 1993.

F. D'Ostilio, *Il diritto amministrativo della Chiesa*, Libreria Editrice Vaticana, Vatican City, 1995.

I. Zuanazzi, *Praesis ut prosis. La funzione amministrativa nella diakonia della Chiesa,* Jovene, Naples, 2005.

J. Miras—E. Baura—J. Canosa, *Compendio de derecho administrativo canónico,* EUNSA, Pamplona, 2001.

In addition to the monographic studies cited in the notes, many works on this subject are gathered in the proceedings of the III International Congress of the *Consociatio studio iuris canonici promovendo* (Pamplona, 10–15 October, 1976): *La norma en el derecho canónico*, EUNSA, Pamplona 1979, 2 vol. See the various studies by Javier Otaduy, *Fuentes, interpretación, personas*, Navarra Gráfica Ediciones, Pamplona, 2002.

On the conception of juridical norms from the perspective of law (right) as that which is just, see J. Hervada, *Lecciones propedéuticas de filosofía del derecho*, EUNSA, Pamplona, 1992, pp. 303–421. The reflections of G. Lo Castro, "L'uomo e la norma," in *Ius Ecclesiae*, 5 (1993), pp. 159–194, are also very helpful.

## Notes

1   On divine revelation from the perspective of fundamental theology, see R. Latourelle, *Teologia della rivelazione*, 9th ed., Cittadella, Assisi, 1991; F. Ocáriz—A. Blanco, *Rivelazione, fede e credibilità: corso di teologia fondamentale*, EDUSC, Rome, 2001.

2   See *Dei Verbum*, nn. 7–10.

3   For example, the teachings of St. John Paul II in the encyclical *Evangelium vitae*, March 25, 1995, on the unlawfulness of the killing of an innocent human being in general, and in particular of abortion and euthanasia (see, respectively, nn. 57, 62, and 65) formally declaring a doctrine that had already been taught infallibly from the ordinary and universal magisterium.

4   For example, regarding the issue of admitting the divorced and remarried to the Eucharistic communion, an attempt was made to contrast the doctrine of magisterial documents such as *Familiaris Consortio*, n. 84, with the codicial discipline of canon 915, as if the latter permitted what the magisterium declared inadmissible (see Pontifical Council for Legislative Texts, Declaration of June 24, 2000, in *Comm.*, 32, 2000, pp. 159–162, which rejects this opposition).

5   In this regard, see St. John Paul II, *Address to the participants in the Day of Study sponsored by the Pontifical Council for Legislative Texts on the 20th anniversary of the promulgation of the Code of Canon Law*, January 24, 2003, in *AAS*, 95 (2003), pp. 333–336, especially n. 3; and id., *Address to the Roman Rota*, January 29, 2005, n. 6, in *AAS* 97 (2005), pp. 165–166.

6   Examples of dogmatic definitions having great juridical importance are those of Vatican Council I on the primacy of jurisdiction of the Roman Pontiff as well as on the infallibility of his *ex cathedra* declarations: see the Dogmatic

Constitution of the Church of Christ *Pastor aeternus*, July 18, 1870, chap. 3, in Denzinger—Hünermann and Fastiggi, Ignatius Press, San Francisco, 2013, 3050–3075.

7    The latter modality has recently been the subject of confirmatory interventions by the Pope himself, including in matters most relevant for canon law such as the impossibility of the priestly ordination of women (see St. John Paul II, apostolic letter *Ordinatio sacerdotalis*, May 22, 1994, in *AAS*, 86, 1994, pp. 545–548) and the incapacity of the pope to dissolve ratified and consummated marriages (see id., *Speech to the Roman Rota*, January 21, 2000, in *AAS*, 92, 2000, pp. 350–355). However, while the first of these declarative interventions is formally definitive, the same did not occur with respect to the second, which obviously does not imply denying its great authority.

8    For example, it appears to us that the question of whether the magisterial authority of episcopal conferences had need of an intervention of human law was actually resolved by means of the *motu proprio* of St. John Paul II *Apostolos suos* (May 21, 1998, in *AAS*, 90, 1998, pp. 641–658). The conferences' possession of such power could neither be inferred from episcopal collegiality nor could it be denied on the basis of the power proper to diocesan bishops. This is explained in the light of the fact that, although based on the principles of divine law, the episcopal conferences are an institutional reality of human creation.

9    With regard to the admission of divorced and remarried to Eucharistic communion, there have been several attempts to overcome the current canonical discipline contrary to this hypothesis on the basis of the use of categories such as equity, mercy, *oikonomia*, etc.

10   This is why a so-called "matrimonial nullity in conscience" is not admissible. The phrase captures the phenomenon in which, despite the absence of externally ascertainable evidence of nullity, an act of ecclesiastical authority is issued on the basis of the subjective conviction of the parties.

11   Given that the 1983 Code introduced very few innovations on this matter, two now classic treatises written after the codification of 1917 are extremely helpful on this topic, containing many references to the canonical tradition on which the rules of the canons are based: A. Van Hove, *De legibus ecclesiasticis*, H. Dessain, Mechliniae—Romae, 1930; and G. Michiels, *Normae generales juris canonici: commentarius libri I codicis juris canonici*, vol. I, 2nd ed., Typis Societatis S. Joannis Evangelistae, Parisiis—Tornaci—Romae, 1949. Michiels in particular constantly refers to the doctrine of the *De legibus* by Francisco Suárez (see number 37, *supra*), so that his approach tends to be focused on the will of the legislator insofar as it produces a moral obligation on the part of the subjects. Although we do not share these voluntaristic and moralistic tendencies, not only can we not forget the enormous influence exerted by Suárez in this matter, but we must also recognize the richness of his doctrine, useful in many aspects even for those who do not follow its approach.

For a comprehensive presentation on the art of legislating and its relationship with the juridical, see E. Baura, "Profili giuridici dell'arte di legiferare nella Chiesa," in Ius Ecclesiae, 19 (2007), pp. 13–36.

12  "Quaedam rationis ordinatio ad bonum commune, ab eo qui curam communitatis habet promulgata," in *Summa Theologiae*, I-II, q. 90, a. 4, c. To understand the meaning of this "ordinatio," it can be helpful to keep in mind the double meaning of the term "order" (and a similar phenomenon occurs in other languages with respective words derived from the Latin term "ordo"): it means at the same time both the rational arrangement or arrangement of things as well as a command or prescription. The latter, in fact, can never be separated from the order of reason from which it springs, and renders it binding, both juridically and morally.

13  This description of ecclesiastical law, insofar as it refers to legislative power, might appear tautological. In reality, however, the law in a technical sense and its distinction from an administrative norm needs formalization, and therefore the formal exercise of legislative power must be present in the act. An examination of the content of the norms alone would not be enough to determine what are laws in a technical sense.

14  This expression, applied to ecclesiastical laws, does not mean in the least a denial of the supernatural nature of ecclesial law, nor the need for faith for adequate canonical knowledge (see number 27, *supra*). E. Corecco's proposal to consider canon law as an *ordinatio fidei*, rather than as an *ordinatio rationis* (see his 1977 article, "'Ordinatio rationis' o 'ordinatio fidei'? Appunti sulla definizione della legge canonica," in Id., *Ius et communio. Scritti di Diritto Canonico*, edited by G. Borgonovo and A. Cattaneo, Piemme—Facoltà di Teologia di Lugano, Casale Monferrato—Lugano, 1997, vol. I, pp. 135–156), is part of the totality of his thought (see number 4, *supra*), tending to conceive the law of the Church as a law only in an analogous sense in respect to the secular law. It is true that the reason of an ecclesiastical legislator must be constantly illuminated by the sense of faith in order to be able to order what is intrinsically supernatural or is at the service of it, but this does not mean that reason is no longer the faculty primarily involved in the legislative work in the Church. After all, faith is not a power alternative to reason, but a supernatural virtue that perfects human reason itself.

15  On this issue and in general for a philosophical-juridical treatment of the rule of law, see J. Hervada, *Lecciones propedéuticas de filosofía del derecho*, EUNSA, Pamplona, 1992, pp. 303–421.

16  See, e.g., canon 210 on the duty of the faithful with respect to their own holiness and that of the Church. On the moral obligation of the laws, see number 51, *infra*.

17  See, for example, canon 767 § 3 regarding weekday homilies, and canon 918 on the reception of sacred communion in the Eucharistic celebration itself.

18 This idea supports the manual prepared by J.I. Arrieta, *Il sistema dell'organizzazione ecclesiastica. Norme e documenti*, Edizioni Università della Santa Croce, 3rd ed., Rome, 2006.

19 Canon 368 references these communities, plus personal circumscriptions such as personal prelatures, military ordinariates, and personal ordinariates for Anglicans. The particular participation in the power of governance that religious institutes and clerical societies of apostolic life of pontifical right receive (see canons 596 § 2 and 732) also entails the legislative function for the general regulation of internal matters related to the sacred order. In order to determine the person who exercises that participation in legislative power, it is necessary to consider the law proper to each institute or society. Usually, it is attributed to the general chapter, the holder of the supreme authority in the institute (see canon 631).

20 A distinction must be made between universality in the proper sense, i.e., the entire Church (thus including the Eastern Churches), and universality within the Latin Church alone (see number 52, *infra*).

21 *Pastor Bonus*, article 18, paragraph 2. See also *General Regulations of the Roman Curia*, (new version) April 30, 1999 (in *AAS*, 91, 1999, pp. 629–699), arts. 125–126. It seems to us that there is a substantial coincidence between the delegation referred to in canon 30 and the approval in specific form (such term distinguishing it from an approval in common form for decisions of greater importance, but which do not fall outside the competence of the dicastery in the context of the administrative function). On this matter, cf. V. Gómez-Iglesias, "La 'aprobación específica' en la *Pastor Bonus* y la seguridad jurídica," in *Fidelium iura*, 3 (1993), pp. 361–423.

22 One thinks, for example, of the numerous practical indications contained in the decrees on bishops (*Christus Dominus*), on priests (*Presbyterorum Ordinis*), on priestly formation (*Optatam Totius*), on religious life (*Perfectae Caritatis*), on the apostolate of the laity (*Apostolicam Actuositatem*), and also of those contained in other conciliar documents

23 The Pontifical Council for Legislative Texts is competent to rule on this congruence, at the request of the interested parties (see *Pastor Bonus*, art. 158).

24 See the collection, with a preliminary survey, of J.T. Martín de Agar—L. Navarro, *Legislazione delle Conferenze Episcopali complementare al C.I.C.*, 2nd ed. updated, Coletti a San Pietro, Rome, 2009.

25 "Erit lex honesta, iusta, possibilis, secundum naturam, secundum consuetudinem patriae, loco temporique conveniens; necessaria, utilis, manifesta quoque, ne aliquid per obscuritatem in captionem contineat, nullo private commodo, sed pro communi civium utilitate conscripta" (*Etymologiarum*, Lib. V, n. 21, in PL, 82, 203; collected in the Decree of Graziano: D 4, c. 2).

26 In civil systems, promulgation is the act by which a head of State formally declares and enforces a law, ordering its publication and the observance of it.

Promulgation in the canonical sense would generally be understood in the civil sense as publication; i.e., in an official journal.

27 Pontifical laws are currently made public usually through the bulletin of the press office of the Holy See (accessible also via the internet) and appear in *L'Osservatore Romano*. In addition, they then spread in different ways (magazines, booklets, collections, etc.) in various languages. However, none of these means constitutes a promulgation, which takes place normally, as we will state immediately below, through the *Acta Apostolicae Sedis*, the distribution of which is rather limited.

28 This occurs when the laws declare divine law, or when they reproduce already existing law (as when they declare the sense of words which are certain in themselves: see canon 16 § 2).

29 Remember the well-known *dictum* of Graziano: "Leges instituuntur cum promulgantur, firmantur cum moribus utentium approbantur" (post c. 3, D. 4). "Laws are instituted when they are promulgated; they are confirmed when they have been approved by the long-standing custom of those who observe them."

30 See, e.g., Y. M.-J. Congar, "La réception comme réalité ecclésiologique," in *Revue des Sciences Philosophiques et Théologiques*, 56 (1972), pp. 369–403; AA.VV., Recezione e comunione tra le Chiese (Atti del Colloquio internazionale di Salamanca, April 8–14, 1996), edited by H. Legrand—J. Manzanares—A. García y García, Italian translation, EDB, Bologna, 1998. See a work of critical synthesis in Javier Otaduy, "Discernir la recepción. Las acepciones del concepto y su relieve en el derecho," in *Fidelium Iura*, 7 (1997), pp. 179–243.

31 One speaks traditionally of "acquired rights," terminology that the *CIC* uses in canon 4 in declaring that, with the entry into force of the 1983 Code, acquired rights that were still in use and were not revoked remained intact, unless expressly revoked by the canons of the same Code. Acquired rights are usually distinguished from "mere expectations," in which the right properly speaking, does not yet exist.

32 These three forms are present in canon 6 § 1, which regulates the relationship between the CIC-1983 and previous laws.

33 It is true that a law coming from a lower legislator cannot contradict what a superior legal or customary norm has prescribed (see canon 135 § 2), but the universal higher law, as a rule, leaves in force a particular or special pre-existing law (whether it comes from superior or inferior legislators). Universal canonical law, therefore, respects disciplinary diversity, unless expressly stated otherwise. The inverse rule, however, was followed when the CIC-1917 came into force (see canon 6, 1º) as that of the Code of 1983 (see c. 6 § 1, 2º), so it is easy to forget the general principle sanctioned by canon 20.

34 For that matter, it does not seem that ecclesiastical authority, by virtue of its legislative power, can command something that is outside the sphere of justice.

In this way, in a negative sense and on principle, one can resolve the traditional canonical dispute regarding the possibility of a law commanding merely internal acts of the faithful.

Moreover, the effect of the moral obligation is not something directly left in the hands of the ecclesiastical authority, as if it could arbitrarily establish it independently of the objective relevance of the same precept of law. Therefore, the traditional expression *graviter onerata conscientia* ("gravely bound in conscience"), not used by the Code, must be understood only as an authoritative declaration of the intrinsic importance of the ordered provision, and not as a direct configuration by the authority of a grave sin in any case of disobedience (see A. Del Portillo, "Morale e diritto," in *Seminarium*, 11, 1971, pp. 736–738).

35 In this sense, canon 21 of the 1917 Code, in accordance with the canonical tradition, prescribed: "Leges latae ad praecavendum periculum generale, urgent, etiamsi in casu peculiari periculum non adsit" (i.e., "laws made in order to protect the faithful from what is commonly dangerous oblige even though in a particular case there is no danger").

36 This lawfulness is obviously also moral, but as a consequence of it being juridical; that is, concerning the external configuration of the relationships of justice.

37 For example, the invalidating efficacy of the canonical form for marriage was introduced by the Council of Trent after having overcome many perplexities.

38 Continuing with the same example regarding marriage, those celebrated without public form, called clandestine, were subject to canonical penalties prior to Trent.

39 See, in general, *Unitatis Redintegratio*, Decree on Ecumenism, Chapter 3, and more specifically n. 16 regarding the recognition of the power of the Eastern Churches, including of course those separated from Rome, to regulate according to their own discipline, always within the limits set forth by divine law, which is stated thus in the text: "memores necessariae unitatis totius Ecclesiae."

40 It is true that through the motu proprio *Omnium in mentem* of Benedict XVI (October 26, 2009, in *AAS*, 102, 2010, pp. 8–10), the norm of the 1983 Code was eliminated according to which Catholics who had separated from the Church by a formal act were exempt from the impediment of disparity of worship and observance of the canonical form (see canons 1086 § 1 and 1117). Nonetheless, we consider that the question of the ecclesial recognition of the natural right to marry is still open with respect to those faithful who, despite having true matrimonial will, do not intend to observe the canonical form. A possible solution would be to demand the latter only for the liceity of the union, not for its validity (in this sense, see M.A. Ortiz, "L'obbligatorietà della forma canonica matrimoniale dopo il m.p. *Omnium in mentem*," in *Ius*

*Ecclesiae*, 22 (2010): pp. 477–492; I. Lloréns, *La "diakonia" de la forma. La forma canónica al servicio de la realidad matrimonial,* EUNSA, Pamplona, 2020.

41  This rule is established according to the most characteristic obligations of canon law; i.e., those of a directly religious nature, such as that of the Sunday precept (see canon 1247). An exception is found, for example, in the abstinence laws, which apply only from the age of fourteen, and with respect to fasting, which is compulsory only for adults under the age of sixty (see canon 1252).

42  In fact, the current Codes, Latin and Eastern, are formally different, although many of their norms are identical or nearly so. There are also some laws, however, that are formally common, that is to say strictly universal, such as *Pastor Bonus* or the apostolic constitution on Catholic universities of St. John Paul II, *Ex corde Ecclesiae*, August 15, 1990, in *AAS*, 82 (1990), pp. 1475–1509. The CCEO, more properly, uses the phrase "common law" to refer not only to the norms of the universal Church, but also to the norms common to all the Eastern Churches (such as CCEO itself). It uses the phrase "particular law" to describe the other particular Oriental norms (see canon 1493).

43  It can also be said that universal laws, by their nature, are personal, and that they oblige everywhere, except in those territories where by either legal or customary exception they are not in force (see canon 12 § 2).

44  These rules are formulated in determining the situation of *peregrini*—i.e., those persons who are away from their place or places of domicile or quasi-domicile—with respect to particular laws (see canon 13 § 2). For the *vagi*—i.e., those who have no domicile or quasi-domicile anywhere—the principle of pure territoriality is adopted; that is, they are subject to all universal and particular laws that are in force in the place where they are located (see canon 13 § 3).

45  Regarding the distinction between culpable and non-culpable ignorance, the manuals of moral theology should be consulted. See, e.g., E. Colom—A. Rodríguez Luño, *Scelti in Cristo per essere santi: elementi di teologia morale fondamentale*, Apollinare studi, Romae, 1999, pp. 305–333.

46  On the realistic way of understanding divine law, see number 31, *supra*.

47  See C.J. Errázuriz M., "Circa l'equiparazione quale uso dell'analogia in diritto canonico," in *Ius Ecclesiae*, 4 (1992), pp. 215–224. In this work we recall the saying "nullum simile est idem," which manifests clearly the realism of traditional European jurists, who knew how to use analogy based on the reality of things. A legal or doctrinal equation attributing the same legal solution to different situations never means a complete identification between these situations. Otherwise, it would be impossible in practice for law or doctrine to formulate comparisons, which always assume the existence of possible exceptions deriving from reality itself or from positive norms. On the concept of

analogy, see the monograph by G. Feliciani, *L'analogia nell'ordinamento canonico*, Giuffrè, Milan, 1968.

48   In the canonical tradition, the *Regulae iuris*, placed at the end of the *Liber Sextus*, are famous, almost all of which are drawn from Roman law (see number 32, *supra*). In addition, in the title *de verborum significatione* (5.40) of the *Liber Extra* there are different interpretative rules. They must still be considered valid to the extent that they reflect common sense and specific traits of the canonical tradition, but not in those situations where they sanctioned contingent choices that were subsequently abandoned by the canonical system. For example, the principle according to which "verba ita sunt intellegenda ut res de qua agitur valere possit potius quam perire" (X. 5.40.25) reflects a characteristic aspect of the prudence of the good jurist, that of bringing the texts back to a plausible sense, instead of rushing to declare them completely useless because of the limitations found. In many of the codicial canons true principles of law are enunciated: one thinks, for example, of those contained in the various canons on ecclesiastical laws (see canons 7–22).

49   The original Latin *communi constantique doctorum* sententia better highlights the doctrinal and scientific nature of this source.

50   The case of a custom *contra legem* or *praeter legem* is different (see canon 26).

51   An allusion to this type of authentic interpretation is found in canon 16 § 1: "Leges authentice interpretatur legislator et is cui potestas authentice interpretandi fuerit ab eodem commissa."

52   They are published in the *AAS* and are often the subject of commentary in canonical journals. The list of interpretations that have appeared so far can be found as an appendix in various annotated editions of the CIC.
   The main problem they pose derives precisely from several factors. First, they are presented as simple interpretations of provisions that modify the existing legal order, despite at times seeming to contradict the provisions of the respective canon. Second, they are not even issued by the legislator himself—although they are confirmed by him. To these are added the rather dry form with which they are traditionally presented: a short question is followed by a laconic "affirmative" or "negative," without any explanation (at most there is sometimes some clarification of the affirmative or negative answer). These problems, linked to a tendentially voluntaristic conception of the law and which identifies it with the juridical, have aroused quite a few discussions in the doctrine on the nature of these interpretations—the value of which seems to be equated with that of the laws, having to be considered as included in the phrase "by way of a law" of canon 16 § 2—and in the way of understanding them and harmonizing them with other laws. Such difficulties perhaps explain the less frequent use of this legal instrument in more recent times. In fact, to modify a law (including Codes) the clearest way is by that of the law itself (for examples of modification and integration of the *CIC*, see number

39, *supra*), and often it can even be unnecessarily problematic to present such law as formally an act of interpretation. For other functions of pure authoritative declaration of what, although clear, is spuriously denied, it is possible to resort to other interventions, of a more argumentative nature, as in fact has already happened (see, for example, note 4).

53  "Non sermoni res, sed rei est sermo subiectus" (X. 5. 40. 6).

54  See, e.g., canons 134 ("Ordinary," "Local Ordinary"), 302 ("clerical association"), 1074 ("public" and "occult" impediment) and many others. However, it is not necessarily true that the law always uses the term in the same sense in which it has been defined in the text itself. For example, given the overall meaning of the text, one can deduce that in canons 1079 § 3, 1080 § 1 and 1082, the legislator seems to depart from the definition of "public" and "occult" impediment that had just been established in canon 1074.

55  From the historical point of view, see the classic monograph by R. Wehrlé, *De la coutume dans le droit canonique. Essai historique s'étendant des origines de l'Église au Pontificat de Pie XI*, Sirey, Paris, 1928. The manuals written after the 1917 Code retain their value: see A. Van Hove, *De consuetudine, De temporis supputatione*, H. Dessain, Mechliniae—Rome 1933; and G. Michiels, *Normae generales juris canonici: commentarius libri I codicis juris canonici*, 2nd ed., Typis Societatis S. Joannis Evangelistae, Parisiis—Tornaci—Rome, 1949, vol. II.

56  See P. Pellegrino, *L'"animus communitatis" e l'"adprobatio legislatoris" nell'attuale dottrina canonistica della consuetudine antinomica*, Giuffrè, Milan, 1995.

57  See Gregory IX, Decretale *Quum tanto* (X. 1. 4.11).

58  On the relationship between customs and the *CIC*, decidedly less favorable to the former if *contra legem*, see canon 5.

59  For a concise view of the current problem, with valid reflections and appropriate bibliographic indications, see Javier Otaduy, "La comunidad como fuente de derecho (presupuestos eclesiológicos y sociales de la costumbre)," in *Ius Ecclesiae*, 10 (1998), pp. 37–87. See also G. Comotti, *La consuetudine nel diritto canonico*, CEDAM, Padua, 1993; E. Baura, *La consuetudine*, in AA.VV., *Fondazione del diritto. Tipologia e interpretazione della norma canonica*, Quaderni della Mendola, 9, edited by the Gruppo Italiano Docenti di Diritto Canonico, Glossa, Milan, 2001, pp. 81–104.

60  Even within the sphere of ecclesiastical power of government (the traditional *iurisdictio*), the operation of custom was allowed. As a singular historical example, see the excellent study of St. Josemaría Escrivá de Balaguer, *La Abadesa de las Huelgas: estudio teológico jurídico*, 3rd ed., Rialp, Madrid, 1988.

61  In this sense, see canon 392 § 2 on the duty of supervision by diocesan bishops.

62  In this context, we examine administrative activity only from the point of view of its impact on the rights and duties in the Church. To further explore

this issue, see E. Labandeira, *Trattato di diritto amministrativo*, Italian translation of the 2nd edition, Giuffrè, Milan, 1994; F. D'Ostilio, *Il diritto amministrativo della Chiesa*, Libreria Editrice Vaticana, Vatican City, 1995; I. Zuanazzi, *Praesis ut prosis. La funzione amministrativa nella diakonia della Chiesa*, Jovene, Naples, 2005; J. Mira—J. Canosa—E. Baura, *Compendio di diritto amministrativo canonico*, Italian translation, EDUSC, Rome, 2007.

63  See the seventh guiding principle for the revision of the Code (in *Communicationes*, 1, 1969, p. 83).

64  See I. Zuanazzi, "Il principio di legalità nella funzione amministrativa canonica," in *Ius Ecclesiae*, 8 (1996), pp. 37–69.

65  It would be better if the terminology of "executive general decree" and "instruction," adopted by the Code, be used in a uniform way, in the first place by the Holy See. There is still a certain confusion of names: for example, documents of a very different nature, some very doctrinal, are called "instructions," and the formal category of "executive general decree" has not been incorporated into practice.

66  Unlike the previous legislation, currently the laws and customs that attribute graces to indeterminate subjects are not called privileges. When the granting of a grace is regulated by the law itself, we usually speak of either explicit or implicit permission from the authority (consider, for example, the possibility of reserving the Most Holy Eucharist: see canons 934–936). It therefore seems that the use of the term tends to be restricted, which in our estimation is a positive thing, given that even though one could recover its etymological meaning, thus defending the legitimacy of a private law that takes into account a diversity of situations, there is nevertheless the risk of a strong connotation—difficult to overcome and pejorative in everyday language—as if privileges were something that are essentially violative of the equality that is required by justice. The complexity of the problem is well presented in the monograph of S. Gherro, *Privilegio, bene comune, e interesse privato*, CEDAM, Padua, 1977.

67  Although the rescript is an act typically characterized by constituting a response to someone's petition (see canon 59 § 1), the category is also extended to the granting of pardons on the initiative of the authority; i.e., without being formally connected to a petition.

68  In the canonical norms it is very frequent that the general precept itself expressly contemplates reasonable exceptions. For example, the general rule according to which the parish priest must reside in the parish house in the vicinity of the church is followed by the enunciation of the requirements of the permission to reside elsewhere when, in particular cases, the local Ordinary grants it (see canon 533 § 1); the obligation of receiving the sacrament of confirmation before contracting marriage is conditioned by the traditional clause "if this can be done without grave inconvenience" (canon 1065 § 1).

69 See what we have said about equity as the justice of the single case: see number 51, *supra*.

70 Sometimes the law itself provides for the possibility of dispensations, as happens with respect to matrimonial impediments under human law (see canons 1073–1094). At other times, a dispensation is not expressly provided for, but due to the nature of the provision in question, the dispensation must be considered to be possible by virtue of the general canons on dispensation.

71 The CIC itself alludes explicitly to the legislator with regard to privileges in general (see canon 76 § 1), and contemplates the case of dispensations given by the legislator (see canon 90 § 1).

72 The main supporters of one and the other thesis were two professors from the University of Navarra respectively: Eduardo Labandeira and Pedro Lombardía. For a summary of the discussion, with conclusions that we follow closely, see E. Baura, *La dispensa canonica dalla legge*, Giuffrè, Milan, 1997, pp. 223–242.

73 See canon 76 § 1 on privileges.

74 In the singular precept that goes beyond the content of the law, it seems evident that there must be a legislative power (see canon 49). The same must be said about the competent authority when adding, in an administrative act, a clause of exemption from the law, from custom, or a restriction of an acquired right (see canon 38).

75 As a monograph after the 1983 *CIC*, see E. Baura, *La dispensa canonica dalla legge*, op. cit. For an in-depth study, well documented from a historical point of view, see S. Berlingò, *La causa pastorale della dispensa*, Giuffrè, Milan, 1978.

76 However, it seems questionable to consider this norm as a necessary consequence of this doctrine. In our opinion, there is a question of government convenience at stake, as evidenced by the existence of exceptions. The prudential solution can only be linked to the historical situation. In any case, however, the autonomy and responsibility proper to the bishops must always remain clear in its substance.

77 This canon concerns the dispensation from the obligation of celibacy for clerics, which is granted only by the Roman Pontiff.

78 It must be pointed out that the belonging of these situations to the field of "autonomy of the faithful" does not mean that they can configure such juridical situations without taking into account the requirements of divine law; nor does it mean that the respective acts and relationships do not have any relevance from the point of view of the ecclesial common good, through which they are, in fact, the subject of acts of the power of jurisdiction. These considerations are obvious when dealing with marriage, and also apply to associative realities, especially to public associations, and even more so to institutes of consecrated life and societies of apostolic life. But the norms proper to all these realities, apart from those of divine law and those that establish special connections with the Church as institution, are the fruit of the autonomy of

the faithful. This autonomy is by no means incompatible with all the specific characteristics of the respective ecclesial realities: the sacramentality of marriage; the origin, heritage and charismatic persistence of many associations, etc.

79 See J. Fornés, "El acto jurídico-canónico (sugerencias para una teoría general)," in *Ius Canonicum*, 49 (1985), pp. 57–89; *L'atto giuridico nel diritto canonico*, Libreria Editrice Vaticana, Vatican City, 2002.

80 The only exception in the terminology of the Code is marriage, which, however, has its own legal regulation as well as its own specificity that goes beyond the purely contractual scope.

81 The ecclesial nature of the employment relationship does not change simply because, as is logical, these contracts are stipulated in such a way that they have civil effects.

82 This canon deals with the aggregation of a cleric to a particular church other than the one in which he remains incardinated. A written agreement is expected between the two diocesan bishops. The cleric himself does not appear among the subjects of the agreement, but the essential presupposition of the transfer (configured as a permission) is his will, so it is logical that he signs the same agreement, as happens in practice.

83 This canon deals with the situation in which a member of the lay faithful participates with a relationship of organic cooperation in the life of a personal prelature, something that may arise in relation to other particular hierarchical structures of the Church. In fact, although we are not talking about a formal convention, it is implicit in the apostolic constitution on military ordinariates: "(…) they belong to the military ordinariate and are under its jurisdiction: (…) 4º All the faithful, both men and women, whether or not they are members of a religious institute, who carry out in a permanent way a task committed to them by the Military Ordinary, or with his consent" (St. John Paul II, Apostolic Constitution *Spirituali militum curae*, April 21, 1986, X , 4º, in *AAS*, 78, 1986, pp. 481–486).

84 One thinks, for example, of an agreement between two associations of the faithful to unite their activities; or of the assignment of a parish to a clerical religious institute or to a society of clerical apostolic life (see canon 520); or of an act by which a diocese assumes responsibility for the parish of another diocese.

85 In this sense, see T. Blanco, *La noción canonica de contrato. Estudio de su vigencia en el CIC de 1983*, EUNSA, Pamplona, 1997.

86 These canons deal with the statutes and regulations of the realities dependent on the Church as an institution (e.g., statutes of an Episcopal Conference, the regulations of a diocesan Synod), and those issued by the faithful in their autonomous sphere, which we have described in the text.